TIME FOR KIDS®

WORLD ATLAS

Keep your world knowledge up-to-the-minute
with news from around the globe at
www.timeforkids.com/kids

Continue your travel adventures online with
TFK Around the World! Explore countries, test your
knowledge and learn words in new languages at
www.timeforkids.com/aroundtheworld

WORLD ATLAS

TIME FOR KIDS World Atlas
PUBLISHER: John Stevenson
EDITOR: Nelida Gonzalez Cutler
DEPUTY EDITOR: Leslie Dickstein
MAPS: Joe LeMonnier. **Additional maps:** Joe Lertola,
Jean Wisenbaugh. **Research:** Kathleen Adams
PHOTOGRAPHY EDITOR: Joan Menschenfreund
CONTRIBUTORS: Claudia Atticot, David Bjerklie, Jeremy Caplan,
Borden Elniff, Jennifer Marino, Butch Phelps, Lisa Jo Rudy,
Kathryn R. Satterfield, Tiffany Sommers, Elizabeth Winchester
COPY EDITORS: Barbara Collier, Steve Levine, Peter McGullam,
Elsie St. Léger
INDEXING: Marilyn Rowland
ART DIRECTION AND DESIGN: Raúl Rodriguez/Rebecca Tachna for
R studio T, NYC
COVER DESIGN: Elliot Kreloff

TIME INC. HOME ENTERTAINMENT
PUBLISHER: Richard Fraiman
GENERAL MANAGER: Steven Sandonato
EXECUTIVE DIRECTOR, MARKETING SERVICES: Carol Pittard
DIRECTOR, RETAIL & SPECIAL SALES: Tom Mifsud
DIRECTOR, NEW PRODUCT DEVELOPMENT: Peter Harper
ASSISTANT DIRECTOR, BRAND MARKETING: Laura Adam
ASSISTANT GENERAL COUNSEL: Dasha Smith Dwin
BOOK PRODUCTION MANAGER: Jonathan Polsky
DESIGN & PREPRESS MANAGER: Anne-Michelle Gallero
RETAIL MANAGER: Bozena Bannett
SPECIAL SALES MANAGER: Ilene Schreider
MARKETING MANAGER: Alexandra Bliss
SPECIAL THANKS: Glenn Buonocore, Suzanne Janso, Robert Marasco,
Brooke McGuire, Mary Sarro-Waite, Adriana Tierno, Alex Voznesenskiy

DOWNTOWN
BOOKWORKS INC.

PRODUCED BY DOWNTOWN BOOKWORKS
PRESIDENT: Julie Merberg
EDITOR: Sarah Parvis
PRODUCTION DESIGNER: mouse+tiger
SPECIAL THANKS: Sara Newberry, Kate Gibson,
Patricia Dublin, Dinah Dunn

Copyright ©2007
Time Inc. Home Entertainment

Published by TIME FOR KIDS Books
Time Inc.
1271 Avenue of the Americas
New York, NY 10020

All rights reserved. No part of this book may be reproduced
in any form or by any electronic or mechanical means, including
information storage and retrieval systems, without permission in
writing from the publisher, except by a reviewer, who may quote
brief passages in a review.

Softcover:
ISBN: 1-933821-94-9
ISBN 13: 978-1-933821-94-8

"TIME For Kids" and the red border design are registered trademarks
of Time Inc.

We welcome your comments and suggestions about TIME FOR KIDS
Books. Please write to us at:
TIME FOR KIDS Books
Attention: Book Editors
P.O. Box 11016
Des Moines, IA 50336-1016

Contents

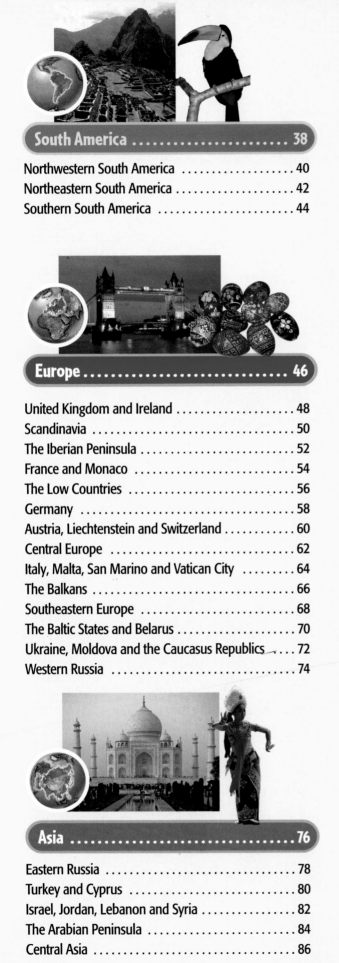

World Guide

The Arctic
12

Scandinavia
50

The Low Countries
56

United Kingdom and Ireland
48

France and Monaco
54

Italy, Malta, San Marino and Vatican City
64

The Iberian Peninsula
52

Western Canada and Alaska
18

Eastern Canada
16

United States of America: Midwest
26

United States of America: West
32

United States of America: New England
22

United States of America: South
28

United States of America: Middle Atlantic
24

United States of America: Southwest
30

Western Africa
106

Mexico and Central America
34

Caribbean
36

Northwestern South America
40

Northeastern South America
42

Southern South America
44

How to Use the TFK World Atlas

Take a trip around the world with the TIME FOR KIDS **World Atlas.** This book divides the world into continents, countries and regions. Each of the book's sections begins with a map of the continent and an explanation of the continent's features. "Wow Zone!" and "Did You Know?" features will introduce interesting information about the people, places and landmarks within a country or region. The "World-at-a-Glance" chapter at the end of the book gives vital statistics for every country in the world. But before you begin to explore the world, take a few moments to find out about planet Earth by reading pages 8 through 11.

Abbreviations

ft	feet
h	hectare
kg	kilogram
I.	island
L.	lake
lb	pound
Mt.	Mount
Mtns.	Mountains
m	meter
mi	mile
NA	not available
R.	River
St.	Saint
sq km	square kilometer
sq mi	square mile
U.K.	United Kingdom

Key to Map Symbols

⊛ state, province or territory capital

✪ country capital

● city

▲ mountain or volcano

Introduction
These paragraphs give a brief overview of the continent's physical and geographic features.

Color Tabs
Each continent has a different color tab so that you can easily locate countries within continents.

Lines of Longitude and Latitude
Lines of longitude run in a north-south direction. Lines of latitude run in an east-west direction.

Continent

Continent Facts
Here you will find the size of the continent, its countries and other information.

Scale
Use the scale to measure distances. The scale is given in kilometers and miles.

Wow Zone!
This is where you will find amazing facts about the continent.

Locator Globe
The globe shows the continent's location in the world.

Introduction
These paragraphs give a brief overview of states, provinces, territories or countries.

Compass Rose
The compass rose will help you locate north, south, east, west and points in between.

Country/Region

Map Grid
A color-coded grid surrounds the country and regional maps. Use the grid to quickly locate places.

Data Bank
Each section has a Data Bank with important information about area, population, the capital and the languages. Look for Data Bank entries about Canadian provinces on pages 16–19 and each state in the United States on pages 22–33.

Locator Globe

Scale

Did You Know?
This is where you will discover surprising facts about the states, provinces, territories or countries.

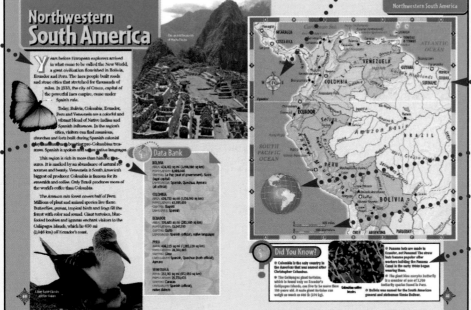

World-at-a-Glance
Turn to pages 122–136 for information about every country in the world. Here you will find facts on the country's flag, area, population, capital, languages, government, religions, literacy rate, currency and main exports.

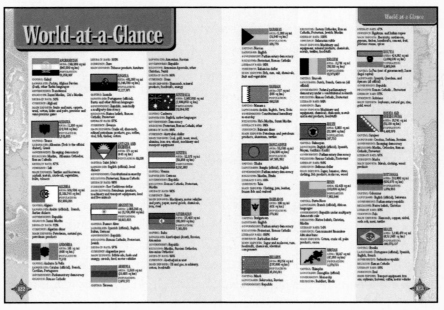

The Living Earth

When did life on Earth begin, and how? What were the conditions that made life possible? Did life arise only once? For centuries, scientists have struggled with these difficult questions.

We know from studying tiny microfossils of simple marine bacteria that life on Earth began at least 3.5 billion years ago. For the first billion years of Earth's history, bacteria were the only life on the planet. Some types of marine bacteria formed large colonies, and their fossil remains, called stromatolites, can be found along the coasts of South Africa and Australia.

Gradually, more complex animals began to evolve in the sea. An explosion in the diversity of animals took place between 500 million and 550 million years ago. This was followed by the appearance of the first creatures with back-bones: fish. The next 100 million years saw the first plants and the first animals and insects to live on land. Dinosaurs appeared nearly 250 million years ago. They ruled Earth until 65 million years ago, when they disappeared. Scientists believe that an asteroid hit Earth and caused mass extinctions.

Today, life in all of its forms and glory is present in every nook and cranny of the globe, from the coldest, darkest depths of the ocean to ice-covered lakes in Antarctica to desolate Himalayan mountaintops. Earthlings now include microscopic flower mites that hitch rides on the beaks of hummingbirds, awesome 100-foot-long blue whales—and humans.

Biologists categorize the amazing diversity of the world's plant and animal life by habitat. The Arctic tundra, for example, with its polar bears and seals, is one habitat. The tropical rain forest along the Amazon River is another. Habitats range from the grasslands of bison and prairie dogs to the coral reefs of clownfish and moray eels. As the number of human beings on the planet grows larger and larger, it is our responsibility to make sure that these habitats and the precious creatures that depend on them are kept healthy and safe.

Major Events in Earth's History

4.5 billion years ago
Earth forms.

3.5 billion years ago
The oldest forms of life, such as bacteria, appear.

2 billion years ago
Simple microbes called protists appear.

1 billion years ago
Plants and fungi emerge.

Atmosphere

Lithosphere

Biosphere

Hydrosphere

Did You Know?

● Earth is made up of four spheres. The atmosphere includes the gases that surround Earth. The biosphere includes all the living organisms. The hydrosphere contains all the planet's water. The lithosphere is Earth's hard crust, which includes the tallest craggy mountains and the dirt in our gardens.

● There have been periods in Earth's history when many plants and animals have died all at once.

These mass extinctions were probably caused by climate change or something like an asteroid hitting Earth.

● Bacteria, the first living things on Earth, are still the most plentiful organisms on the planet. They are found on land, in water and in the air.

● Each type of plant and animal is called a species. Biologists use the word *biodiversity* to describe the many different species on Earth. Even though scientists have identified only 1.5 million species, there may be as many as 10 million to 30 million in the world.

600 million years ago
More complex soft-bodied animals emerge.

500 million years ago
Animals with backbones (jawless fish) emerge.

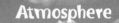

7 million years ago
Human ancestors emerge.

Weather and Climate

When it comes to the day's forecast, climate is what you expect and weather is what you get. You can expect that it will be hot in Houston in July and cold in Chicago in January. It's impossible to know whether it will be sunny or raining or what the temperature will be.

The Tinuy-An Falls
in the Philippines

The Sahara Desert

The Sun is the ultimate climate and weather machine for our planet. The Sun's energy doesn't fall evenly on Earth—and that makes all the difference in the world! The tilt of our planet as it orbits the Sun causes the four seasons and contributes to the patterns of air circulation that create wet and dry seasons in parts of the world. Because Earth is curved, the Sun's rays hit the planet at different angles. Places located near the equator get more direct sunlight and more intense heat. The Sun also drives the weather on a daily basis. The collision of warm and cold air can produce a spring shower or a swarm of tornados. The circulation patterns in oceans also play a role in creating weather conditions. Some ocean currents keep Northern Europe warm. Other currents fuel hurricanes and monsoons.

Climate is stable from year to year. But over long periods of time, climate can change dramatically. Fifteen thousand years ago, large parts of Europe, Canada and the United States were stuck in a long, deep freeze called the Ice Age. Scientists are now busy taking the planet's temperature and measuring polar ice caps and mountaintop glaciers to determine how much our climate is changing. Scientists believe that the burning of fossil fuels is causing global warming.

Earth's atmosphere is divided into five layers: the troposphere, 0 mi to 7 mi (0 km to 11 km) high, where our weather occurs; the stratosphere, 7 mi to 30 mi (11 km to 48 km) high; the mesosphere, 30 mi to 50 mi (48 km to 80 km); the thermosphere, 50 mi to 300 mi (80 km to 483 km) high; and the exosphere, at 300 mi to 500 mi (483 km to 804 km) and above, the edge of outer space.

Did You Know?

● The end of the Ice Age, about 10,000 years ago, was also the time of giant animals such as the mastodon, the woolly mammoth and the saber-toothed tiger. We know from fossils that Ice Age peoples used stone spears to hunt animals. Did these animals disappear because of overhunting or because the climate was getting warmer? Scientists don't know.

A glacier in Antarctica

● In the past million years, ice ages have been common. It is the warm periods between them, such as the one we are in now, that are unusual. Some scientists believe that the next ice age is right around the corner. Don't worry: That could be about 10,000 years away!

● Is Earth getting warmer? The average worldwide surface temperature has been above normal for the past 25 years. The 10 warmest years on record for at least a century also occurred during that time. This warming trend is a concern to a lot of scientists—and to polar bears, too!

The Changing Planet

The earth is 4.5 billion years old. Like all other planets, it was formed from dust and debris by the powerful pull of the Sun's gravity. Scientists believe a smaller planet crashed into Earth when it was still a ball of molten rock. This collision created our moon. Gradually, the surface of Earth cooled and hardened. But most of the planet is still molten. What we think of as solid ground is only the outer layer, or the crust, less than 50 mi (80 km) thick. In some places it is only a couple of miles (kilometers) thick.

The Earth's crust is on the move. Think of it as a giant jigsaw puzzle floating on a hot lava ball that is nearly 8,000 mi (13,000 km) across! The slowly shifting pieces of crust are called tectonic plates. Scientists believe that 220 million years ago, our seven continents were actually squashed together into one supercontinent called Pangaea. Right now, the plates that meet in the middle of the Atlantic Ocean are pulling apart. That movement makes the Atlantic grow an inch wider each year.

Even though shifting plates move as slowly as snails, the shifts create dramatic results. Mountains are caused by plates crashing into one another. Earthquakes happen when two plates grinding against each other suddenly slip. Volcanoes are spots where the molten rock beneath the crust leaks out, sometimes explosively. And though we can't see them, many of the most spectacular formations on earth—from the biggest mountains to the deepest canyons—are actually underneath the water of the oceans, which covers two-thirds of the planet.

Many of the world's volcanoes are clustered in the Ring of Fire, a region surrounding the Pacific Ocean. The region outlines a tectonic plate, one of seven major movable pieces of the earth's crust.

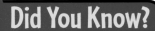

Did You Know?

● In 1999, a team of scientists used satellite equipment to calculate a more accurate height for Mount Everest. The new height is 29,035 ft (8,850 m) above sea level. That is 7 ft (2 m) higher than before.

● Volcanoes can form where two plates meet. They can also form as the sea-floor plate passes over a "hot spot," an area where the crust is thin and the molten rock below has broken through. As the moving crust passes over the hot spot, volcanoes form, sometimes one after another. This is how the Hawaiian Islands were formed.

● There are thousands of volcanic eruptions each year. Most of them are minor. Many occur underwater. In 1963, an underwater eruption created a new island near Iceland.

● The Richter scale measures the strength of earthquakes. The scale goes from a magnitude 0 to 9, with 9 being the strongest quake. An earthquake measuring 8 on the Richter scale is 10 times more powerful than a quake that measures 7. In 1908, a magnitude-8 earthquake nearly destroyed San Francisco, California.

Karimsky Volcano, Russia

Arctic

The Arctic region is the northernmost place on the planet. Strictly speaking, it is the area that falls inside the Arctic Circle. But many scientists define the Arctic as the area centered around the North Pole, including everything north of the tree line (the point beyond which no trees can grow). That region includes parts of Alaska, Canada, Greenland, Iceland, Russia and Norway.

The Arctic climate is cold and harsh. Winter at the North Pole lasts six months, and the sun never rises! The average temperature is about −22°F (−33°C). Summer at the top of the world is nearly opposite, with six months of constant daylight and relatively mild temperatures of around 32°F (0°C).

Despite the forbidding environment, some hardy animals—including humans!—thrive in the frozen north. Giant polar bears, walruses, seals and some 23 other animal species survive year-round in the polar climate. The people of the Arctic, including the Inuit of North America, the Lapps (Sami) of Scandinavia and the Nenets and Chukchis of Russia, have also adapted to their surroundings. It is not possible to grow food, so nourishment must come from land and sea animals. In the past, native Arctic communities were isolated from the rest of the world. But in recent years, tourism and the discovery of oil and mineral deposits have started to bring more outsiders to the region.

Night Lights: The aurora borealis dances across the Alaskan sky.

Regional Facts

ARCTIC CIRCLE AREA: 8,000,000 sq mi (21,000,000 sq km)
ARCTIC OCEAN AREA: 5,427,000 sq mi (14,056,000 sq km)
ARCTIC OCEAN DEPTH: 13,123 ft (4,000 m)
LOWEST POINT: Fram Basin, 15,305 ft (4,665 m)
LARGEST ISLAND: Greenland, 836,222 sq mi (2,166,086 sq km)

Polar bears can weigh as much as 1,000 lbs (453 kg)!

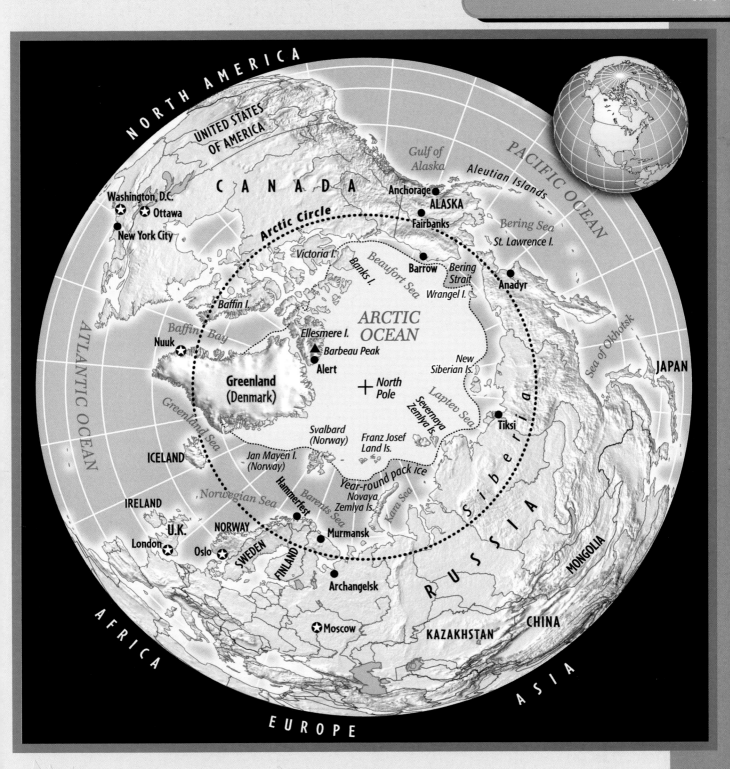

NORTH AMERICA

UNITED STATES
OF AMERICA

C A N A D A

*Gulf of
Alaska*

PACIFIC OCEAN

Aleutian Islands

Washington, D.C.
Ottawa
New York City

Anchorage
ALASKA
Fairbanks

Arctic Circle

Bering Sea

St. Lawrence I.

Victoria I.

Banks I.

Beaufort Sea

Barrow

*Bering
Strait*

Anadyr

Baffin I.

Wrangel I.

ARCTIC
OCEAN

*New
Siberian Is.*

Sea of Okhotsk

Baffin Bay

Nuuk

Ellesmere I.
▲ *Barbeau Peak*
Alert

JAPAN

ATLANTIC
OCEAN

**Greenland
(Denmark)**

+ *North
Pole*

Laptev Sea

*Severnaya
Zemlya Is.*

Tiksi

Greenland Sea

*Svalbard
(Norway)*

*Franz Josef
Land Is.*

Siberia

ICELAND

*Jan Mayen I.
(Norway)*

Year-round pack ice

*Novaya
Zemlya Is.*

Kara Sea

IRELAND

Norwegian Sea

Hammerfest

Barents Sea

R U S S I A

U.K.
London

NORWAY

Murmansk

Oslo
SWEDEN

FINLAND

MONGOLIA

A F R I C A

Archangelsk

CHINA

Moscow

KAZAKHSTAN

A S I A

E U R O P E

Wow Zone!

● Ilulissat, also called Jakobshavn, is the third-largest town in Greenland. The town is home to 4,000 people and some 6,000 sled dogs!

● The word Arctic comes from the Greek word *arktos*, which means "bear." It refers to the northern constellation of stars called Bear.

● The Arctic Ocean is the smallest ocean in the world.

● The aurora borealis, or northern lights, can be seen in the Arctic night sky. It is caused by solar winds interacting with Earth's atmosphere.

Dogsledding is an Arctic mode of transportation.

13

North America

The Grand Canyon in Arizona

Stretching 9 million square miles (24 million sq km), North America is the world's third-biggest continent. The region extends from the icy Arctic Ocean in the north to the warm, turquoise waters of the Caribbean Sea. In between lies nearly every landscape imaginable: massive glaciers, snow-covered mountains, vast canyons, fertile plains and tropical rain forests.

North America is made up of 23 nations, including Canada, the world's second-largest country, and the United States, the world's third-largest country. The continent is rich in natural resources—abundant water, minerals and fertile soil—and has one of the world's most developed economies. North Americans have a higher income per person than those living on any other continent.

Beyond its physical beauty, North America is also known for its dynamic cities. From New York City to Los Angeles, Mexico City to Vancouver, world-class museums, universities and concert halls beckon those hungry for cultural and intellectual fare.

Continent Facts

AREA: 9.361,791 sq mi (24,247,039 sq km)

COUNTRIES AND TERRITORIES: Antigua and Barbuda, Anguilla (U.K.), Aruba (Netherlands), Bahamas, Barbados, Belize, Bermuda (U.K.), Canada, Cayman Islands (U.K.), Costa Rica, Cuba, Dominica, Dominican Republic, El Salvador, Greenland (Denmark), Grenada, Guadeloupe (France), Guatemala, Haiti, Honduras, Jamaica, Martinique (France), Mexico, Montserrat (U.K.), Netherlands Antilles (Netherlands), Nicaragua, Panama, Puerto Rico (U.S.), Saint Barthélemy (Guadeloupe), Saint Kitts and Nevis, Saint Lucia, Saint Maarten/Saint Martin (Netherlands Antilles/ Guadeloupe), Saint Vincent and the Grenadines, Trinidad and Tobago, Turks and Caicos (U.K), United States, Virgin Islands (U.S. and U.K.)

HIGHEST POINT: Mount McKinley (Denali), Alaska, 20,320 ft (6,194 m)

LOWEST POINT: Death Valley, California, 282 ft (86 m) below sea level

LARGEST LAKE: Lake Superior, 31,820 sq mi (82,414 sq km)

LONGEST RIVER: Missouri-Mississippi river system, 3,710 mi (5,971 km)

LARGEST COUNTRY: Canada, 3,855,085 sq mi (9,984670 sq km)

SMALLEST COUNTRY: Saint Kitts and Nevis, 101 sq mi (262 sq km)

Wow Zone!

● The oldest rocks in the world are from Canada. Scientists believe they are close to 4 billion years old!

● Greenland is the world's largest island. It is nearly covered with ice.

● Lake Superior, on the U.S.–Canadian border, is the world's largest freshwater lake.

● The Everglades covers about 4 million acres (1.6 million hectares) in southwestern Florida. It is home to more than 400 species of birds, 25 species of mammals, 60 species of amphibians and reptiles and 125 species of fish.

● North America includes two of the world's most populous cities, New York City and Mexico City. Both have populations in excess of 8 million.

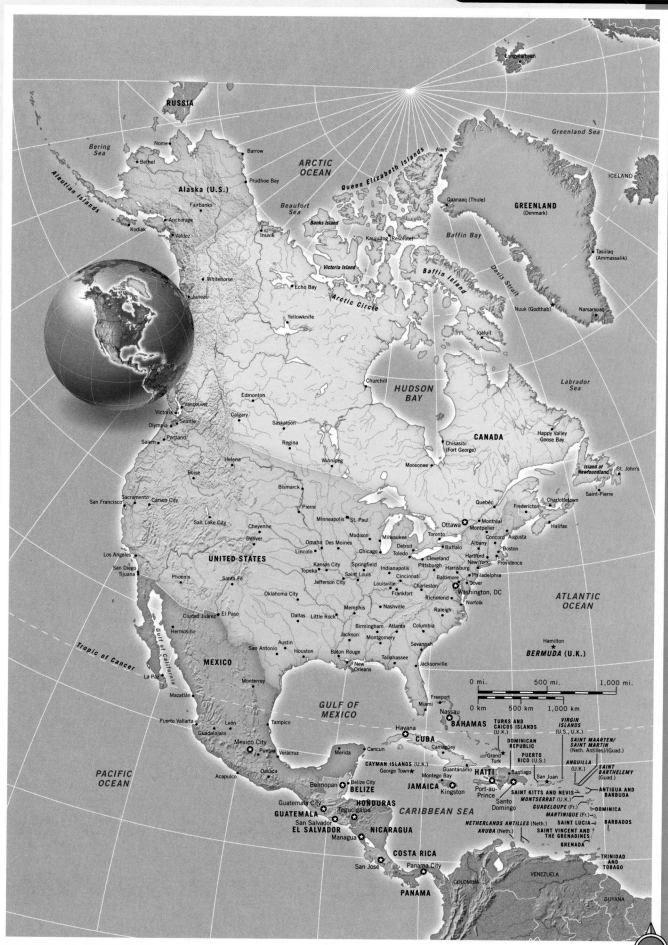

RUSSIA

Bering Sea

Nome
Bethel
Barrow

ARCTIC OCEAN

Prudhoe Bay

Alaska (U.S.)

Beaufort Sea

Fairbanks
Anchorage
Kodiak
Valdez

Inuvik

Aleutian Islands

Banks Island

Kaujuitog (Resolute)

Victoria Island

Greenland Sea

Alert

Queen Elizabeth Islands

Qaanaaq (Thule)

GREENLAND
(Denmark)

ICELAND

Baffin Bay

Whitehorse
Echo Bay
Juneau

Arctic Circle

Yellowknife

Baffin Island

Davis Strait

Tasiilaq
(Ammassalik)

Nuuk (Godthab)
Narsarsuaq

Iqaluit

Edmonton

Churchill

HUDSON BAY

Labrador Sea

Vancouver
Victoria
Olympia
Seattle
Salem
Portland

Calgary

Saskatoon

Regina

Helena

Winnipeg

Chisasibi
(Fort George)

CANADA

Moosonee

Happy Valley
Goose Bay

Island of Newfoundland

St. John's

Saint-Pierre

Boise

Bismarck

San Francisco
Sacramento
Carson City

Pierre

Quebéc

Charlottetown

Fredericton

Salt Lake City

Minneapolis
St. Paul

Madison
Milwaukee

Detroit

Toronto

Ottawa
Montréal
Montpelier
Concord
Augusta

Halifax

Cheyenne

Denver

Omaha Des Moines

Chicago
Toledo

Cleveland

Buffalo

Albany
Boston

Los Angeles

Lincoln

UNITED STATES

Santa Fe

Kansas City
Topeka

Jefferson City

Springfield
Saint Louis

Indianapolis

Pittsburgh
Cincinnati

Hartford
New York
Providence

San Diego
Tijuana

Phoenix

Louisville
Frankfort

Harrisburg
Baltimore
Philadelphia
Dover

Charleston

Washington, DC

ATLANTIC OCEAN

Oklahoma City

Memphis
Nashville

Richmond
Norfolk

Raleigh

Ciudad Juárez El Paso

Dallas
Little Rock

Birmingham
Atlanta

Columbia

Hermosillo

Jackson
Montgomery

Savannah

Hamilton

BERMUDA (U.K.)

San Antonio
Austin

Houston

Baton Rouge

Tallahassee

Jacksonville

New
Orleans

MEXICO

Tropic of Cancer

Gulf of California

La Paz

Monterrey

GULF OF MEXICO

Freeport
Miami

Mazatlán

Nassau

BAHAMAS

Puerto Vallarta
León
Tampico

Havana

CUBA

TURKS AND
CAICOS ISLANDS
(U.K.)

VIRGIN
ISLANDS
(U.S., U.K.)

Guadalajara

Mexico City
Puebla
Veracruz

Merida

Cancun

Camaguey

DOMINICAN
REPUBLIC

SAINT MAARTEN/
SAINT MARTIN
(Neth. Antilles)/(Guad.)

PACIFIC OCEAN

Acapulco

Oaxaca

CAYMAN ISLANDS (U.K.)
George Town

Grand
Turk

Guantánamo

PUERTO
RICO (U.S.)

San Juan

ANGUILLA
(U.K.)

SAINT
BARTHELEMY
(Guad.)

Montego Bay

HAITI

Santiago

Belmopan

Belize City

BELIZE

JAMAICA

Kingston

Port-au-
Prince

SAINT KITTS AND NEVIS
MONTSERRAT (U.K.)

ANTIGUA AND
BARBUDA

Guatemala City

GUATEMALA

Tegucigalpa

HONDURAS

CARIBBEAN SEA

Santo
Domingo

GUADELOUPE (Fr.)
MARTINIQUE (Fr.)

DOMINICA

San Salvador

EL SALVADOR

NICARAGUA

NETHERLANDS ANTILLES (Neth.)
ARUBA (Neth.)

SAINT LUCIA

SAINT VINCENT AND
THE GRENADINES

BARBADOS

Managua

COSTA RICA

GRENADA

San José

Panama City

VENEZUELA

TRINIDAD
AND
TOBAGO

PANAMA

COLOMBIA

GUYANA

0 mi.   500 mi.   1,000 mi.

0 km   500 km   1,000 km

Eastern Canada

Niagara's Horseshoe Falls

Measuring nearly 4 million sq mi (10 million sq km), Canada is the world's second-largest country. Only Russia is larger. Canada is divided into ten provinces and three territories. It stretches from the Atlantic Ocean in the east to the Pacific Ocean in the west. More than half of Canada's population lives in the eastern region. The east is also the location of the country's capital, Ottawa, and its two largest cities, Montreal and Toronto. Many of Canada's early settlers were from France and Britain. Both countries believed that Canada should belong to them, which led to years of war and conflict. In 1763, at the end of the Seven Years' War, France was forced to give its Canadian territory to Britain. In 1867, Canada's colonies joined to form the Dominion of Canada. The country's government included a governor general, who represented Britain's monarch.

Canadians today are proud of their freedom, but they have not forgotten their heritage. French is spoken by about one-third of the population; Britain's queen is still pictured on some Canadian money; and the customs and traditions of native people are valued and respected.

Data Bank

CANADA
AREA: 3,855,085 sq mi (9,984,670 sq km)
POPULATION: 32,623,490
CAPITAL: Ottawa
LANGUAGES: English, French (both official)

Eastern Canada's Provinces

ONTARIO
AREA: 412,582 sq mi (1,068,587 sq km)
POPULATION: 12,686,952
CAPITAL: Ottawa

NEW BRUNSWICK
AREA: 28,345 sq mi (73,433 sq km)
POPULATION: 749,168
CAPITAL: Fredericton

NEWFOUNDLAND AND LABRADOR
AREA: 156,185 sq mi (404,519 sq km)
POPULATION: 509,677
CAPITAL: St. John's

NOVA SCOTIA
AREA: 21,425 sq mi (55,491 sq km)
POPULATION: 934,405
CAPITAL: Halifax

PRINCE EDWARD ISLAND
AREA: 2,184 sq mi (5,657 sq km)
POPULATION: 138,519
CAPITAL: Charlottetown

QUÉBEC
AREA: 594,860 sq mi (1,553,637 sq km)
POPULATION: 7,651,531
CAPITAL: Québec

Ice fishing is a popular hobby in parts of Canada.

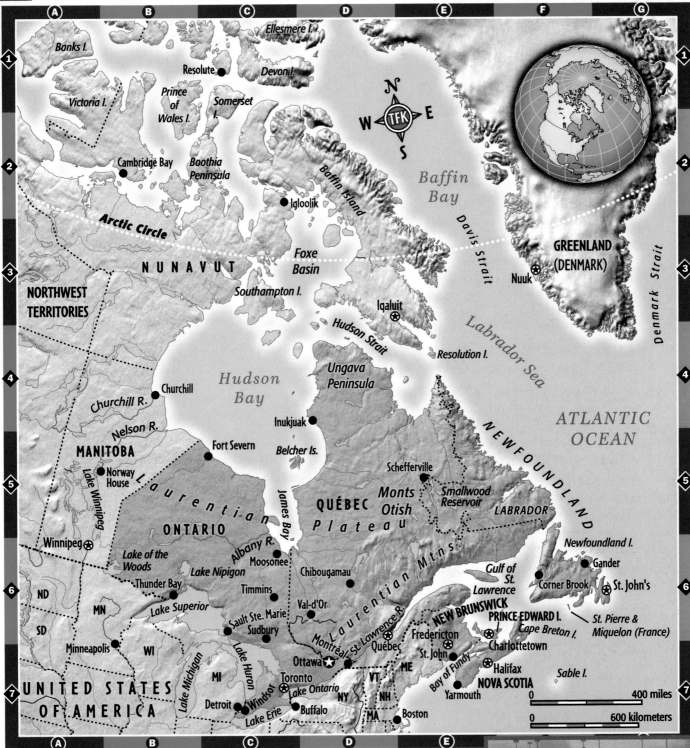

Banks I.
Ellesmere I.
Devon I.
Resolute
Victoria I.
Prince of Wales I.
Somerset I.
Cambridge Bay
Boothia Peninsula
Igloolik
Baffin Island
Baffin Bay
Davis Strait
GREENLAND (DENMARK)
Nuuk
Arctic Circle
NUNAVUT
Foxe Basin
NORTHWEST TERRITORIES
Southampton I.
Iqaluit
Hudson Strait
Resolution I.
Labrador Sea
Denmark Strait
Hudson Bay
Ungava Peninsula
Churchill
Churchill R.
Nelson R.
MANITOBA
Norway House
Fort Severn
Inukjuak
Belcher Is.
Laurentian
James Bay
Schefferville
Smallwood Reservoir
NEWFOUNDLAND
ATLANTIC OCEAN
Lake Winnipeg
Winnipeg
ONTARIO
QUÉBEC
Monts Otish Plateau
LABRADOR
Lake of the Woods
Albany R.
Moosonee
Lake Nipigon
Chibougamau
Laurentian Mtns
Newfoundland I.
Gander
Gulf of St. Lawrence
Corner Brook
St. John's
ND
Thunder Bay
Timmins
Val-d'Or
Lake Superior
MN
Sault Ste. Marie
Sudbury
Montréal
St. Lawrence R.
Québec
NEW BRUNSWICK
PRINCE EDWARD I.
Cape Breton I.
St. Pierre & Miquelon (France)
SD
Minneapolis
WI
Fredericton
St. John
Charlottetown
Ottawa
MI
Lake Huron
Lake Michigan
Toronto
Lake Ontario
VT
ME
Bay of Fundy
Halifax
Sable I.
UNITED STATES OF AMERICA
Detroit
Windsor
Lake Erie
Buffalo
NY
NH
MA
Boston
Yarmouth
NOVA SCOTIA

N W E S TFK

| 0 | 400 miles |
| 0 | 600 kilometers |

Did You Know?

● Canada has the world's longest coastline. Its length of 151,614 mi (244,000 km) would circle the earth more than six times!

● In winter, the Rideau Canal, in Ottawa, is the world's longest skating rink. It is 4.8 mi (7.72 km) long.

● Canada is considered the birthplace of ice hockey. More than half the players in the U.S.'s National Hockey League are Canadian.

● Niagara Falls has two sides, one in Canada and one in the United States. The Canadian Falls, or Horseshoe Falls, is 170 ft (52 m) high. As much as 40 million gal of water (151 million l) rushes over the rim of the Canadian Falls each minute.

● The word *Canada* is from an Iroquois Indian word that means "community."

Winter Wonderland: The Rideau Canal is a giant ice-skating rink.

Western Canada and Alaska

S nowcapped mountains, icy glaciers, grassy prairies and fertile farmland are the landscapes that cover the vast area that makes up western Canada. This region has four provinces and three territories. Nunavut—a sprawling region of tundra, Arctic islands and frozen fjords—was carved out of the Northwest Territories in 1999.

Vancouver is Canada's third-largest city.

Most of western Canada's residents live near the country's southern border, where temperatures are milder. Alberta, Saskatchewan and Manitoba are known for their oil and gas reserves, plentiful fields of wheat and large cattle ranches. British Columbia, which is Canada's westernmost province, features the beautiful city of Vancouver.

West of Canada lies Alaska. It is the largest state in the United States but has the fewest people per square mile. In 1867, the U.S. bought Alaska from Russia for $7.2 million. Many people thought it was a foolish purchase. But they changed their minds when gold was discovered in 1896. Today, oil is Alaska's largest industry.

Data Bank

Western Canada's Provinces

ALBERTA
AREA: 255,285 sq mi (661,188 sq km)
POPULATION: 3,375,763
CAPITAL: Edmonton

BRITISH COLUMBIA
AREA: 366,255 sq mi (948,600 sq km)
POPULATION: 4,310,452
CAPITOL: Victoria

MANITOBA
AREA: 250,934 sq mi (650.930 sq km)
POPULATION: 1,177,765
CAPITAL: Winnipeg

SASKATCHEWAN
AREA: 251,700 sq mi (651,903 sq km)
POPULATION: 985,386
CAPITAL: Regina

NORTHWEST TERRITORIES
AREA: 532,643 sq mi (1,379,028 sq km)
POPULATION: 41,861
CAPITAL: Yellowknife

NUNAVUT
AREA: 772,260 sq mi
(2,000,671 sq km)
POPULATION: 30,782
CAPITAL: Iqaluit

YUKON TERRITORY
AREA: 207,076 sq mi (536,327 sq km)
POPULATION: 31,229
CAPITAL: Whitehorse

U.S. State

ALASKA
AREA: 656,424 sq mi (1,700,135 sq km)
POPULATION: 670,053
CAPITAL: Juneau
MOTTO: North to the Future

RUSSIA Anadyr

Arctic Circle

St. Lawrence I.

Bering Sea

Aleutian Islands

Eagle totem
in Ketchikan, Alaska

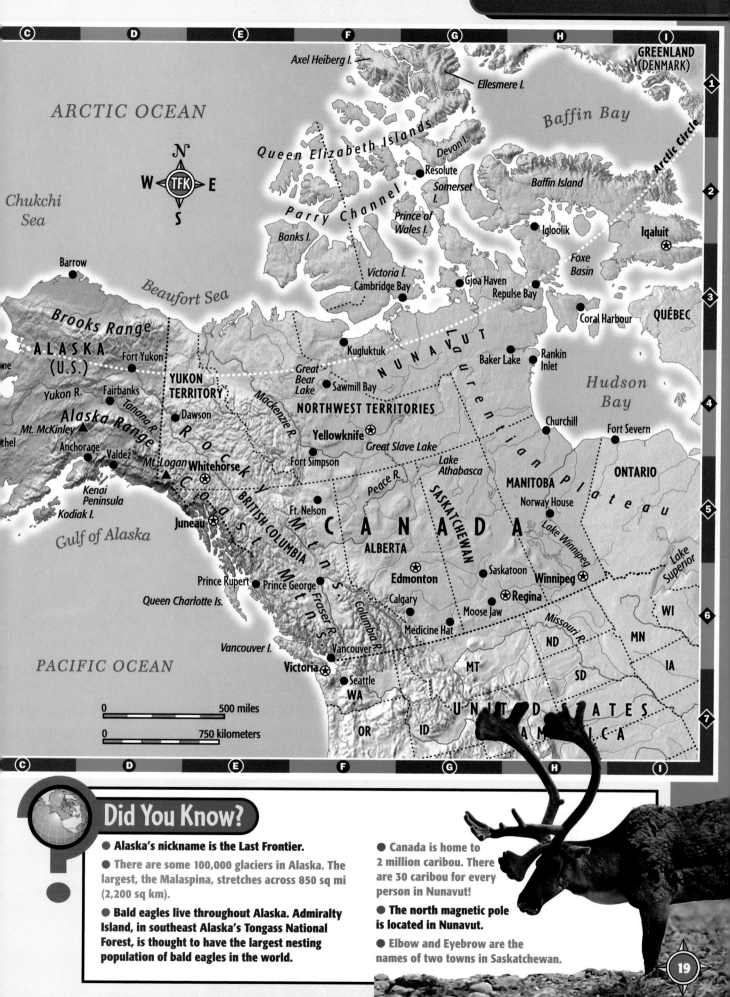

C   D   E   F   G   H   I

GREENLAND
(DENMARK)

ARCTIC OCEAN

Axel Heiberg I.

Ellesmere I.

1

Baffin Bay

Queen Elizabeth Islands

Chukchi
Sea

N
W · TFK · E
S

Devon I.

Resolute

Baffin Island

Arctic Circle

2

Somerset
I.

Banks I.

Prince of
Wales I.

Iqaluit

Parry Channel

Igloolik

Foxe
Basin

Barrow

Beaufort Sea

Victoria I.
Cambridge Bay

Gjoa Haven

Repulse Bay

QUÉBEC

3

Brooks Range

Coral Harbour

ALASKA
(U.S.)

Fort Yukon

Kugluktuk

Hudson
Bay

4

ne

Yukon R.

Fairbanks

YUKON
TERRITORY

Dawson

Great
Bear
Lake

Sawmill Bay

NORTHWEST TERRITORIES

Baker Lake

Rankin
Inlet

Mt. McKinley

Alaska Range

Tanana R.

Mackenzie R.

Yellowknife

Great Slave Lake

Churchill

Fort Severn

thel

Anchorage

Valdez

Mt. Logan

Whitehorse

Fort Simpson

Lake
Athabasca

ONTARIO

5

Kenai
Peninsula

Kodiak I.

BRITISH COLUMBIA

Ft. Nelson

Peace R.

CANADA

SASKATCHEWAN

MANITOBA

Norway House

Gulf of Alaska

Juneau

Rocky

ALBERTA

Lake Winnipeg

Lake
Superior

Prince Rupert

Prince George

Edmonton

Saskatoon

Winnipeg

Queen Charlotte Is.

Fraser R.

Columbia R.

Calgary

Regina

WI

6

Medicine Hat

Moose Jaw

Missouri R.

MN

Vancouver I.

Vancouver

ND

IA

PACIFIC OCEAN

Victoria

Seattle

WA

MT

SD

7

OR

ID

UNITED STATES
AMERICA

0   500 miles

0   750 kilometers

C   D   E   F   G   H   I

United States of America

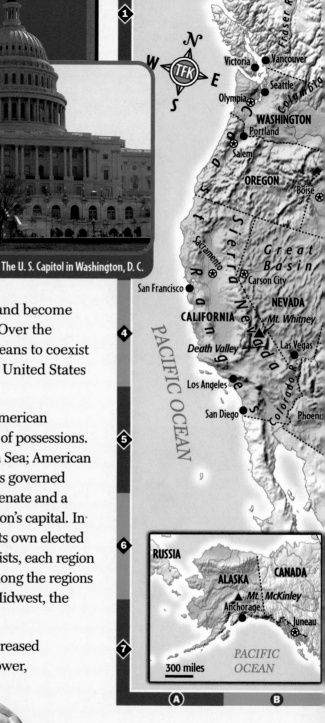

The United States of America stretches across the North American continent and beyond. It includes a vast range of climates and geographic regions, from temperate forests to arid deserts. In 1776, the 13 original British colonies revolted against their rulers and formed a new nation. Since the Revolution, the United States has grown to 50 states and become a destination for immigrants from around the world. Over the centuries, these very diverse cultures have found a means to coexist in a democracy. For this reason, the population of the United States is often referred to as a "melting pot" of people.

The United States includes 49 states on the North American continent, one state in the Pacific Ocean and a number of possessions. Puerto Rico and the Virgin Islands are in the Caribbean Sea; American Samoa and Guam are in the Pacific Ocean. The nation is governed by an elected President and a Congress, made up of a Senate and a House of Representatives. Washington, D.C., is the nation's capital. In addition to the President and Congress, each state has its own elected government. Although an American national culture exists, each region has its own particular accent, customs and cuisines. Among the regions are New England, the Middle Atlantic, the South, the Midwest, the Southwest and the West.

Since its founding, the United States has steadily increased in physical size and political power. Today, as a superpower, the nation wields a great deal of economic and cultural influence around the world.

The U. S. Capitol in Washington, D. C.

Data Bank

UNITED STATES OF AMERICA
AREA: 3,717,776 sq mi (9,629,091 sq km)
POPULATION: 299,398,484
CAPITAL: Washington, D.C.
LANGUAGES: English, Spanish

Monumental Presidents:
Mount Rushmore in South Dakota

Did You Know?

Benjamin Franklin thought the wild turkey would be a more appropriate symbol!

● The United States is the third-largest country in the world by size and population.

● The bald eagle is the national bird of the United States and a symbol for the nation. With its 7-ft (2-m) wingspan and powerful beak and talons, the eagle is an impressive bird of prey. Still, not all the Founding Fathers wanted the eagle to represent the country.

● Mount Rushmore National Memorial is an enormous sculpture blasted and drilled into the side of a mountain in the Black Hills of South Dakota. The monument, which was completed in 1941, depicts Presidents George Washington, Thomas Jefferson, Theodore Roosevelt and Abraham Lincoln.

● The motto of the United States is *E pluribus unum*, which means "From many, one."

United States of America
New England

Nestled between Canada, New York and the Atlantic Ocean are the six states that make up New England. Each state has its own special identity. But they share many features, including snowcapped mountains that beckon skiers during the winter; miles of scenic coastline; marshy bogs where cranberries grow; spectacular fall foliage; and bustling cities and towns.

The Atlantic Ocean forms the eastern border of all but Vermont, which is landlocked. Connecticut, Massachusetts, Maine, New Hampshire and Rhode Island touch the ocean.

Much of America's colonial history is anchored in New England. Plymouth Colony, in Massachusetts, was the first permanent European settlement in New England. The first battles of the American Revolution took place in Concord, Massachusetts, near Boston. Historically, trade, fishing and shipbuilding were important revenue sources for the region. But tourism, banking and industry have emerged as the major moneymakers for these Northeastern states.

Beacon of Light: Portland Head Light in Maine

The purple finch is New Hampshire's state bird.

Data Bank

CONNECTICUT
AREA: 4,845 sq mi (12,550 sq km)
POPULATION: 3,504,809
CAPITAL: Hartford
MOTTO: *Qui transtulit sustinet* (He who transplanted still sustains)

MAINE
AREA: 30,865 sq mi (79,941 sq km)
POPULATION: 1,321,574
CAPITAL: Augusta
MOTTO: *Dirigo* (I lead)

MASSACHUSETTS
AREA: 7,838 sq mi (20,300 sq km)
POPULATION: 6,437,193
CAPITAL: Boston
MOTTO: *Ense petit placidam sub libertate quietem* (By the sword we seek peace, but peace only under liberty)

NEW HAMPSHIRE
AREA: 8,969 sq mi (23,231 sq km)
POPULATION: 1,314,895
CAPITAL: Concord
MOTTO: Live free or die

RHODE ISLAND
AREA: 1,045 sq mi (2,707 sq km)
POPULATION: 1,067,610
CAPITAL: Providence
MOTTO: Hope

VERMONT
AREA: 9,249 sq mi (23,955 sq km)
POPULATION: 623,908
CAPITAL: Montpelier
MOTTO: Vermont, freedom and unity

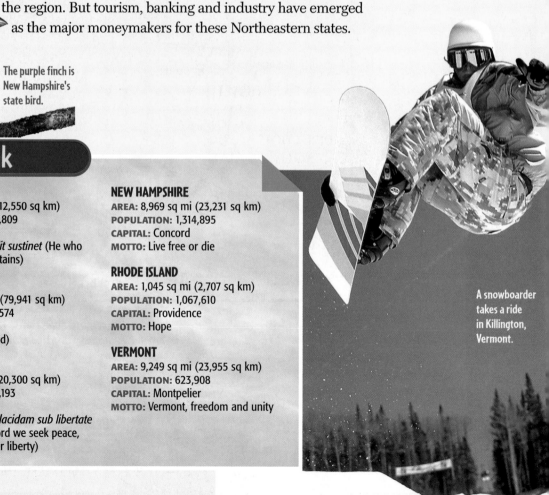

A snowboarder takes a ride in Killington, Vermont.

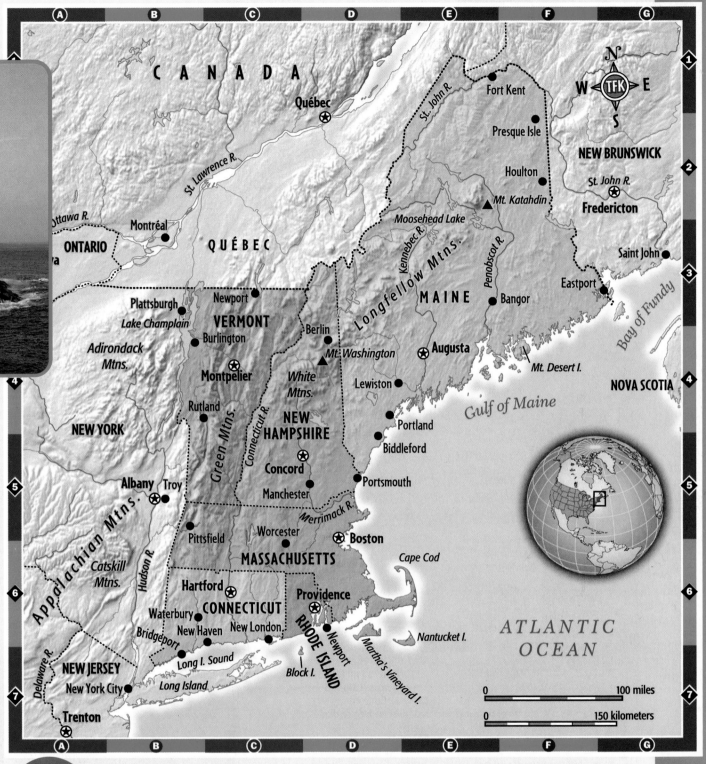

A B C D E F G

CANADA

Québec

St. Lawrence R.

Ottawa R.

Montréal

ONTARIO

QUÉBEC

Plattsburgh

Lake Champlain

VERMONT

Burlington

Newport

Adirondack
Mtns.

Montpelier

Rutland

NEW YORK

Green Mtns.

Albany Troy

Connecticut R.

Berlin

White
Mtns.

Mt. Washington

NEW
HAMPSHIRE

Concord

Manchester

Merrimack R.

Worcester

Pittsfield

MASSACHUSETTS

Hartford

Waterbury CONNECTICUT

Bridgeport New Haven New London

Appalachian Mtns.

Catskill
Mtns.

Hudson R.

NEW JERSEY

New York City

Delaware R.

Trenton

Long I. Sound

Long Island

St. John R.

Fort Kent

Presque Isle

NEW BRUNSWICK

Houlton

St. John R.

Mt. Katahdin

Fredericton

Moosehead Lake

Kennebec R.

Penobscot R.

Longfellow Mtns.

MAINE

Saint John

Eastport

Bangor

Bay of Fundy

Augusta

Mt. Desert I.

NOVA SCOTIA

Lewiston

Gulf of Maine

Portland

Biddeford

Portsmouth

Boston

Cape Cod

Providence

Newport

RHODE ISLAND

Block I.

Martha's Vineyard I.

Nantucket I.

ATLANTIC
OCEAN

N
W TFK E
S

0   100 miles

0   150 kilometers

A B C D E F G

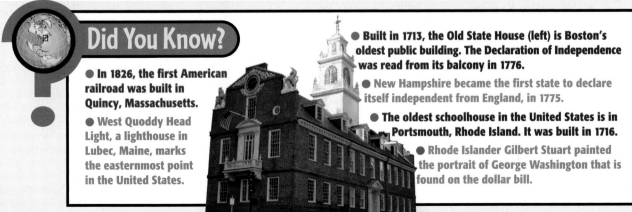

Did You Know?

● In 1826, the first American railroad was built in Quincy, Massachusetts.

● West Quoddy Head Light, a lighthouse in Lubec, Maine, marks the easternmost point in the United States.

● Built in 1713, the Old State House (left) is Boston's oldest public building. The Declaration of Independence was read from its balcony in 1776.

● New Hampshire became the first state to declare itself independent from England, in 1775.

● The oldest schoolhouse in the United States is in Portsmouth, Rhode Island. It was built in 1716.

● Rhode Islander Gilbert Stuart painted the portrait of George Washington that is found on the dollar bill.

United States of America
Middle Atlantic

The Middle Atlantic region is the most ethnically diverse, densely populated area of the United States. From New York to Delaware, people of every race and religion live in a colorful, cultural mix.

New York City is the nation's largest city, with more than 8 million residents. It is home to the United Nations and many international companies and organizations. It is also the country's financial capital. Philadelphia, the fifth-largest city in the U.S., is the birthplace of the nation. It was there that the Declaration of Independence was drafted in 1776 and the U.S. Constitution was written in 1787. Washington, D.C., the nation's capital, lies on the Potomac River, nestled between Maryland and Virginia. Washington is a federal city rather than a state; it belongs to the entire nation.

New York City's famous skyline

Outside the big cities, the Middle Atlantic region has fertile farmland. Pennsylvania has the largest rural population in the United States and is a major producer of milk, eggs and poultry. Farmland covers some 20% of New Jersey.

Industry and tourism are equally important to the region. New Jersey and Delaware are major pharmaceutical and chemical manufacturers. Maryland, famous for its delicious fresh crabs and shellfish, also produces many electronic goods and metals. New York City, with its theaters and museums, draws many visitors.

Data Bank

DELAWARE
AREA: 1,955 sq mi (5,153 sq km)
POPULATION: 853,476
CAPITAL: Dover
MOTTO: Liberty and independence

MARYLAND
AREA: 9,775 sq mi (25,316 sq km)
POPULATION: 5,615,727
CAPITAL: Annapolis
MOTTO: *Fatti maschii, parole femine*
(Manly deeds, womanly words)

NEW JERSEY
AREA: 7,419 sq mi (19,215 sq km)
POPULATION: 8,724,560
CAPITAL: Trenton
MOTTO: Liberty and prosperity

NEW YORK
AREA: 47,224 sq mi (122,310 sq km)
POPULATION: 19,306,183
CAPITAL: Albany
MOTTO: *Excelsior* (Ever upward)

PENNSYLVANIA
AREA: 44,820 sq mi (116,083 sq km)
POPULATION: 12,440,621
CAPITAL: Harrisburg
MOTTO: Virtue, liberty and independence

WASHINGTON, D.C.
AREA: 68 sq mi (177 sq km)
POPULATION: 581,530
MOTTO: *Justitia omnibus* (Justice to all)

Maryland's Chesapeake Bay at sunset

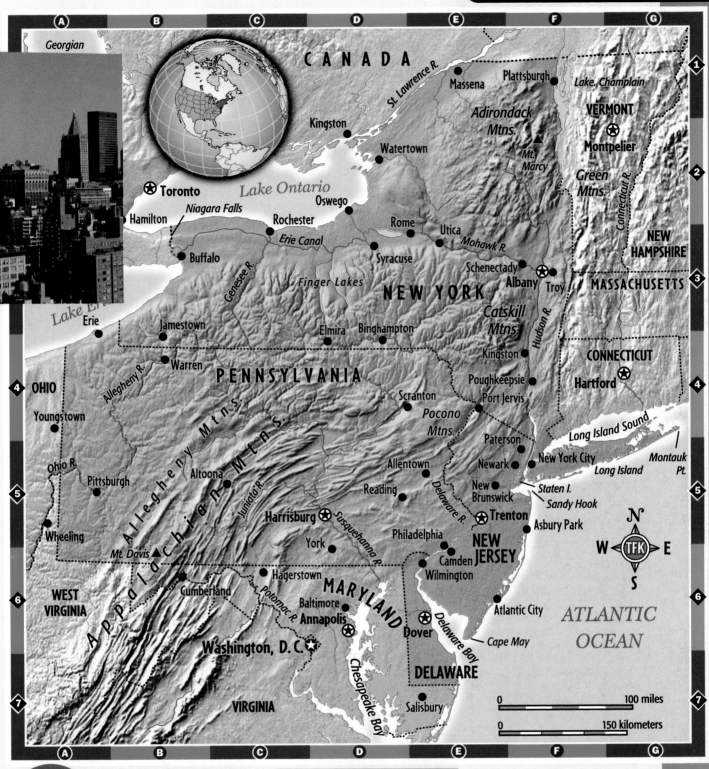

Georgian

CANADA

Massena
Plattsburgh
Lake Champlain

St. Lawrence R.

Kingston

Adirondack
Mtns.

VERMONT
⊛ Montpelier

Watertown

Mt.
Marcy ▲

Green
Mtns.

Connecticut R.

NEW
HAMPSHIRE

⊛ Toronto

Niagara Falls

Lake Ontario

Oswego

Hamilton

Rochester

Rome

Utica

Mohawk R.

Buffalo

Erie Canal

Syracuse

Schenectady
⊛ Albany   Troy

MASSACHUSETTS

Genesee R.

Finger Lakes

NEW YORK

Catskill
Mtns.

Hudson R.

Lake Erie

Erie

Jamestown

Elmira   Binghampton

Kingston

CONNECTICUT

Poughkeepsie

Hartford ⊛

OHIO

Warren

Allegheny R.

PENNSYLVANIA

Scranton

Port Jervis

Pocono
Mtns.

Long Island Sound

Youngstown

Paterson

Long Island

Montauk
Pt.

Ohio R.

Allentown

Newark

New York City

Pittsburgh

Altoona

Reading

Allegheny Mtns.

Appalachian Mtns.

Juniata R.

Delaware R.

New
Brunswick

Staten I.

Sandy Hook

Wheeling

Mt. Davis ▲

Harrisburg ⊛

Susquehanna R.

Trenton ⊛

Asbury Park

N
W ⊛TFK E
S

York

Philadelphia

NEW
JERSEY

Camden

Hagerstown

Wilmington

WEST
VIRGINIA

Cumberland

Potomac R.

MARYLAND

Baltimore

Atlantic City

Annapolis ⊛

Dover ⊛

Delaware Bay

ATLANTIC
OCEAN

Washington, D.C. ⊛

Cape May

Chesapeake Bay

DELAWARE

VIRGINIA

Salisbury

0   100 miles
0   150 kilometers

Did You Know?

● Annapolis, Maryland, is home to the U.S. Naval Academy. It was founded in 1845.

● Delaware, the second-smallest state, was the first to ratify the U.S. Constitution, in 1787.

● New Jersey has the highest population density of any state in the nation.

● The Liberty Bell (left), housed in Philadelphia, Pennsylvania, cracked in 1835 when it was rung to announce the death of Supreme Court Chief Justice John Marshall.

● In 1961, the 23rd Amendment to the U.S. Constitution gave the citizens of Washington, D.C., the right to vote. Washington's residents cast their first ballots for President and Vice President in 1964.

United States of America
Midwest

A Great Lake:
Boats on Lake Michigan in Chicago

Tucked in the middle of the United States between the East Coast and the West Coast are the 12 states that make up the Midwest. Much of the terrain in the Midwest is flat. Rich, fertile soil and an abundance of crops have earned the region its nickname, the nation's breadbasket. Farmers here grow wheat, oats, corn and potatoes, among other crops.

The population of the Midwest grew dramatically in the 19th century. People from the Eastern states moved there as well as immigrants from Germany, Sweden and Norway. Today, the population, especially in large urban centers, is ethnically and culturally diverse.

Chicago is the biggest city in the Midwest and the nation's third largest. The city serves as a major hub for train and airline passengers. One of the country's tallest buildings, the Sears Tower, looms over Chicago's imposing skyline. Other large cities contribute to the vitality of the region. The U.S. automobile industry is based in Detroit, Michigan. Each year, Indianapolis, Indiana, hosts the Indianapolis 500, a car race.

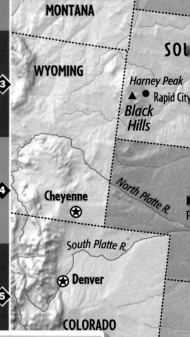

MONTANA

WYOMING

Harney Peak
▲ ● Rapid City
Black Hills

NO

SOU

Cheyenne ✪

North Platte R.

South Platte R.

✪ Denver

COLORADO

XAS

miles

neters

Data Bank

ILLINOIS
AREA: 55,593 sq mi (143,987 sq km)
POPULATION: 12,831,970
CAPITAL: Springfield
MOTTO: State sovereignty, national union

INDIANA
AREA: 35,870 sq mi (92,904 sq km)
POPULATION: 6,313,520
CAPITAL: Indianapolis
MOTTO: The crossroads of America

IOWA
AREA: 55,875 sq mi (144,716 sq km)
POPULATION: 2,982,085
CAPITAL: Des Moines
MOTTO: Our liberties we prize and our rights we will maintain

KANSAS
AREA: 81,823 sq mi (211,922 sq km)
POPULATION: 2,764,075
CAPITAL: Topeka
MOTTO: Ad astra per aspera (To the stars through difficulties)

MICHIGAN
AREA: 56,809 sq mi (147,135 sq km)
POPULATION: 10,095,643
CAPITAL: Lansing
MOTTO: Si quaeris peninsulam amoenam circumspice (If you seek a pleasant peninsula, look around you)

MINNESOTA
AREA: 79,617 sq mi (206,207 sq km)
POPULATION: 5,167,101
CAPITAL: Saint Paul
MOTTO: L'Etoile du nord (The north star)

NEBRASKA
AREA: 76,878 sq mi (199,113 sq km)
POPULATION: 1,768,331
CAPITAL: Lincoln
MOTTO: Equality before the law

NORTH DAKOTA
AREA: 70,704 sq mi (183,123 sq km)
POPULATION: 635,867
CAPITAL: Bismarck
MOTTO: Liberty and union, now and forever: one and inseparable

OHIO
AREA: 40,953 sq mi (106,067 sq km)
POPULATION: 11,478,006
CAPITAL: Columbus
MOTTO: With God all things are possible

SOUTH DAKOTA
AREA: 75,898 sq mi (196,575 sq km)
POPULATION: 781,919
CAPITAL: Pierre
MOTTO: Under God the people rule

WISCONSIN
AREA: 97,105 sq mi (251,501 sq km)
POPULATION: 5,556,506
CAPITAL: Madison
MOTTO: Equal rights

Amber Waves of Grain:
A farm near Salina, Kansas

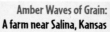

Did You Know?

- South Dakota is the home of the Sioux Indians. The Sioux greeting *How, kola!* means "Hello, friend!"
- Chewing gum was invented in Ohio in 1869.
- Minnesota has more recreational boats per person than any other state. There is about one boat for every six people.

- Michigan's shoreline is longer than that of any other state except Alaska.
- Kool-Aid is the official soft drink of Nebraska. It was invented in Hastings in 1927.
- Wisconsin produces more milk than any other state.

27

United States of America
South

Old Kentucky Home: Horses at play on a farm

At one time, the states that make up the Southern part of the United States were best known for their rolling fields of cotton, tobacco, soy beans and other vegetables. In the 1800s, cotton was king. Plantation owners relied on slave labor to grow and harvest the crop. From 1861 to 1865, the Southern states fought the Northern states in the bloody and destructive Civil War.

Today, agriculture is still an important industry. But Southern cities such as Atlanta, Georgia, and Miami, Florida, are commercial, industrial and cultural centers. In Miami as well as New Orleans, Louisiana, and Nashville, Tennessee, the sounds of uniquely Southern music set the rhythm and pace for this section of the nation.

Southerners are proud of their region's scenic beauty. The Great Smoky Mountains National Park in North Carolina and Tennessee attracts more than 9 million visitors each year. The park has more than 800 mi (1,290 km) of trails. Everglades National Park in Florida is the only subtropical preserve in North America. It is the only place in the world where alligators and crocodiles live side by side.

Data Bank

A riverboat on the Mississippi River

ALABAMA
AREA: 50,750 sq mi (131,443 sq km)
POPULATION: 4,599,030
CAPITAL: Montgomery
MOTTO: *Audemus jura nostra defendere* (We dare defend our rights)

ARKANSAS
AREA: 52,075 sq mi (134,874 sq km)
POPULATION: 2,810,872
CAPITAL: Little Rock
MOTTO: *Regnat populus* (The people rule)

FLORIDA
AREA: 54,153 sq mi (140,256 sq km)
POPULATION: 18,089,888
CAPITAL: Tallahassee
MOTTO: In God we trust

GEORGIA
AREA: 57,919 sq mi (150,010 sq km)
POPULATION: 9,363,941
CAPITAL: Atlanta
MOTTO: Wisdom, justice and moderation

KENTUCKY
AREA: 39,732 sq mi (102,907 sq km)
POPULATION: 4,206,074
CAPITAL: Frankfort
MOTTO: United we stand, divided we fall

LOUISIANA
AREA: 43,566 sq mi (112,836 sq km)
POPULATION: 4,287,768
CAPITAL: Baton Rouge
MOTTO: Union, justice and confidence

MISSISSIPPI
AREA: 46,914 sq mi (121,506 sq km)
POPULATION: 2,910,540
CAPITAL: Jackson
MOTTO: *Virtute et armis* (By valor and arms)

MISSOURI
AREA: 68,898 sq mi (178,446 sq km)
POPULATION: 5,842,713
CAPITAL: Jefferson City
MOTTO: *Salu populi suprema lex esto* (The welfare of the people shall be the supreme law)

NORTH CAROLINA
AREA: 48,718 sq mi (126,180 sq km)
POPULATION: 8,856,505
CAPITAL: Raleigh
MOTTO: *Esse quam videri* (To be rather than to seem)

SOUTH CAROLINA
AREA: 30,111 sq mi (77,988 sq km)
POPULATION: 4,321,249
CAPITAL: Columbia
MOTTO: *Animis opibusque parati* (Prepared in mind and resources) and *Dum spiro spero* (While I breathe, I hope)

TENNESSEE
AREA: 41,220 sq mi (106,759 sq km)
POPULATION: 6,038,803
CAPITAL: Nashville
MOTTO: Agriculture and commerce

VIRGINIA
AREA: 39,598 sq mi (102,558 sq km)
POPULATION: 7,642,884
CAPITAL: Richmond
MOTTO: *Sic semper tyrannis* (Thus always to tyrants)

WEST VIRGINIA
AREA: 24,087 sq mi (62,384 sq km)
POPULATION: 1,818,470
CAPITAL: Charleston
MOTTO: *Montani semper liberi* (Mountaineers are always free)

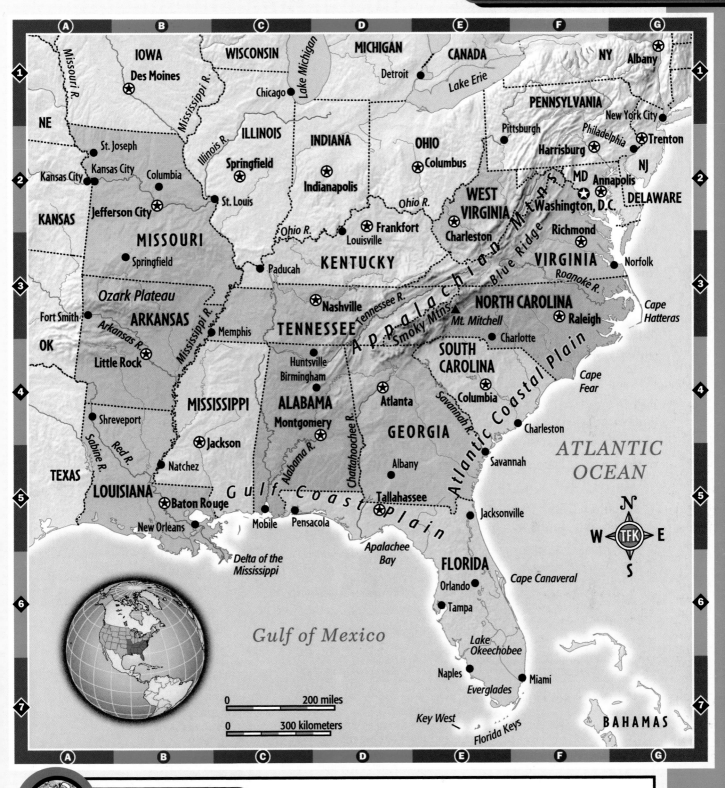

IOWA
Des Moines
WISCONSIN
MICHIGAN
Detroit
Lake Erie
CANADA
NY
Albany
NE
Chicago
Lake Michigan
Missouri R.
Mississippi R.
PENNSYLVANIA
New York City
Pittsburgh
Philadelphia
Trenton
ILLINOIS
INDIANA
OHIO
Harrisburg
NJ
Illinois R.
St. Joseph
Springfield
Indianapolis
Columbus
MD
Annapolis
DELAWARE
Kansas City
Kansas City
Columbia
St. Louis
WEST
VIRGINIA
Washington, D.C.
KANSAS
Jefferson City
Ohio R.
Frankfort
Louisville
Charleston
Richmond
MISSOURI
Paducah
KENTUCKY
Virginia
Norfolk
Springfield
Ozark Plateau
Appalachian Mts.
Blue Ridge
Roanoke R.
Cape Hatteras
Fort Smith
ARKANSAS
Arkansas R.
Mississippi R.
Nashville
Tennessee R.
Smoky Mtns.
Mt. Mitchell
NORTH CAROLINA
Raleigh
OK
Memphis
TENNESSEE
Charlotte
Little Rock
Huntsville
Birmingham
SOUTH
CAROLINA
Atlantic Coastal Plain
Cape Fear
MISSISSIPPI
ALABAMA
Atlanta
Columbia
Shreveport
Montgomery
GEORGIA
Charleston
Jackson
Chattahoochee R.
Savannah R.
Savannah
ATLANTIC
OCEAN
Red R.
Sabine R.
Natchez
Alabama R.
Albany
TEXAS
LOUISIANA
Gulf Coast Plain
Tallahassee
Jacksonville
Baton Rouge
N
New Orleans
Mobile
Pensacola
W TFK E
S
Delta of the
Mississippi
Apalachee
Bay
FLORIDA
Cape Canaveral
Orlando
Gulf of Mexico
Tampa
Lake
Okeechobee
Naples
Miami
Everglades
BAHAMAS
0   200 miles
Key West
0   300 kilometers
Florida Keys

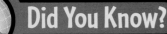

Did You Know?

- Jamestown, Virginia, was the first permanent English settlement in North America.

- Panthers live in the Florida Everglades. There are fewer than 50 panthers left in the wild.

- In 1860, South Carolina was the first state to secede from the Union. Mississippi, Florida, Alabama, Georgia, Louisiana, Texas, Virginia, Arkansas, Tennessee and North Carolina joined it to form the Confederacy that fought against the North in the Civil War.

- Coca-Cola was first bottled in Vicksburg, Mississippi, in 1894.

- The Grand Ole Opry is the world's longest-running live radio show.

- *Mississippi* is a Native American word meaning "great water."

United States of America
Southwest

The Southwest is a region of dry desert and high plains. It is rich in Native American and Hispanic culture. Geographically, the region is dominated by Texas, the second-largest state in the U.S. and an industrial giant. When it comes to oil production and cattle ranching, the Lone Star State leads the nation. Texas is also tops in farmland and in the production of cotton and cottonseed oil. The state is home to the Johnson Space Center in Houston.

Arizona's Montezuma Castle was built by Sinagua Indians more than 600 years ago.

To the north of Texas lies Oklahoma, another state that struck it rich with oil. Farming and cattle ranching are also vital to the state's economy. Wheat is Oklahoma's main crop. Oklahoma's Native American population—273,230—is second only to California's—333,346.

In New Mexico and Arizona, pueblos (flat-roofed stone or adobe dwellings) still dot the desert landscape, along with giant saguaro cacti. Many American Indians live in the area, including people belonging to the Hopi, Zuni and Navajo tribes. Arizona is perhaps best known for the Grand Canyon, the world's largest gorge. Carved by the Colorado River over 6 million to 10 million years ago, the etched rocky walls turn brilliant shades of red, orange and yellow at sunset each day.

Data Bank

ARIZONA
AREA: 113,642 sq mi (296,400 sq km)
POPULATION: 6,166,318
CAPITAL: Phoenix
MOTTO: *Ditat deus* (God enriches)

NEW MEXICO
AREA: 121,365 sq mi (314,334 sq km)
POPULATION: 1,954,599
CAPITAL: Santa Fe
MOTTO: *Crescit eundo* (It grows as it goes)

OKLAHOMA
AREA: 68,679 sq mi (177,880 sq km)
POPULATION: 3,579,212
CAPITAL: Oklahoma City
MOTTO: *Labor omnia vincit* (Labor conquers all things)

TEXAS
AREA: 261,914 sq mi (678,358 sq km)
POPULATION: 23,507,783
CAPITAL: Austin
MOTTO: Friendship

OREG

NEVADA

Carson City

CALIFORNIA

Los Angeles

San Diego

Tijuana

PACIFIC OCEAN

Mission Control at Houston's Johnson Space Center

IDAHO

WYOMING

Cheyenne

NEBRASKA

North Platte R.

IOWA

Missouri R.

Great Salt Lake

Salt Lake City

Denver

Lincoln

Topeka

Kansas City

Missouri R.

Kansas City

UTAH

KANSAS

Kansas City

MISSOURI

Great Basin

N W E S TFK

COLORADO

Arkansas R.

Colorado R.

Colorado Plateau

Great Plains

ARKANSAS

Grand Canyon

egas

Humphreys Peak

Santa Fe

Gallup

Oklahoma City

Tulsa

Canadian R.

Flagstaff

Albuquerque

Amarillo

OKLAHOMA

Ouachita Mtns.

ARIZONA

Sacramento Mtns.

NEW MEXICO

Lawton

Red R.

Phoenix

Black Range

Lubbock

Dallas

Sabine R.

Colorado R.

Gila R.

Sierra Blanca

Brazos R.

Fort Worth

Tyler

LA

Yuma

Llano Estacado

TEXAS

Waco

Tucson

Douglas

El Paso

Pecos R.

Colorado R.

Davis Mtns.

Edwards Plateau

Austin

Houston

Galveston

Gulf Coastal Plain

Sierra Madre Occidental

Chihuahua

Rio Grande

San Antonio

Hermosillo

Nueces R.

Corpus Christi

Laredo

Baja California

Gulf of California

MEXICO

Sierra Madre Oriental

Gulf of Mexico

Monterrey

Matamoros

| 0 | | 300 miles |

| 0 | | 450 kilometers |

Did You Know?

● The Chapel of San Miguel, built in Santa Fe, New Mexico, in the 17th century, is known as the oldest church in the United States.

● The cowboy hat is based on the Mexican sombrero. The first cowboys raised cattle in Texas when the state still belonged to Mexico.

● In the 1830s, what is now Oklahoma was set aside as Indian Territory for Native Americans. Today the state is still home to more than 60 tribes.

● The Grand Canyon measures 277 mi (446 km) long, up to 18 mi (29 km) wide and more than 5,000 ft (1,500 m) deep. Some 4 million people visit the gorge each year!

United States of America
West

El Capitan in Yosemite National Park

The Mississippi River forms a natural boundary between the American East and the American West. Before the 1840s, very few pioneers had ventured beyond the Mississippi. By 1900, settlers had built cities all across the West and were laying claim to Indian territories. The Gold Rush of 1849 brought an avalanche of miners to California. The following year, California became the first state west of the Mississippi.

Stories of the Old West are part of the heritage of the United States. So, too, are the natural wonders of the region. The area's towering mountains, wide deserts, canyons and waterfalls inspired the creation of the U.S. National Park System, which includes Yellowstone in Montana and Yosemite in California.

The most western of all states, Hawaii, did not become a state until 1959. Located in the South Pacific, Hawaii is a string of volcanic islands with its own history and culture.

The Seattle Space Needle

PACIFIC OCEAN

0 — 300 mi
0 — 450 kilometers

HAWAII

Kauai
Oahu
Honolulu
Molokai
Lanai

PACIFIC OCEAN

50 miles

Data Bank

CALIFORNIA
AREA: 155,973 sq mi (403,970 sq km)
POPULATION: 36,457,549
CAPITAL: Sacramento
MOTTO: Eureka! (I have found it!)

COLORADO
AREA: 103,730 sq mi (268,660 sq km)
POPULATION: 4,753,377
CAPITAL: Denver
MOTTO: Nil sine numine (Nothing without providence)

HAWAII
AREA: 6,423 sq mi (16,637 sq km)
POPULATION: 1,285,498
CAPITAL: Honolulu
MOTTO: Ua mau ke ea o ka aina i ka pono (The life of the land is perpetuated in righteousness)

IDAHO
AREA: 82,751 sq mi (214,325 sq km)
POPULATION: 1,466,465
CAPITAL: Boise
MOTTO: Esto perpetua (It endures forever)

MONTANA
AREA: 145,556 sq mi (376,991 sq km)
POPULATION: 944,632
CAPITAL: Helena
MOTTO: Oro y plata (Gold and silver)

NEVADA
AREA: 109,806 sq mi (284,397 sq km)
POPULATION: 2,495,529
CAPITAL: Carson City
MOTTO: All for our country

OREGON
AREA: 96,003 sq mi (248,647 sq km)
POPULATION: 3,700,758
CAPITAL: Salem
MOTTO: Alis volat propriis (She flies with her own wings)

UTAH
AREA: 82,168 sq mi (212,816 sq km)
POPULATION: 2,550,063
CAPITAL: Salt Lake City
MOTTO: Industry

WASHINGTON
AREA: 66,582 sq mi (172,448 sq km)
POPULATION: 6,395,798
CAPITAL: Olympia
MOTTO: Al-ki (By and by)

WYOMING
AREA: 97,105 sq mi (251,501 sq km)
POPULATION: 515,004
CAPITAL: Cheyenne
MOTTO: Equal rights

C D E F G H I

CANADA

Vancouver
Victoria
Olympic Mtns.
WASHINGTON
Seattle
Olympia ☆
Mt. Rainier ▲
Mt. St. Helens (volcano) ▲
Portland
Salem ☆
Eugene
Columbia R.
Spokane
Moscow
Snake R.
Missoula
Great Falls
Milk R.
Missouri R.
MONTANA
Helena ☆
Billings
Yellowstone R.
NORTH DAKOTA
Missouri R.
Cascade Range
Bitterroot Range
Salmon R.
IDAHO
Boise
Idaho Falls
Snake R.
Yellowstone National Park
Cody
Bighorn R.
Sheridan
SOUTH DAKOTA
Klamath Falls
OREGON
Coastal Ranges
Eureka
Jackson
Casper
WYOMING
ROCKY
Green River
Cheyenne ☆
N. Platte R.
NEBRASKA
Humboldt R.
Great Salt Lake
Ogden
Elko
Ely
Salt Lake City ☆
Green R.
Boulder
S. Platte R.
Denver ☆
KANSAS
Reno
Carson City ☆
Great Basin
UTAH
COLORADO
Mtns.
Mt. Elbert ▲
▲ Pikes Peak
Arkansas R.
Pueblo
Sacramento Valley
Sierra Nevada
Sacramento ☆
NEVADA
Zion National Park
Bryce Canyon National Park
Colorado R.
Colorado Plateau
San Francisco
Oakland
Modesto
San Joaquin Valley
Fresno
Death Valley
Las Vegas
CALIFORNIA
Bakersfield
Mt. Whitney
Mojave Desert
Lake Mead
Grand Canyon
NEW MEXICO
Santa Fe ☆
TEXAS
Maui
Santa Barbara
Los Angeles
Salton Sea
San Bernardino
ARIZONA
Phoenix ☆
Gila R.
Rio Grande
awaii
Hilo
Mauna Kea (volcano)
San Diego
Tijuana
El Paso

MEXICO

C D E F G H I

1 2 3 4 5 6 7

Did You Know?

- The San Andreas Fault is a huge crack in the earth's crust that stretches for 600 mi (966 km) through the state of California. The fault causes dozens of earthquakes each year.

- The Seattle Space Needle, built in 1962 for the Century 21 Exposition, is a marvel of engineering. It includes a revolving restaurant and a gas torch that is 600 ft (183 m) high.

- Hawaii is famous for its huge, tubular waves, which are great for surfers.

- The hula originated in Hawaii as a dance to honor the gods.

- The ten national forests in Idaho cover 20.4 million acres (8.2 million hectares).

Mexico and Central America

Just south of the United States lies Mexico and Central America, the narrow landmass that connects North America and South America. From Mexico's dry plateaus to Costa Rica's tropical rain forests, this is an area of varied terrain and climate.

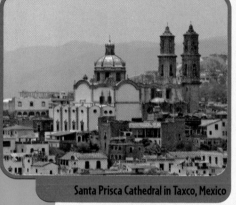
Santa Prisca Cathedral in Taxco, Mexico

Mexico was once home to several great civilizations, including the Mayan and the Aztec. Today, Mexico's language, food, culture and architecture reflect its rich history: magnificent temples and pyramids mix with sleek skyscrapers and luxurious beachfront resorts. Mexico City, the nation's capital, is the oldest continuously inhabited city in the Western Hemisphere.

To the south of Mexico sit the seven small countries that make up Central America: Belize, Costa Rica, El Salvador, Guatemala, Honduras, Nicaragua and Panama. Combined, they are less than half the size of Mexico. Rare and exotic wildlife can be found throughout the region. In tiny Costa Rica alone, there are 850 species of birds, 136 species of snakes and 1,500 species of orchids.

Data Bank

MEXICO
AREA: 761,600 sq mi (1,972,550 sq km)
POPULATION: 107,449,525
CAPITAL: Mexico City
LANGUAGES: Spanish, Mayan, Nahuatl, other native languages

BELIZE
AREA: 8,867 sq mi (22,966 sq km)
POPULATION: 287,730
CAPITAL: Belmopan
LANGUAGES: English (official), Creole, Spanish, Mayan, Garifuna

COSTA RICA
AREA: 19,730 sq mi (51,100 sq km)
POPULATION: 4,075,261
CAPITAL: San José
LANGUAGES: Spanish (official), English

EL SALVADOR
AREA: 8,124 sq mi (21,040)
POPULATION: 6,822,378
CAPITAL: San Salvador
LANGUAGES: Spanish, Nahuatl

GUATEMALA
AREA: 42,042 sq mi (108,890 sq km)
POPULATION: 12,293,545
CAPITAL: Guatemala City
LANGUAGES: Spanish, native languages

HONDURAS
AREA: 43,278 sq mi (112,090 sq km)
POPULATION: 7,326,496
CAPITAL: Tegucigalpa
LANGUAGES: Spanish, Amerindian dialects

NICARAGUA
AREA: 49,998 sq mi (129,494 sq km)
POPULATION: 5,570,129
CAPITAL: Managua
LANGUAGES: Spanish (official), English and native languages on Atlantic coast

PANAMA
AREA: 30,193 sq km (78,200 sq km)
POPULATION: 3,191,319
CAPITAL: Panama City
LANGUAGES: Spanish (official), English

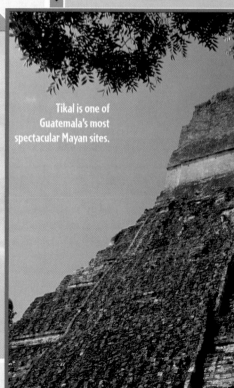
Tikal is one of Guatemala's most spectacular Mayan sites.

Mexico and Central America

C **D** **E** **F** **G** **H** **I**

NM OK AR TN NC

UNITED STATES OF AMERICA

El Paso TX

Chihuahua

MS AL GA FL

Mississippi R.

LA

Houston

New Orleans

Miami

ATLANTIC OCEAN

Gulf of Mexico

SC

1

2

3

Río Grande

M E X I C O Laredo
Nuevo Laredo

Durango Monterrey Matamoros

Guadalajara León

Santiago R.

Paricutín

Sierra Madre Oriental

Mexican Plateau

Tampico

Mexico City

Citlaltépetl

Puebla

Veracruz

Bay of Campeche

Mérida

Campeche

Yucatán Peninsula

Cancun

Chichén Itzá (ruin)

Yucatán Channel

Havana

CUBA

JAMAICA

Kingston

Caribbean Sea

4

Oaxaca

Acapulco

Sierra Madre del Sur

Gulf of Tehuantepec

Tajumulco Volcano

GUATEMALA

Guatemala City

San Salvador

EL SALVADOR

Cobán

Belize City

Belmopan

BELIZE

Gulf of Honduras

HONDURAS

San Pedro Sula

Tegucigalpa

NICARAGUA

León

Managua

Lake Nicaragua

Granada

Puerto Cabezas

Bluefields

5

PACIFIC OCEAN

San José

Puntarenas

COSTA RICA

David

Puerto Limón

Colón

Panama Canal

Panama City

PANAMA

6

7

0 ————— 400 miles

0 ————— 600 kilometers

N W TFK E S

D **E** **F** **G** **H** **I**

Did You Know?

Costa Rica's Arenal volcano

● There are nearly 100 volcanoes in Mexico and Central America.

● The Panama Canal, which connects the Atlantic and Pacific oceans, took more than ten years and some 56,000 workers to build. The U.S. owned it from 1914 until December 31, 1999, when it was given to the Panamanian people.

● At its narrowest point, in Panama, Central America is just 50 mi (80 km) wide.

● Some of the largest and possibly oldest Mayan ruins can be found in Tikal, Guatemala. The ancient site has thousands of structures, including spectacular temples and pyramids that were used in the first *Star Wars* movie.

● Belize's barrier reef, the largest in the Western Hemisphere, stretches across 185 mi (298 km).

Caribbean

Just Beachy: The Dominican Republic

FLORIDA (U.S.)

Miami

Straits of Florida

Havana ✪

Pinar del Río

Cienfuegos

I. of Pines

Cayman Is. (U.K.)

The Caribbean Islands, also called the West Indies, are known for their sparkling blue waters, white sand beaches and gentle tropical breezes. The multiethnic people of the Caribbean are proud of their contributions to the fields of literature, dance and music.

There are thousands of islands in the Caribbean, including 13 nations and many colonial dependencies, territories and possessions. Just 90 mi (145 km) off the coast of Florida lies the Caribbean's largest island, Cuba. Since 1960, relations between the governments of Cuba and the United States have been strained.

Data Bank

The West Indies

AREA: The islands of the West Indies are an archipelago approximately 2,000 mi (3,200 km) long. There are four island chains in the West Indies: the Bahamas, the Greater Antilles and the eastern and southern islands of the Lesser Antilles.
POPULATION: 34.5 million
LANGUAGES: Spanish, French, English, Dutch, Creole, local dialects

Countries

ANTIGUA AND BARBUDA
AREA: 171 sq mi (443 sq km)
POPULATION: 69,108
CAPITAL: Saint John's
LANGUAGES: English (official), local dialects

BARBADOS
AREA: 166 sq mi (431 sq km)
POPULATION: 279,912
CAPITAL: Bridgetown
LANGUAGE: English

BAHAMAS
AREA: 5,380 sq mi (13,940 sq km)
POPULATION: 303,770
CAPITAL: Nassau
LANGUAGE: English

CUBA
AREA: 42,803 sq mi (110,860 sq km)
POPULATION: 11,382,820
CAPITAL: Havana
LANGUAGE: Spanish

DOMINICA
AREA: 290 sq mi (754 sq km)
POPULATION: 68,910
CAPITAL: Roseau
LANGUAGES: English (official), French patois

DOMINICAN REPUBLIC
AREA: 18,815 sq mi (48,730 sq km)
POPULATION: 9,183,984
CAPITAL: Santo Domingo
LANGUAGE: Spanish

GRENADA
AREA: 133 sq mi (344 sq km)
POPULATION: 89,703
CAPITAL: Saint George's
LANGUAGES: English (official), French patois

HAITI
AREA: 10,714 sq mi (27,750 sq km)
POPULATION: 8,308,504
CAPITAL: Port-au-Prince
LANGUAGES: French, Creole (both official)

JAMAICA
AREA: 4,244 sq mi (10,991 sq km)
POPULATION: 2,758,124
CAPITAL: Kingston
LANGUAGES: English, patois English

SAINT KITTS AND NEVIS
AREA: 101 sq mi (261 sq km)
POPULATION: 39,129
CAPITAL: Basseterre
LANGUAGE: English

SAINT LUCIA
AREA: 238 sq mi (616 sq km)
POPULATION: 168,458
CAPITAL: Castries
LANGUAGES: English (official), French patois

SAINT VINCENT AND THE GRENADINES
AREA: 150 sq mi (389 sq km)
POPULATION: 117,848
CAPITAL: Kingstown
LANGUAGES: English, French patois

TRINIDAD AND TOBAGO
AREA: 1,980 sq mi (5,128 sq km)
POPULATION: 1,065,842
CAPITAL: Port-of-Spain
LANGUAGES: English (official), Hindi, French, Spanish, Chinese

U.S. Territories

PUERTO RICO (Commonwealth)
AREA: 3,515 sq mi (9,104 sq km)
POPULATION: 3,927,776
CAPITAL: San Juan
LANGUAGES: Spanish, English

VIRGIN ISLANDS (Unincorporated territory)
AREA: 135 sq mi (349 sq km)
POPULATION: 108,605
CAPITAL: Charlotte Amalie
LANGUAGES: English (official), Creole, Spanish

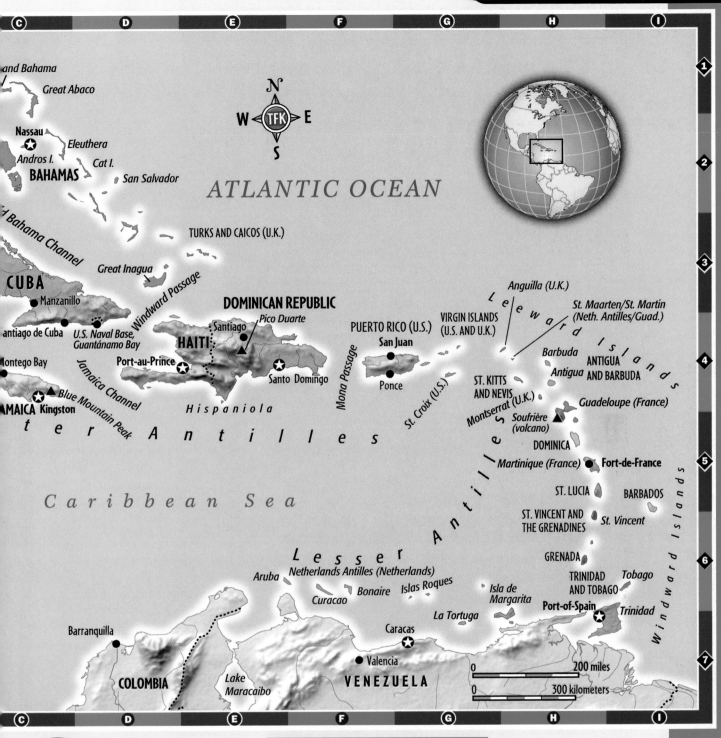

ATLANTIC OCEAN

and Bahama
Great Abaco
Nassau ✪
Eleuthera
Andros I.
Cat I.
San Salvador
BAHAMAS

d Bahama Channel

Great Inagua

TURKS AND CAICOS (U.K.)

CUBA
Manzanillo
antiago de Cuba
U.S. Naval Base,
Guantánamo Bay

Montego Bay

Jamaica Channel

AMAICA Kingston
▲ Blue Mountain Peak

Windward Passage

DOMINICAN REPUBLIC
Santiago
Pico Duarte ▲
HAITI
Port-au-Prince ✪
Santo Domingo ✪

Hispaniola

ter Antilles

Mona Passage

PUERTO RICO (U.S.)
San Juan ●
Ponce ●

VIRGIN ISLANDS
(U.S. AND U.K.)

St. Croix (U.S.)

Anguilla (U.K.)

Leeward Islands

St. Maarten/St. Martin
(Neth. Antilles/Guad.)

Barbuda

ANTIGUA AND BARBUDA
Antigua

ST. KITTS AND NEVIS

Montserrat (U.K.)
Soufrière ▲
(volcano)

Guadeloupe (France)

DOMINICA

Martinique (France) ● **Fort-de-France**

ST. LUCIA

ST. VINCENT AND
THE GRENADINES   St. Vincent

BARBADOS

GRENADA

Lesser Antilles

Windward Islands

Caribbean Sea

L e s s e r

Aruba
Netherlands Antilles (Netherlands)
Curacao
Bonaire
Islas Roques

Isla de
Margarita
La Tortuga

TRINIDAD AND TOBAGO
Tobago
Port-of-Spain ✪   Trinidad

Barranquilla ●

Caracas ✪

Valencia ●

COLOMBIA

Lake
Maracaibo

VENEZUELA

0   200 miles
0   300 kilometers

Did You Know?

Havana, Cuba, is the Caribbean's largest city.

● The nations of Haiti and the Dominican Republic share the island of Hispaniola.

● When Christopher Columbus reached the island of Hispaniola in 1492, he believed he was just west of India. That's why the region is called the West Indies.

● The islands of the Caribbean are divided into three long chains called the Bahama Islands,

the Greater Antilles and the Lesser Antilles. The Lesser Antilles includes the Windward and Leeward Islands.

● The native people of the islands are the Taíno and Carib Indians.

● The Bermuda Triangle, also known as the Devil's Triangle, is an area between Bermuda, Puerto Rico and Florida. Many ships and aircraft have mysteriously disappeared in the Bermuda Triangle.

South America

South America, the world's fourth-largest continent, is a region of contrasts and extremes. The world's longest mountain range, the Andes, stretches along the continent's western coast. Even though the equator crosses South America and four-fifths of the continent is located in the tropics, the tall peaks of the Andes remain cold and snow covered year-round. To the east of the Andes lies the world's largest tropical rain forest. The waters of the mighty Amazon River have their source in the mountains of Peru. The river flows across Peru and into Brazil. The Amazon River Basin is hot, humid and rainy. The Atacama Desert in northern Chile is cold and extremely dry.

South America's broad range of climate and terrain offers ideal conditions for a wide variety of plant and animal life. Colorful birds, giant snakes, monkeys and jaguars are among the many creatures that make their home in the lush rain forest. At the southern tip of the continent, seals, penguins and whales swim in the waters of the Southern Ocean. Animals that are found nowhere else on earth, such as Darwin finches and giant tortoises, can be seen on Ecuador's Galápagos Islands.

A toucan in Brazil

Angel Falls in Venezuela

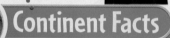

Continent Facts

NUMBER OF COUNTRIES AND TERRITORIES: 12 countries—Argentina, Bolivia, Brazil, Chile, Colombia, Ecuador, Guyana, Paraguay, Peru, Suriname, Uruguay, Venezuela; three territories—Falkland Islands (U.K.), French Guiana (France), South Georgia and the South Sandwich Islands (U.K.)

AREA: 6,878,000 sq mi (17,814,000 sq km)

LONGEST RIVER: Amazon River, 4,000 mi (6,400 km)

LONGEST MOUNTAIN RANGE: Andes Mountains, 5,500 mi (8,900 km)

HIGHEST PEAK: Mount Aconcagua in Argentina, 22,834 ft (6,960 m)

Wow Zone!

● At a length of about 2,700 mi (4,345 km) and an average width of 110 mi (177 km), Chile is the world's longest, thinnest country.

● The Atacama Desert in Chile is the driest place in the world. In some parts of the desert, rain has never been recorded!

● Ushuaia (oo-*sway*-yah), at the southern tip of Argentina, is the southernmost city in the world. It is just 745 mi (1,199 km) from Antarctica.

● At 3,212 ft (979 m), Angel Falls (Salto Angel), in Venezuela, is the highest waterfall in the world.

● Lake Titicaca, right, located 12,500 ft (3,810 m) above sea level between Bolivia and Peru, is the largest fresh-water lake in South America. It is also the highest lake in the world in which large ships can navigate.

● The Amazon River Basin is home to a third of the world's plant and animal species.

CUBA

JAMAICA   HAITI   DOMINICAN REPUBLIC   Puerto Rico (U.S.)   ANTIGUA AND BARBUDA

BELIZE   SAINT KITTS AND NEVIS   GUADELOUPE

HONDURAS   CARIBBEAN SEA   DOMINICA

NICARAGUA   SAINT LUCIA   BARBADOS

COSTA RICA   PANAMA   Aruba   GRENADA   SAINT VINCENT AND THE GRENADINES   ATLANTIC OCEAN

TRINIDAD AND TOBAGO

Barranquilla   Maracaibo   Caracas

Cartagena   Lake Maracaibo   Ciudad Guayana   Georgetown   Paramaribo

Medellín   Orinoco River   VENEZUELA   GUYANA   Cayenne

Bogotá   SURINAME   FRENCH GUIANA

Cali   COLOMBIA   Negro River   Macapá

Esmeraldas   Putumayo River   Manaus   Amazon River   Belém   São Luís   Parnaíba

Equator   Quito   AMAZON   Santarém   Fortaleza

ECUADOR   Iquitos   Benjamin Constant   BASIN

Guayaquil   Amazon River   Natal

Piura   PERU   Cruzeiro do Sul   Selvas   Pôrto Velho   Madeira River   Recife

Trujillo   Ucayali River   Cobija   Riberalta   BRAZIL   Maceió

Lima   Cusco   Xingu River   Tocantins River   São Francisco River   Salvador

Lake Titicaca   La Paz   BOLIVIA   Brasília   Araguaia River

Arequipa   Cochabamba   Santa Cruz   Brazilian Highlands   Belo Horizonte

Arica   Sucre   Paraguay River   Paraná River   São Paulo   Rio de Janeiro

Iquique   PARAGUAY   São Paulo   Curitiba

PACIFIC OCEAN   Antofagasta   Asunción

Formosa   Ciudad del Este

San Miguel de Tucumán   Resistencia   Encarnación   Pôrto Alegre

Paraná River   Salto

CHILE   Córdoba   URUGUAY   ATLANTIC OCEAN

Valparaíso   Rosario   Buenos Aires   Montevideo

Santiago   Río de la Plata

ARGENTINA   Mar del Plata

Concepción   Bahía Blanca

Andes Mts.

Puerto Montt

Comodoro Rivadavia

Strait of Magellan   Stanley

Río Gallegos   **Falkland Is.**

Punta Arenas   **(Islas Malvinas)**

Ushuaia   (Administered by U.K.; claimed by Argentina)

Cape Horn

0 mi.   500 mi.   1,000 mi.

0 km   500 km   1,000 km

Northwestern South America

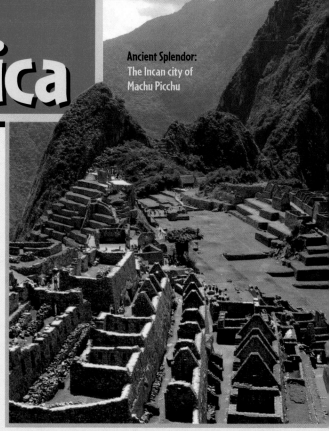

Ancient Splendor:
The Incan city of
Machu Picchu

Years before European explorers arrived in what came to be called the New World, a great civilization flourished in Bolivia, Ecuador and Peru. The Inca people built roads and stone cities that stretched for thousands of miles. In 1533, the city of Cuzco, capital of the powerful Inca empire, came under Spain's rule.

Today, Bolivia, Colombia, Ecuador, Peru and Venezuela are a colorful and vibrant blend of Native Indian and Spanish influences. In the region's cities, visitors can find mansions, churches and forts built during Spanish colonial days and museums boasting pre-Columbian treasures. Spanish is spoken and so are native languages.

This region is rich in more than historic treasures. It is marked by an abundance of natural resources and beauty. Venezuela is South America's biggest oil producer. Colombia is famous for its emeralds and coffee. Only Brazil produces more of the world's coffee than Colombia.

The Amazon rain forest covers half of Peru. Millions of plant and animal species live there. Butterflies, pumas, tropical birds and frogs fill the forest with color and sound. Giant tortoises, blue-footed boobies and iguanas enchant visitors on the Galápagos Islands, which lie 650 mi (1,046 km) off Ecuador's coast.

A blue-footed booby and her babies

Data Bank

BOLIVIA
AREA: 424,162 sq mi (1,098,580 sq km)
POPULATION: 8,989,046
CAPITAL: La Paz (seat of government), Sucre (legal capital)
LANGUAGES: Spanish, Quechua, Aymara (all official)

COLOMBIA
AREA: 439,733 sq mi (1,138,910 sq km)
POPULATION: 43,593,035
CAPITAL: Bogotá
LANGUAGE: Spanish

ECUADOR
AREA: 109,483 sq mi (283,560 sq km)
POPULATION: 13,547,510
CAPITAL: Quito
LANGUAGES: Spanish (official), native languages

PERU
AREA: 496,223 sq mi (1,285,220 sq km)
POPULATION: 28,302,603
CAPITAL: Lima
LANGUAGES: Spanish, Quechua (both official), Aymara

VENEZUELA
AREA: 352,141 sq mi (912,050 sq km)
POPULATION: 25,730,435
CAPITAL: Caracas
LANGUAGES: Spanish (official), native dialects

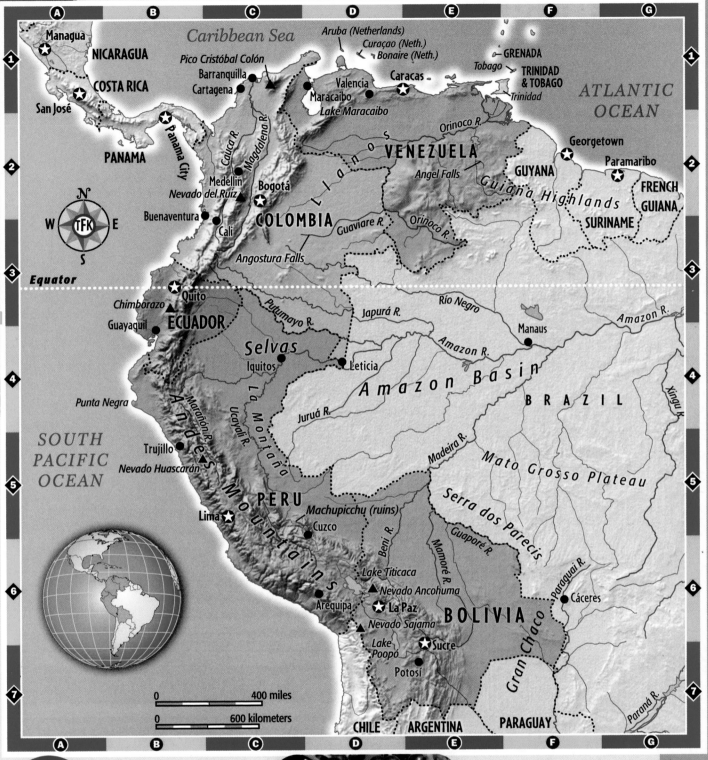

Caribbean Sea

NICARAGUA

Managua

COSTA RICA

San José

PANAMA

Panama City

Pico Cristóbal Colón

Barranquilla

Cartagena

Medellín

Nevado del Ruiz

Buenaventura

Cali

Bogotá

COLOMBIA

Cauca R.

Magdalena R.

Llanos

Aruba (Netherlands)

Curaçao (Neth.)

Bonaire (Neth.)

Valencia

Maracaibo

Lake Maracaibo

Caracas

VENEZUELA

Orinoco R.

Angel Falls

GRENADA

Tobago

TRINIDAD & TOBAGO

Trinidad

ATLANTIC OCEAN

Georgetown

GUYANA

Paramaribo

SURINAME

FRENCH GUIANA

Guiana Highlands

Guaviare R.

Orinoco R.

Angostura Falls

N W E S

TFK

Equator

Chimborazo

Quito

ECUADOR

Guayaquil

Putumayo R.

Japurá R.

Río Negro

Amazon R.

Manaus

Selvas

Iquitos

Leticia

La Montaña

Marañón R.

Ucayali R.

Juruá R.

Amazon R.

Amazon Basin

BRAZIL

Xingu R.

Punta Negra

Andes

SOUTH PACIFIC OCEAN

Trujillo

Nevado Huascarán

PERU

Lima

Mountains

Machupicchu (ruins)

Cuzco

Madeira R.

Mato Grosso Plateau

Serra dos Parecis

Guaporé R.

Beni R.

Mamoré R.

Lake Titicaca

Nevado Ancohuma

Arequipa

La Paz

Nevado Sajama

BOLIVIA

Sucre

Lake Poopó

Potosí

Gran Chaco

Paraguai R.

Cáceres

Paraná R.

CHILE

ARGENTINA

PARAGUAY

0 — 400 miles

0 — 600 kilometers

Did You Know?

Colombian coffee berries

● Colombia is the only country in the Americas that was named after Christopher Columbus.

● The Galápagos giant tortoise, which is found only on Ecuador's Galápagos Islands, can live to be more than 150 years old. A male giant tortoise can weigh as much as 600 lbs (270 kg).

● Panama hats are made in Ecuador, not Panama! The straw hats became popular after workers building the Panama Canal in the early 1900s began wearing them.

● The giant blue morpho butterfly is a member of one of 3,700 butterfly species found in Peru.

● Bolivia was named for the South American general and statesman Simón Bolívar.

41

Northeastern South America

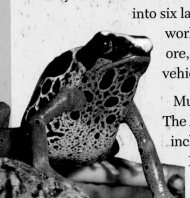

A woman from French Guiana in traditional dress

Every spring, the people of Rio de Janeiro, in Brazil, throw the world's biggest party, called Carnival. It is a four-day extravaganza that brings together people from all backgrounds and cultures. Brazil is the fifth most populous nation on earth and South America's biggest country. But more than 75% of Brazil's people are crowded into six large cities. Brazil is one of the world's top producers of steel, iron ore, tin, gold, emeralds, motor vehicles, coffee and sugar.

Much of Brazil is untamed wilderness. The Amazon jungle is home to millions of rare plants and animals, including 1,600 kinds of birds. Sadly, in the past 100 years, about 13% of the original forest has been destroyed.

The Blue Poison Arrow Frog is found in Suriname.

Brazil shares a border with every nation in South America except Chile and Ecuador. To Brazil's north are the small countries of Suriname and Guyana and the territory of French Guiana. Guyana, the only English-speaking nation on the continent, gained its independence from Britain in 1966. Nine years later, neighboring Suriname gained its independence from the Netherlands. Most of French Guiana, which is a department of France, is unsettled wilderness.

Data Bank

BRAZIL
AREA: 3,286,470 sq mi (8,511,965 sq km)
POPULATION: 188,078,227
CAPITAL: Brasília
LANGUAGES: Portuguese (official), Spanish, English, French

FRENCH GUIANA (Department of France)
AREA: 35,135 sq mi (91,000 sq km)
POPULATION: 199,509
CAPITAL: Cayenne
LANGUAGE: French

GUYANA
AREA: 83,000 sq mi (214,970 sq km)
POPULATION: 767,245
CAPITAL: Georgetown
LANGUAGES: English, Amerindian dialects, Creole, Hindi, Urdu

SURINAME
AREA: 63,039 sq mi (163,270 sq km)
POPULATION: 439,117
CAPITAL: Paramaribo
LANGUAGES: Dutch (official), Surinamese, English

Sugarloaf Mountain looms over the bay in Rio de Janeiro, Brazil.

VENEZUELA

COLOMBIA

Orinoco R.

GUYANA
Georgetown
Kaieteur Fall

SURINAME
Paramaribo

FRENCH GUIANA
Cayenne

Guiana Highlands

Lethem

Branco R.

Equator

Pico da Neblina

Japurá R.
Río Negro

Amazon Basin

Amazon R.

Manaus

Amazon R.

Canal do Norte

Canal do Sul-Perigoso

Marajó I.

Belém

São Luis

Fortaleza

Benjamin Constant

Selvas

Juruá R.

Borba

Tapajós R.

Madeira R.

Xingu R.

BRAZIL

Catingas

São Francisco R.

Recife

Porto Velho

Serra dos Parecis

Guaporé R.

Araguaia R.

Tocantins R.

Campos

PERU

La Montaña

Lake Titicaca

La Paz

BOLIVIA

Mato Grosso
Plateau

Brasília

Brazilian
Highlands

Salvador

Andes Mountains

Lake Poopó

Sucre

Campo
Grande

Serra de Amambai

Belo Horizonte

Pico da Bandeira

Gran Chaco

PARAGUAY

Paraná R.

Asunción

Iguazú Falls

Curitiba

Paraíba R.

São Paulo
Serra do Mar
Rio de Janeiro

CHILE

PACIFIC OCEAN

ARGENTINA

Paraná R.

Uruguay R.

Pôrto Alegre

URUGUAY

ATLANTIC
OCEAN

N W TFK E S

0   500 miles

0   750 kilometers

Did You Know?

- Brazil was originally called Pau Brasil by Europeans. Pau Brasil is a wood, found only in Brazil's forests, that is used to make a red dye.

- Nearly a third of Brazilians are kids.

- More than 80 kinds of monkeys live in the Amazon jungle. Brazil has more primate species than any other country.

One of Brazil's endangered golden lion tamarins

- Until 1938, France sent prisoners to colonies in French Guiana. Devil's Island, in the Atlantic Ocean, housed the most notorious prison.

- The Potaro River in Guyana comes to a sheer 741-ft (226-m) drop at Kaieteur Falls.

Southern South America

The city of Buenos Aires is a bustling urban area with many parks.

The countries of southern South America—Argentina, Chile, Paraguay and Uruguay—form a long, geographically diverse triangle stretching from Chile's hot, dry Atacama Desert across Argentina's rolling grasslands (called pampas) to the frigid lands of Tierra del Fuego near Antarctica. Much of the region is abundant in natural resources.

At the center of the triangle is the landlocked country of Paraguay. The people of Paraguay take great pride in their heritage. Many are more comfortable speaking the native language Guarani than Spanish.

Millions of immigrants from Spain, Italy, France and other European nations settled in Argentina, Chile and Uruguay. The wide boulevards of Argentina's capital, Buenos Aires, and the cosmopolitan flair of Uruguay's capital, Montevideo, show a strong European influence.

Perito Moreno Glacier in Argentina

Polynesians were the first inhabitants of Easter Island, which is located in the Pacific Ocean 2,300 mi (3,750 km) west of Chile's capital, Santiago. The remote island is famous for its giant stone statues called *maoi*.

Did You Know?

● The Perito Moreno Glacier, located at the southern tip of Argentina, is 20 mi (32 km) long!

● Argentines call the Falkland Islands the Malvinas. In 1982, Argentina went to war against Britain over ownership of the islands.

● Dinosaur fossils have been found all over Patagonia, in southern Argentina.

● Portunol, which is spoken near the Uruguay-Brazil border, is a language that mixes Portuguese and Spanish.

● Easter Island is one of the most isolated places on earth. It is equidistant from Chile and Tahiti.

Data Bank

ARGENTINA
AREA: 1,068,296 sq mi (2,766,890 sq km)
POPULATION: 39,921,833
CAPITAL: Buenos Aires
LANGUAGES: Spanish (official), English, Italian, German

CHILE
AREA: 292,258 sq mi (756,950 sq km)
POPULATION: 16,134,219
CAPITAL: Santiago
LANGUAGE: Spanish

PARAGUAY
AREA: 157,046 sq mi (406,750 sq km)
POPULATION: 6,506,464
CAPITAL: Asunción
LANGUAGES: Spanish, Guarani (both official)

URUGUAY
AREA: 68,038 sq mi (176,220 sq km)
POPULATION: 3,431,932
CAPITAL: Montevideo
LANGUAGES: Spanish, Portunol

Easter Island *maoi*

SOUTH
PACIFIC
OCEAN

BOLIVIA
☆ Sucre
Arica ●
Altiplano
Antofagasta ●
Llullaillaco Volcano ▲
CHILE
Salta ●
Gran Chaco
PARAGUAY
Pilcomayo R.
Formosa ●
Asunción ☆
Paraná R.
BRAZIL
São Paulo ●
Rio de Janeiro ●
Cabo de São Tomé
Serra do Mar

ARGENTINA
Córdoba ●
Paraná R.
Uruguay R.
Rosario ●
Salto ●
Porto Alegre ●
URUGUAY
Pampas
Mendoza ●
Mount Aconcagua ▲
Valparaíso ●
Santiago ☆
Juan Fernández Is. (Chile)
Salado R.
Buenos Aires ●
Rio de la Plata
Montevideo ☆

SOUTH
ATLANTIC
OCEAN

Concepción ●
Colorado R.
San Matías Gulf
Chubut R.
Chonos Archipelago
San Jorge Gulf
Patagonia
Andes Mountains

N
W TFK E
S

Limit of Drift Ice

Strait of Magellan
Falkland Islands (U.K.) (Malvinas)
Stanley ●
South Georgia Island (U.K.)
Tierra del Fuego
Punta Arenas ●
Cape Horn

Drake Passage
Elephant Island
South Orkney Islands (U.K.)
South Shetland Islands

SOUTHERN   OCEAN

Antarctic Peninsula
Graham Land
0   500 miles
0   700 kilometers

Antarctic Circle
Palmer Land
ANTARCTICA
Weddell Sea

45

Europe

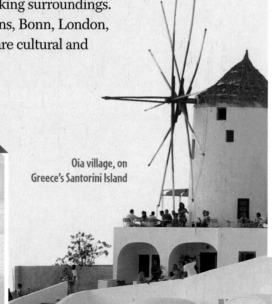

Fjord near Flam, Norway

Technically, Europe is not really a continent. Most geographers consider Europe to be a part of a larger area called Eurasia. The Ural and the Caucasus mountains separate Europe from Asia. The countries to the west of the mountains are part of Europe, and the countries to the east of the mountains make up Asia. Russia and Turkey are considered part of both Europe and Asia. A tiny portion of Azerbaijan also lies in Europe.

By area, Europe is the second-smallest of the continents. But by population, it is the third largest. It is also one of the richest. Four out of the five wealthiest countries in the world—Luxembourg, Switzerland, Liechtenstein and Norway—are in Europe. (Japan, in Asia, is the only non-European country to make that top five list!)

Europe is also rich in natural resources and beauty. From Scandinavia's frozen fjords to Greece's sun-drenched islands, Europeans enjoy breathtaking surroundings. Large, bustling cities such as Athens, Bonn, London, Paris, Madrid, Rome and Vienna are cultural and industrial centers.

Continent Facts

AREA: 3,997,929 sq mi (10,354,636 sq km)

NUMBER OF COUNTRIES: 44 countries—Albania, Andorra, Austria, Belarus, Belgium, Bosnia and Herzegovina, Bulgaria, Croatia, Czech Republic, Denmark, Estonia, Finland, France, Germany, Greece, Hungary, Iceland, Ireland, Italy, Latvia, Liechtenstein, Lithuania, Luxembourg, Macedonia, Malta, Moldova, Monaco, Montenegro, Netherlands, Norway, Poland, Portugal, Romania, Russia, San Marino, Serbia, Slovakia, Slovenia, Spain, Sweden, Switzerland, Turkey, Ukraine, United Kingdom, Vatican City

HIGHEST PEAK: Mount Elbrus, in Russia, 18,481 ft (5,633 m)

LONGEST RIVER: Volga River, in Russia, 2,293 mi (3,689 km)

LARGEST COUNTRY: Russia

SMALLEST COUNTRY: Vatican City (Holy See), .17 sq mi (.44 sq km)

Oia village, on Greece's Santorini Island

Arctic Circle

FAROE ISLANDS
(Denmark)
• Torshavn

SHETLAND ISLANDS

ORKNEY
ISLANDS

Tromso
Kiruna
Murmansk
Pechora

ASIA

Lulea
Oulu
Arkhangel'sk

Umea
FINLAND

NORWAY
Bergen
Oslo
Stavanger

Tampere
Turku Helsinki

St. Petersburg

RUSSIA

Izhevsk

Trondheim

Glasgow
Aberdeen
Edinburgh

SWEDEN
Göteborg

Stockholm

BALTIC
SEA

Tallinn
ESTONIA

Riga
LATVIA

Moscow

Nizhniy Novgorod
Kazan

Samara

NORTH
SEA
DENMARK
Alborg
Copenhagen
Malmö

LITHUANIA
Vilnius
Kaliningrad
RUSSIA

Smolensk

Minsk

Lipetsk

Saratov

UNITED
KINGDOM
iverpool Leeds
hester
Sheffield
ingham
London

NETHERLANDS
Amsterdam
The Hague
Rotterdam

Hamburg
Bremen

GERMANY

Berlin
Poznan

POLAND
Warsaw

Gdansk

BELARUS
Homyel'

Voronezh

Volgograd

KAZAKHSTAN

Calais Lille
Le Havre
Brussels
BELGIUM
LUXEMBOURG
Luxembourg
Paris

Antwerp
Essen
Dusseldorf
Cologne
Bonn
Frankfurt

Wroclaw
Lodz

Brest

Kiev

Kharkiv

Voroshilovgrad

Rostov

FRANCE

Strasbourg
Dijon
LIECHTENSTEIN
Geneva Bern
SWITZERLAND
Lyon

Stuttgart
Munich
Vaduz
Zürich

Prague
CZECH
REPUBLIC
Brno
Bratislava
SLOVAKIA

Krakow

L'viv
Derazhnya

UKRAINE

Gorlovka
Makeyevka
Zhdanov

AUSTRIA
Vienna
Budapest
HUNGARY

Chisinau
Iasi
MOLDOVA

Odessa
Mykolaiva
Kerch'
Simferopol'
Sevastopol'

Groznyy

eaux
louse
Turin Milan
Genoa

Ljubljana
SLOVENIA
Trieste
CROATIA
Zagreb
Arad

ROMANIA

Belgrade
Craiova
Bucharest
Constanta

Marseille
MONACO
ANDORRA
Bastia
ITALY
Corsica
Florence
SAN
MARINO
BOSNIA AND
HERZEGOVINA
Sarajevo
MONTENEGRO
Podgorica
Nis
SERBIA
Sofia
BULGARIA

Varna

BLACK SEA

elona
jorca

Vatican
City
Rome
Bari

ADRIATIC
SEA

Tirane
Korce
MACEDONIA
Skopje
Thessaloniki
Istanbul

Sardinia
Naples

ALBANIA
Volos

GREECE

Izmir

TURKEY

RANEAN SEA
Cagliari
Palermo
Messina
Sicily
Valletta
MALTA

Kerkira
Athens

Crete

CYPRUS

SYRIA

IRAN

LEBANON

IRAQ

Wow Zone!

● At 15,771 ft (4,807 m), Mont Blanc in the French Alps is the highest mountain in Western Europe.

● Finland has about 55,000 lakes and nearly 180,000 islands.

● There are no snakes in Ireland. You won't find any snakes in New

Mont Blanc, France

Zealand or at the North and South Poles either!

● With a population of 32,270 and an area of .75 sq mi (1.95 sq km), Monaco has the highest population density of any country in the world.

● Amsterdam, in the Netherlands, has about 1,300 bridges.

United Kingdom and Ireland

Ireland is often called the Emerald Isle. The English sing of "England's green and pleasant shores." Both lands have a wet, temperate climate, which makes the soil fertile—and green! Over the centuries, these lands have been farmed and mined for coal and minerals. The lush farms, gardens and forests of the region continue to impress visitors.

Britain, Northern Ireland and several smaller islands are all part of a nation called the United Kingdom, which is also referred to as Britain. England, Scotland and Wales are located on the island of Britain, which is the eighth-largest island in the world. Ireland is a separate island. While England, Scotland, Wales and Northern Ireland are all governed by one democratic system, the southern part of Ireland, called the Republic of Ireland, is a separate nation.

The Emerald Isle: A green pasture in Ireland

Huge stone structures like Stonehenge, barrows (burial mounds), ruined castles and crumbling stone walls tell some of the area's history. The islands were first inhabited 7,000 years ago. Ancient peoples, including Druids and Celts, built mysterious stone circles that fascinate us today. Roman Emperor Julius Caesar invaded the region in 54 B.C., and the Romans ruled until 410 B.C. They too built structures. Then came the Middle Ages, the time of knights and castles. Dozens of little kingdoms fought each other, forming and breaking alliance after alliance. It was not until 1707 that England, Scotland and Wales joined together to form the United Kingdom. By the 19th century, a huge British Empire circled the globe. Today, that empire is nearly gone. But the United Kingdom and Ireland are each part of the European Union, which is made up of 25 countries.

London's Tower Bridge was completed in 1894.

Data Bank

UNITED KINGDOM
AREA: 94,525 sq mi (244,820 sq km)
POPULATION: 60,609,153
CAPITAL: London
LANGUAGES: English, Welsh, Gaelic

IRELAND
AREA: 27,136 sq mi (70,280 sq km)
POPULATION: 4,062,235
CAPITAL: Dublin
LANGUAGES: English, Irish (Gaelic)

ATLANTIC OCEAN

North Sea

NORWAY

Stavanger

Shetland Is.

Fair Isle

Orkney Is.

Isle of Lewis

Ben Hope

Outer Hebrides

Inner Hebrides

Moray Firth

Loch Ness

Spey R.

Aberdeen

Ben Nevis

Grampian Mtns.

Dundee

Glasgow

Islay

Clyde R.

Edinburgh

SCOTLAND

North Channel

NORTHERN IRELAND (U.K.)

Donegal Bay

Lake Neagh

Belfast

Tyne R.

UNITED KINGDOM

Isle of Man

Irish Sea

Central Plain

Galway

REPUBLIC OF IRELAND

Dublin

Leeds

Liverpool

Manchester

Eastern Plain

Trent R.

The Wash

Aran Is.

Shannon R.

Midland Plain

Norwich

Amsterdam

NETHERLANDS

Limerick

Cambrian Mtns.

Severn R.

Birmingham

Blackwater R.

Waterford

Carrantuohill

WALES

Cardiff

ENGLAND

London

Cork

St. George's Channel

Swansea

Bristol

Thames R.

Dover

Strait of Dover

BELGIUM

Brussels

Southampton

Calais

ATLANTIC OCEAN

Bristol Channel

Isle of Wight

English Channel

Land's End

Plymouth

FRANCE

0   150 miles

0   200 kilometers

Is. of Scilly

Channel Islands (U.K.)

Cherbourg

Guernsey

Seine R.

Jersey

Did You Know?

● At its height in the 19th century, the British Empire included one-fourth of the earth's surface.

● One out of every eight residents of the United Kingdom lives in London.

● The Royal Observatory in Greenwich, England, is the home of Greenwich Mean Time (GMT) and the Prime Meridian of the world—a line of longitude that separates the eastern and western hemispheres of the earth. That means that Greenwich is at longitude 0 degrees.

● At 4,407 ft (1,343 m), Ben Nevis, in Scotland, and at 3,560 ft (1,085 m), Mount Snowdon, in Snowdonia National Park in Wales, are the highest points in Britain.

● Bagpipes were actually brought to Scotland by the Romans, who discovered them in the Middle East.

Scandinavia

The midnight sun over Reykjavik, Iceland

In the far north of Europe are the seafaring nations of Denmark, Sweden, Norway, Iceland and Finland. All five share a similar history, culture and climate. Only Norway and Sweden form the Scandinavian Peninsula, but all five countries are often grouped under the headings Scandinavia or Nordic nations.

Though winters are harsh where Scandinavia overlaps the Arctic Circle, the climate in the rest of the region is less severe. Surrounding waters keep temperatures from becoming bitterly cold. Because Scandinavia is so far north, summers in the region can have daylight almost around the clock. In winter, darkness often falls after only a few hours of twilight.

Although each of the Scandinavian countries has its own history and language, all of Scandinavia shares the legacy of the Vikings. Beginning in about 800 A.D., these warrior-sailors from Denmark, Sweden and Norway built open sailing ships that ventured as far as what is known today as North America. They also visited Finland and laid claim to some of its islands. As the Vikings traveled the seas, they conquered and claimed other lands, including Iceland, Greenland, Britain, France, Russia, Belgium and Holland. Gradually, the Vikings became part of the communities they conquered.

Today, all the Scandinavian nations are members of the European Union, and all enjoy a high standard of living. Cities such as Oslo, Copenhagen and Stockholm are international cultural centers.

Data Bank

DENMARK
AREA: 16,639 sq mi (43,094 sq km)
POPULATION: 5,450,661
CAPITAL: Copenhagen
LANGUAGES: Danish, Faroese, Greenlandic, German

FINLAND
AREA: 130,127 sq mi (337,030 sq km)
POPULATION: 5,231,372
CAPITAL: Helsinki
LANGUAGES: Finnish, Swedish (both official)

ICELAND
AREA: 39,768 sq mi (103,000 sq km)
POPULATION: 299,388
CAPITAL: Reykjavik
LANGUAGES: Icelandic, English, Nordic languages, German

NORWAY
AREA: 125,181 sq mi (324,220 sq km)
POPULATION: 4,610,820
CAPITAL: Oslo
LANGUAGE: Norwegian

SWEDEN
AREA: 173,731 sq mi (449,964 sq km)
POPULATION: 9,016,596
CAPITAL: Stockholm
LANGUAGE: Swedish

Reindeer Games: Most reindeer are semi-domesticated, but wild ones can still be found in Norway.

ICELAND
Arctic Circle
Horn · Grimsey I. · Fontur
Húna Bay
Akureyri
ICELAND
Hvítá R.
Faxa Bay · Vatnajökull
Keflavik ☆ Reykjavik
Hvannadalshnúkur
Hekla (volcano)
Surtsey I.
100 miles

North Cape
Barents Sea
Norwegian Sea · Hammerfest · Tana
Tromso · Finnmark Plateau · Lake Inari · Murmansk
Mt. Haltia
Narvik · Muonio R. · Arctic Circle
Mt. Kebnekaise · Kemi R.
ATLANTIC OCEAN
Kölen Mtns. · Lule R. · Lulea · Oulu
Skelleftea · Oulu R.
Faroe Is. (Denmark)
Trondheim Fjord · Angerman R. · FINLAND
Ålesund · Trondheim · SWEDEN · Vaasa
Östersund · Lake Saimaa
NORWAY · Tampere · Lake Ladoga
Shetland Is. (U.K.) · Glittertind Peak · Gulf of Bothnia
Bergen · Turku · Helsinki
Hardanger Fjord · Klar R. · Dal R. · Aland Is. · St. Petersburg
Drammen · Oslo · Gulf of Finland
North Sea · Karlstad · Uppsala · Tallinn
SCOTLAND · Stavanger · Lake Vänern · Stockholm · ESTONIA · RUSSIA
Otra R. · Lake Vättern · Norrköping
Arendal · Gulf of Riga
Kristiansand · Skagerrak · Göteborg · Gotland · Baltic Sea · Riga · LATVIA
Kattegat · Öland
Ålborg · LITHUANIA
DENMARK · Vilnius · BELARUS
Esbjerg · Odense · Malmö · Bornholm (Denmark)
Kaliningrad · RUSSIA
Copenhagen
Kiel · Gdansk · 0 · 300 miles
ENGLAND · GERMANY · POLAND · 0 · 450 kilometers

Did You Know?

● The Lapp, or Sami, people live in northern Norway, Sweden, Finland and Russia.

● Reykjavik, the capital of Iceland, is the northernmost national capital in the world.

● In his will, Swedish inventor and businessman Alfred Nobel

established the Nobel Prizes. They were first awarded in 1901. The prizes reward leaders in the fields of physics, chemistry, medicine, literature, economics and peace.

● Danish storyteller Hans Christian Andersen wrote "The Little Mermaid." A statue of the mermaid watches over the harbor of the Danish capital, Copenhagen.

● Sweden is famous for the smorgasbord, a buffet including all kinds of foods, such as pickled and smoked fish.

The Iberian Peninsula

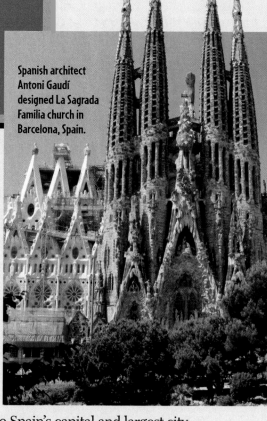

Spanish architect Antoni Gaudí designed La Sagrada Família church in Barcelona, Spain.

Poets and writers have often likened Spain to a fortress. The snowcapped Pyrenees Mountains have protected Spain as well as its smaller neighbors on Europe's Iberian Peninsula—Portugal and Andorra. But the mountains have also separated the countries from the rest of the European continent.

The geography of the peninsula, which ranges from high plateaus and mountains to Mediterranean and Atlantic coastlines, presents varying climates. The north is the wettest; the central region, home to Spain's capital and largest city, Madrid, is dry and, in the winter, cold. The coasts experience mild winter temperatures. Summer is hot almost everywhere. The sunny beaches and resorts are popular tourist destinations.

At the peninsula's southern tip is the British territory of Gibraltar. It is only about eight miles from Africa. The influence of Moors from North Africa, who conquered the Iberian Peninsula in the 8th century, is reflected in some of the region's architecture. Throughout the area, great works of art adorn magnificent cathedrals and museums.

Fiestas occur at intervals all year. The lively celebrations, which honor everything from saints to the changing seasons, often include parades and fireworks. Spain is also known for flamenco dancing and bullfighting, one of the country's most popular sporting events.

Olé: Flamenco dancers in Seville, Spain

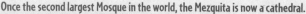

Once the second largest Mosque in the world, the Mezquita is now a cathedral.

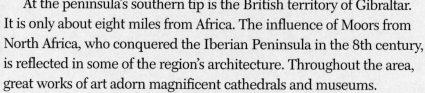

Data Bank

ANDORRA
AREA: 181 sq mi (468 sq km)
POPULATION: 71,201
CAPITAL: Andorra la Vella
LANGUAGES: Catalan (official), French, Castilian, Portuguese

PORTUGAL
AREA: 35,672 sq mi (92,391 sq km)
POPULATION: 10,605,870
CAPITAL: Lisbon
LANGUAGE: Portuguese

SPAIN
AREA: 194,896 sq mi (504,782 sq km)
POPULATION: 40,397,842
CAPITAL: Madrid
LANGUAGES: Castilian Spanish, Catalan, Galician, Basque

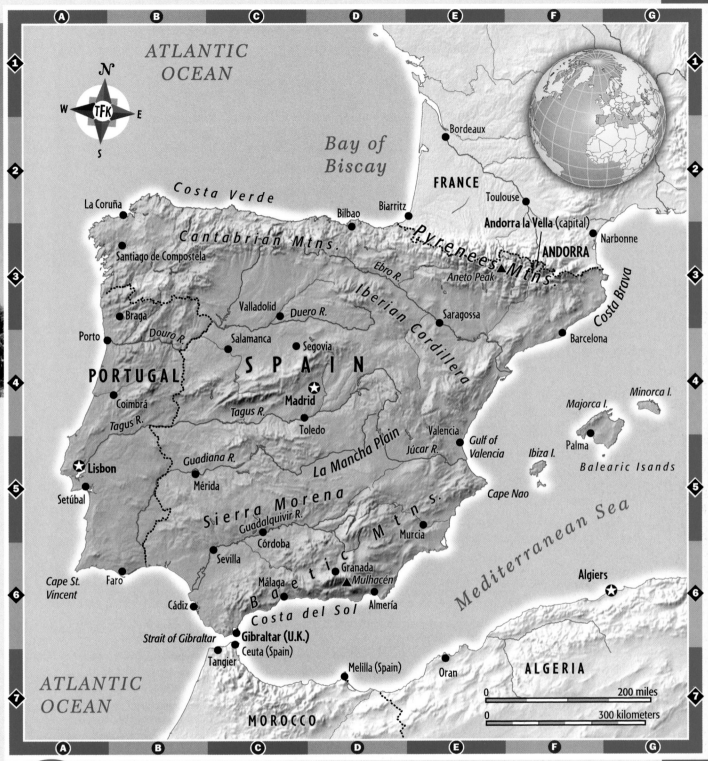

ATLANTIC OCEAN

Bay of Biscay

FRANCE

Bordeaux

Toulouse

La Coruña

Costa Verde

Bilbao

Biarritz

Andorra la Vella (capital)

Narbonne

Cantabrian Mtns.

Santiago de Compostela

Pyrenees Mtns.

ANDORRA

Ebro R.

Aneto Peak

Costa Brava

Braga

Valladolid

Duero R.

Iberian Cordillera

Saragossa

Porto

Douro R.

Salamanca

Segovia

Barcelona

PORTUGAL

SPAIN

Madrid

Minorca I.

Majorca I.

Coimbrá

Tagus R.

Toledo

Valencia

Palma

Tagus R.

Guadiana R.

La Mancha Plain

Júcar R.

Gulf of Valencia

Ibiza I.

Balearic Isands

Lisbon

Mérida

Cape Nao

Setúbal

Sierra Morena

Guadalquivir R.

Baetic Mtns.

Mediterranean Sea

Córdoba

Murcia

Cape St. Vincent

Faro

Sevilla

Granada

Mulhacén

Algiers

Málaga

Almería

Cádiz

Costa del Sol

Strait of Gibraltar

Gibraltar (U.K.)

Ceuta (Spain)

Tangier

Melilla (Spain)

Oran

ALGERIA

ATLANTIC OCEAN

MOROCCO

0   200 miles

0   300 kilometers

N W E S TFK

Did You Know?

The Rock of Gibraltar

- About one-third of the world's cork oak trees grow in Portugal. The country produces about half the world's cork.

- *Don Quixote*, written by Spanish author Miguel de Cervantes in the early 1600s, is considered to be the first modern novel.

- At midnight on New Year's Eve, Spaniards eat one grape with each chime of the clock. The grapes are said to bring luck for the next 12 months.

- Spain is the world's leading producer of olive oil. In 2003, 865,000 metric tons of it were made.

- Spanish-born Pablo Picasso is considered the founder of modern art.

- Spain, under the Terms of the Treaty of Utrecht of 1713, ceded Gibraltar to Britain in perpetuity.

France and Monaco

France is a feast for the senses. The sights, scents and flavors of Western Europe's largest country have been celebrated for hundreds of years. The French are proud of their nation's history and culture. They treasure their artistic and architectural accomplishments and savor their country's fine cuisine and flair for fashion.

Paris, the City of Light, is France's capital and cultural center. The city sits on the banks of the Seine River and is a magnet for writers and artists. It is considered to be one of the world's most romantic cities and an ideal place to people-watch at a sidewalk café.

Most of France's 60 million residents live in cities or towns, but much of the country is fertile farmland. Grapes of all varieties are among the country's main products. France is one of the world's leading wine producers.

In southern France, the resort towns of Nice and Cannes grace the French Riviera. Monaco, the world's second-smallest country, hugs the border with Italy. Monaco is known for its casinos.

Tourists flock to the Eiffel Tower in Paris.

Monte Carlo, in Monaco, is packed with resorts and hotels.

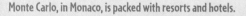

Data Bank

FRANCE
AREA: 211,208 sq mi (547,030 sq km)
POPULATION: 62,752,136
CAPITAL: Paris
LANGUAGE: French

MONACO
AREA: .75 sq mi (1.95 sq km)
POPULATION: 32,543
CAPITAL: Monaco
LANGUAGES: French (official), English, Italian, Monégasque

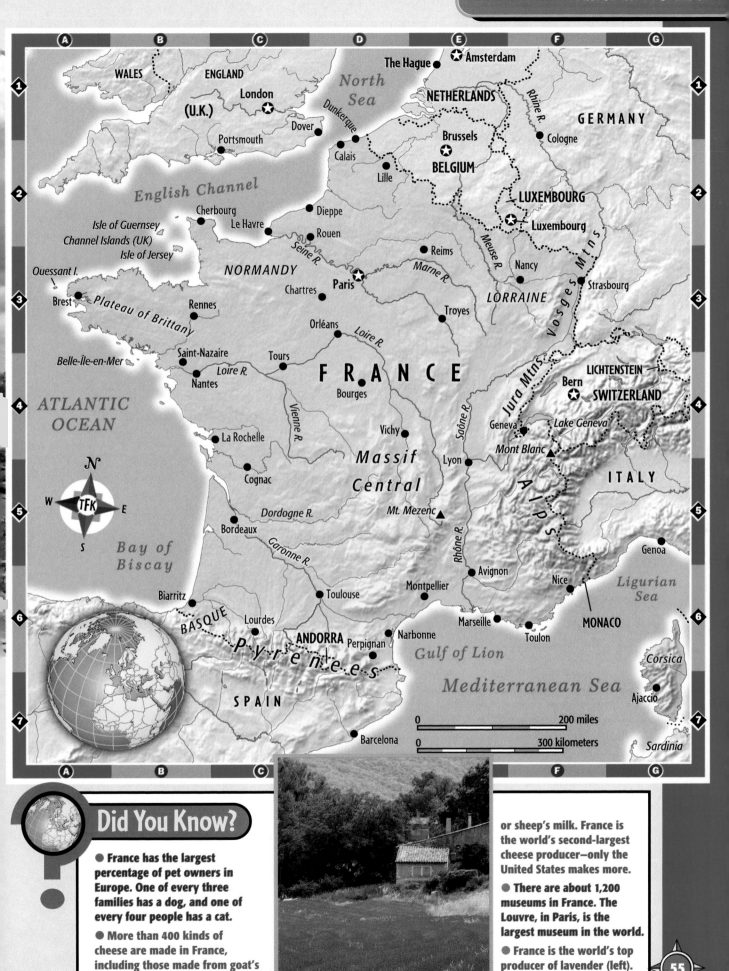

The Hague · ☆ Amsterdam

WALES · ENGLAND · North Sea · NETHERLANDS · GERMANY

London ☆ · Dover · Dunkerque · Brussels ☆ · Cologne · Rhine R.

(U.K.) · Portsmouth · Calais · BELGIUM

Lille

English Channel · LUXEMBOURG

Cherbourg · Dieppe · Luxembourg ☆ · Meuse R. · Vosges Mtns

Isle of Guernsey · Le Havre · Rouen · Reims · Nancy

Channel Islands (UK) · Seine R. · Marne R. · LORRAINE · Strasbourg

Isle of Jersey · NORMANDY

Ouessant I. · Chartres · Paris ☆ · Troyes

Brest · Plateau of Brittany · Rennes · Orléans · Loire R.

Belle-Île-en-Mer · Saint-Nazaire · Tours · F R A N C E · Jura Mtns · LICHTENSTEIN · Bern ☆ · SWITZERLAND

Loire R. · Bourges · Mont Blanc ▲

ATLANTIC · Nantes · Vienne R. · Saône R. · Geneva · Lake Geneva

OCEAN · La Rochelle · Vichy · Lyon · A l p s · ITALY

Massif · Mt. Mezenc ▲ · Rhône R.

N · Cognac · Central

W · TFK · E · Dordogne R. · Genoa

S · Bordeaux · Garonne R. · Avignon · Nice · **Ligurian Sea**

Bay of Biscay · Montpellier · Toulon

Biarritz · Toulouse · Marseille · MONACO

BASQUE · Lourdes · Narbonne

ANDORRA · Perpignan · **Gulf of Lion** · Corsica

P y r e n e e s · **Mediterranean Sea** · Ajaccio

S P A I N

Barcelona · 0 — 200 miles · 0 — 300 kilometers · Sardinia

Did You Know?

● **France has the largest percentage of pet owners in Europe. One of every three families has a dog, and one of every four people has a cat.**

● **More than 400 kinds of cheese are made in France, including those made from goat's** or sheep's milk. France is the world's second-largest cheese producer—only the United States makes more.

● **There are about 1,200 museums in France. The Louvre, in Paris, is the largest museum in the world.**

● **France is the world's top producer of lavender (left).**

The Low Countries

Belgium, the Netherlands and Luxembourg are often called the Low Countries. It is a fitting name for this densely populated region, as much of its land lies either below, or just slightly above, sea level. The terrain seems endlessly flat, which is perfect for bicycling, a favorite activity and popular mode of transportation. Travel by boat is also essential. Thousands of rivers and canals connect gabled cities, quaint villages and bountiful farmland throughout the region.

Waterway: Amsterdam, in the Netherlands, has more than 150 canals.

Flower Power: Tulips bloom across the Dutch landscape.

The Low Countries produce some of the world's finest flowers, cheeses and chocolates. The Netherlands (commonly called Holland) is the world's flower hub. It is host to flower festivals and auctions and exports more blossoms than any other nation. Belgium's capital, Brussels, is called the capital of Europe. A uniquely multicultural city, it houses the headquarters of the European Union (E.U.) as well as NATO (the North Atlantic Treaty Organization).

Luxembourg, one of the world's smallest countries, is tucked just below Belgium. Despite its size—998 sq mi (2,586 sq km)—it is an important worldwide banking center. Luxembourg also houses the E.U.'s financial headquarters.

Some of the world's most famous painters came from the Low Countries. Hieronymus Bosch, Rembrandt van Rijn, Johannes Vermeer and Vincent van Gogh were all from the Netherlands; Jan van Eyck, Pieter Brueghel the Elder and Peter Paul Rubens were all from Belgium.

Say Cheese: Holland is famous for its delicious butter and cheese.

Data Bank

BELGIUM
AREA: 11,781 sq mi (30,510 sq km)
POPULATION: 10,379,067
CAPITAL: Brussels
LANGUAGES: Dutch, French, German (all official)

LUXEMBOURG
AREA: 998 sq mi (2,586 sq km)
POPULATION: 474,413
CAPITAL: Luxembourg
LANGUAGES: Luxembourgish, German, French

NETHERLANDS
AREA: 16,033 sq mi (41,526 sq km)
POPULATION: 16,491,461
CAPITAL: Amsterdam
LANGUAGES: Dutch, Frisian (both official)

Baltic Sea

DENMARK

Copenhagen

Kiel Bay

North Frisian Is.

Nord Ostsee Canal

Fehmarn I.

Rügen

Pomeranian Bay

Mecklenburg Bay

Kiel

Rostock

East Frisian Is.

Hamburg

Lake Müritz

Oder R.

West Frisian Is.

North Sea

Weser R.

Elbe R.

North German Plain

Bremen

Berlin

POLAND

Amsterdam

NETHERLANDS

Teutoburg Forest

Hannover

Mittelland Canal

Magdeburg

Oder R.

Rhine R.

Münster

Brocken Peak

Harz Mtns.

Leipzig

Elbe R.

Ruhr Valley

Dortmund

Dresden

Dusseldorf

Rhine R.

Essen

GERMANY

Cologne

BELGIUM

Bonn

Erfurt

Brussels

Erzegebirge

Liège

Eifel

Wiesbaden

Fichtelberg

Prague

Luxembourg

Moselle R.

Frankfurt am Main

Main R.

CZECH REPUBLIC

LUXEMBOURG

Hunsrück

Haardt Mtns.

Würzberg

Nürnberg

Bohemian Forest

Heidelberg

Danube R.

Rhine R.

Stuttgart

Augsburg

Isar R.

Danube R.

FRANCE

Swabian Jura

Ulm

BAVARIA

Vienna

Black Forest

Munich

Salzburg

Lake Constance

AUSTRIA

LIECHTENSTEIN

Bavarian Alps

Watzmann

SWITZERLAND

Zugspitze

0   100 miles

0   150 kilometers

N
W TFK E
S

Did You Know?

● Many world-renowned classical composers hail from Germany, including Johann Sebastian Bach and Ludwig van Beethoven.

● The Oktoberfest in Munich, Germany, is one of the world's largest festivals. The first annual Oktoberfest was held in 1810 to celebrate a royal wedding.

An Oktoberfest float

● German physicist Daniel Gabriel Fahrenheit invented the alcohol thermometer in 1709, the mercury thermometer in 1714 and the Fahrenheit scale in 1724.

● On April 12, 1990, Germany inched into the *Guinness World Records* book for a traffic jam of 18 million cars on the East German–West German border.

Austria, Liechtenstein and Switzerland

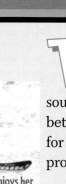

The Alps are a huge chain of mountains that stretches across 750 mi (1,207 km), from the Austrian capital of Vienna to southern Italy. The mountains form a barrier between Northern and Southern Europe. But for centuries, passes cut through the Alps have provided Europeans with trade routes.

Switzerland, which contains more of the Alps than any other nation, is renowned for its magnificent landscapes. It is a politically neutral nation, and many international organizations, including the United Nations and the Red Cross, are based there. There is no official Swiss language; instead, the Swiss speak the languages of the countries that surround them: German, French and Italian.

Between Switzerland and Austria lies the tiny nation of Liechtenstein. After World War I, Liechtenstein allied itself with Switzerland. That close connection is still strong, and Switzerland represents Liechtenstein diplomatically. Liechtenstein is a constitutional monarchy. It is governed by a prince, but the people are represented by an elected parliament.

Just east of Switzerland and Liechtenstein is Austria. The Danube, Europe's second-longest river, passes through Austria's capital city, Vienna. More than 40% of Austria is covered in forests and woodlands, which make it attractive to international tourists.

Alpine Fun: A skier enjoys her day on the mountain.

The Hofburg Palace in Vienna, Austria, is home to the Spanish Riding School, Vienna Boys' Choir, National Library and several museums.

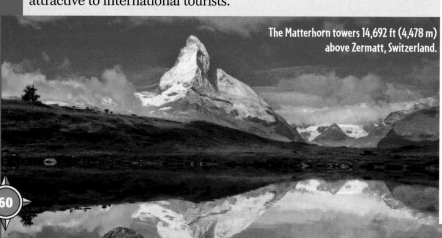

The Matterhorn towers 14,692 ft (4,478 m) above Zermatt, Switzerland.

Data Bank

AUSTRIA
AREA: 32,375 sq mi (83,858 sq km)
POPULATION: 8,192,880
CAPITAL: Vienna
LANGUAGE: German

LIECHTENSTEIN
AREA: 62 sq mi (160 sq km)
POPULATION: 33,987
CAPITAL: Vaduz
LANGUAGES: German (official), Alemannic dialect

SWITZERLAND
AREA: 15,942 sq mi (41,290 sq km)
POPULATION: 7,523,934
CAPITAL: Bern
LANGUAGES: German, French, Italian, Romansch (all official)

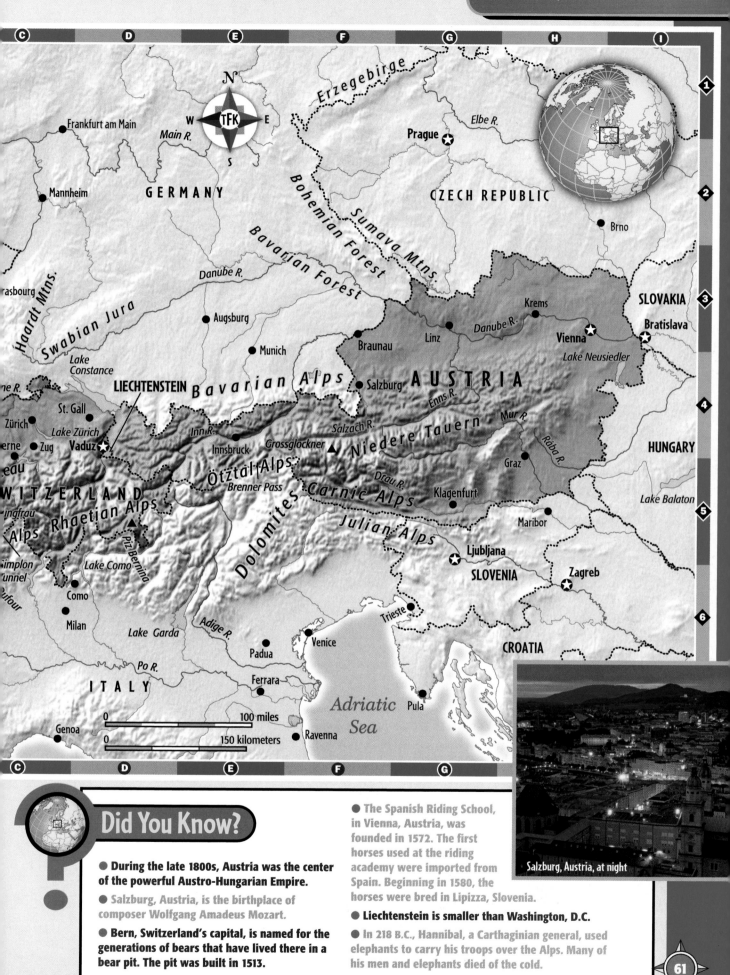

C   D   E   F   G   H   I

1

Erzegebirge

Frankfurt am Main

Main R.

N
W · TFK · E
S

GERMANY

Mannheim

2

Elbe R.

Prague ✪

CZECH REPUBLIC

Brno

SLOVAKIA

3

Danube R.

Augsburg

Bavarian Forest

Sumava Mtns.

Bohemian Forest

Krems

Danube R.

Vienna ✪

Bratislava ✪

rasbourg

Haardt Mtns.

Swabian Jura

Munich

Braunau

Linz

Lake Neusiedler

Lake Constance

LIECHTENSTEIN

Bavarian Alps

Salzburg

AUSTRIA

4

St. Gall

ne R.

Zürich

Enns R.

Mur R.

HUNGARY

Lake Zürich

rne   Zug   **Vaduz** ✪

Inn R.

Salzach R.

Niedere Tauern

eau

Innsbruck

Grossglockner ▲

Graz

Rába R.

WITZERLAND

ingfrau

Rhaetian Alps

Ötztal Alps

Brenner Pass

Drau R.

Klagenfurt

Maribor

Lake Balaton

5

Alps

Piz Bernina ▲

Carnic Alps

Julian Alps

implon unnel

Lake Como

Dolomites

Ljubljana ✪

SLOVENIA

Zagreb ✪

ufour

Como

Milan

Lake Garda

Adige R.

Trieste

6

Po R.

Venice

CROATIA

ITALY

Padua

Ferrara

Adriatic Sea

Pula

0   100 miles

0   150 kilometers

Genoa

Ravenna

C   D   E   F   G

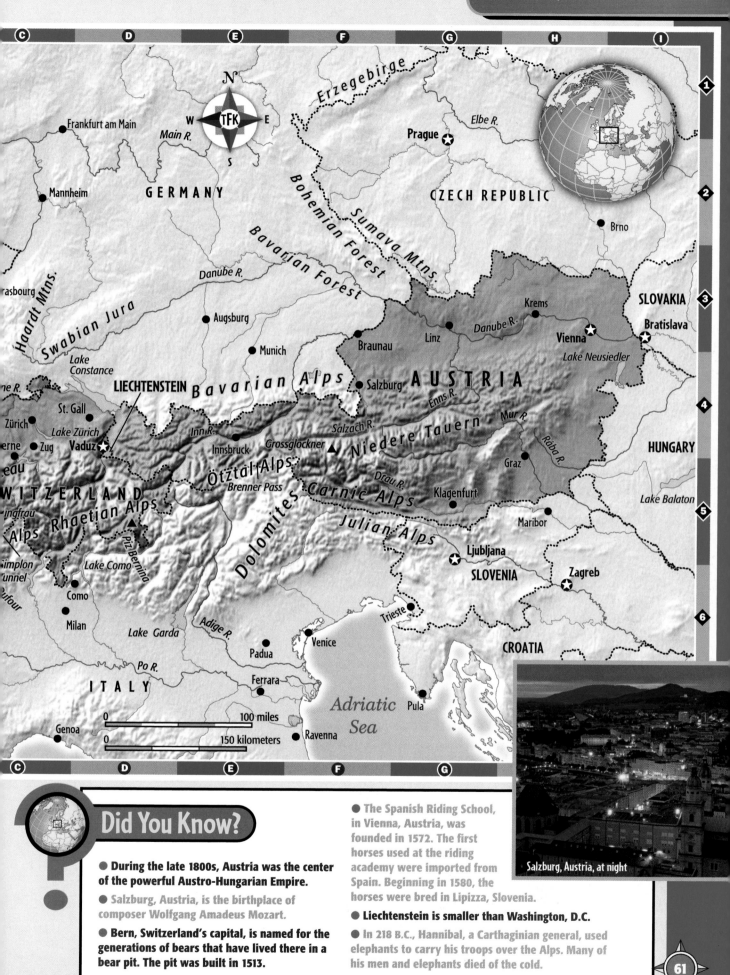

Salzburg, Austria, at night

Did You Know?

● During the late 1800s, Austria was the center of the powerful Austro-Hungarian Empire.

● Salzburg, Austria, is the birthplace of composer Wolfgang Amadeus Mozart.

● Bern, Switzerland's capital, is named for the generations of bears that have lived there in a bear pit. The pit was built in 1513.

● The Spanish Riding School, in Vienna, Austria, was founded in 1572. The first horses used at the riding academy were imported from Spain. Beginning in 1580, the horses were bred in Lipizza, Slovenia.

● Liechtenstein is smaller than Washington, D.C.

● In 218 B.C., Hannibal, a Carthaginian general, used elephants to carry his troops over the Alps. Many of his men and elephants died of the cold.

Central Europe

The great plains of Poland, the mountains of the Czech Republic and the beautiful landscapes of Hungary and Slovakia add beauty to this region's rich, historical character. Architectural masterpieces are common throughout each country. Prague Castle, in the Czech Republic's capital, is one of the largest castles in the world. More castles decorate the Czech Republic's landscape, illustrating the nation's grand heritage. Museums in Budapest, Hungary, are decorated with ornate details that are symbolic of the country's love of art and design. Slovakia has its share of impressive monuments as well as an array of modern buildings that demonstrate its stature as a growing, vibrant country.

Once a part of the communist bloc of nations, much of central Europe has adopted a more progressive, enterprising economy in recent years. But some of the advances in manufacturing have led to problems. For example, Poland is struggling with high levels of air and water pollution; its government is looking for new solutions to these challenges.

Each year, more and more tourists visit the region. Some travelers come to hear the captivating folk music of Hungary, others to taste the delicious foods of Warsaw, Poland. As the countries grow more cosmopolitan, each strives to become an integral part of a new, unified Europe while maintaining its own unique character and flavor.

The Blue Danube: Parliament in Budapest, Hungary

Old Town Square in Prague, Czech Republic

Data Bank

CZECH REPUBLIC
AREA: 30,450 sq mi (78,866 sq km)
POPULATION: 1,0235,455
CAPITAL: Prague
LANGUAGE: Czech

HUNGARY
AREA: 35,919 sq mi (93,030 sq km)
POPULATION: 9,981,334
CAPITAL: Budapest
LANGUAGE: Hungarian

POLAND
AREA: 120,727 sq mi (312,685 sq km)
POPULATION: 38,536,869
CAPITAL: Warsaw
LANGUAGE: Polish

SLOVAKIA
AREA: 18,859 sq mi (48,845 sq km)
POPULATION: 5,439,448
CAPITAL: Bratislava
LANGUAGES: Slovak (official), Hungarian

Baltic Sea

LITHUANIA

Vistula Spit · Kaliningrad · RUSSIA

Pomeranian Bay · Koszalin · Gdansk · Elblag

Oder-Haff · Szczecin

Oder R.

Northern European Plain · *Masuria* · Grodno · Bialystok

Berlin

GERMANY · *Warta R.* · Bydgoszcz · Torun · *Vistula R.* · *Narew R.* · *Bug R.* · BELARUS

Oder R. · Poznan · Plock · **P O L A N D** · Warsaw

Zielona Góra · Kalisz · Lódz · Radom · *Lubelska Hills* · Lublin

Dresden · Wroclaw · *Malopolska Hills* · *Vistula R.* · *San R.*

Erzegebirge · *Sudety Mtns.* · Mt. Snezka · Zabrze · Kraków · *Bug R.*

Bohemian Forest · Prague · *Elbe R.* · Katowice · Lviv · *Dniester R.*

Plzen · **BOHEMIA** · Ostrava · **B e s k i d s** · UKRAINE

CZECH REPUBLIC · *Morava R.* · *Carpathian Mtns.*

Sumava Mtns. · **MORAVIA** · Brno · Zlín · ▲ *Gerlachovsky Peak* · Kosice

Danube R. · Zilina · **S L O V A K I A** · Miskolc · *Tisza R.*

Váh R. · Nitra · **The Great Alföld**

BAVARIA · *Danube R.* · ▲ Mount Kékes

Munich · Vienna · Bratislava

AUSTRIA · Gyor · *Danube R.* · Budapest · Debrecen · TRANSYLVANIA

A l p s · Graz · *Bakony Mtns.* · **H U N G A R Y** · Cluj-Napoca

ITALY · Lake Balaton · *Mecsek Mtns.* · *Danube R.* · Szeged · ROMANIA

SLOVENIA · Ljubljana · Zagreb · Pécs · Venice · Trieste · CROATIA

Danube R.

N · W · **TFK** · E · S

0 — 150 miles
0 — 200 kilometers

Did You Know?

● In 1918, a union of Czech and Slovak lands was formed. The nation of Czechoslovakia existed until January 1, 1993, when the Czechoslovakian federation was dissolved.

● The composer and pianist Bedrich Smetana (1824–1884) lived in Prague. Known for his operas and symphonic poems, he was one of the first Czech composers to write in his native tongue. The Czech composer Antonin Dvořák (1841–1904) wrote many classical pieces, including *Symphony No. 9 in E Minor (New World)* based on American folk music.

● One of the continent's biggest herds of European bison lives in Poland's Bialowieska Forest.

● Composer Frédéric Chopin was born in Poland.

● Almost 80% of Slovakia sits more than 2,460 ft (750 m) above sea level.

Chopin monument in Warsaw

Italy, Malta, San Marino and Vatican City

St. Peter's Basilica is the heart of Vatican City.

Although Italy did not become a unified nation until 1861, Italians are understandably proud of their region's ancient history. The city of Rome, which was founded in 625 B.C., was the center of the Roman Empire. At the height of its power, the empire extended across much of Europe and northern Africa and portions of Asia. Roman monuments, aqueducts and amphitheaters can still be found throughout the land.

Italy is as magnificent now as it was in the past. The country is divided into 20 regions, each with its own unique flavor, big cities and attractions. Rome, Italy's capital and largest city, is located in Lazio. Milan, in Lombardy, is a world-famous fashion center. Florence, in Tuscany, is known for its museums and galleries and as the birthplace of the Renaissance, which was a time of great artistic and scientific growth. Many people consider Venice, in the Veneto region, the world's most beautiful city.

Italy is a long, boot-shaped peninsula. At the top of the boot, the Alps form a border that separates Italy from France, Switzerland, Austria and Slovenia. The rest of Italy is surrounded by seas—the Ligurian, Tyrrhenian, Mediterranean, Ionian and Adriatic. The Apennine Mountains form a backbone that extends down the peninsula. Italy includes two large islands, Sardinia and Sicily, and several small islands. Lying between Sicily and Africa is the tiny island nation of Malta. Sharing the Italian peninsula are San Marino and Vatican City. The Vatican, or Holy See (*see* means "cathedral town"), is the home of the Pope, the head of the Roman Catholic Church.

Data Bank

ITALY
AREA: 116,305 sq mi (301,230 sq km)
POPULATION: 58,133,509
CAPITAL: Rome
LANGUAGES: Italian (official), German, French, Slovene

MALTA
AREA: 122 sq mi (316 sq km)
POPULATION: 400,214
CAPITAL: Valletta
LANGUAGES: Maltese, English (both official)

SAN MARINO
AREA: 24 sq mi (61 sq km)
POPULATION: 29,251
CAPITAL: San Marino
LANGUAGE: Italian

VATICAN CITY (HOLY SEE)
AREA: .17 sq mi (.44 sq km)
POPULATION: 932
CAPITAL: None
LANGUAGES: Latin, Italian, others

A gondola ride in Venice, Italy

A **B** **C** **D** **E** **F** **G**

1

LIECHTENSTEIN

SWITZERLAND

Brenner Pass

AUSTRIA

HUNGARY

Danube R.

Geneva

Lake Como

A L P S

Mt.Dufour

Mont Blanc

Piz Bernina

Dolomites

Ljubljana

SLOVENIA

Zagreb

CROATIA

Belgrade

N
W   TFK   E
S

2

FRANCE

A L P S

Milan

Lake Garda

Ticino R.

Po R.

Piave R.

Venice

Gulf of Venice

Trieste

Rijeka (Fiume)

2

Turin

Tanaro R.

Po R.

Verona

Padua

ITALY

Reno R.

Ravenna

Bologna

SAN MARINO

BOSNIA AND HERZEGOVINA

Sarajevo

SERBIA

3

Genoa

Ligurian Sea

Pisa

Florence

Arno R.

Ancona

Adriatic Sea

Split

Dubrovnik

Podgorica

3

Marseille

Nice

MONACO

Capri

Elba I.

TUSCANY

Lake Trasimeno

A p e n n i n e s

Mt. Corno

Pescara

MONTENEGRO

4

Corsica (France)

Bastia

Tuscan Archipelago

Tiber R.

Rome

Bari

Tirana

ALBANIA

4

Ajaccio

Strait of Bonifacio

VATICAN CITY

Naples

Ischia

Mt. Vesuvius (volcano)

Salerno

PUGLIA

Brindisi

Strait of Orantoa

5

Sardinia

Mount Marmora

Tyrrhenian Sea

Taranto

Gulf of Taranto

Corfu (Greece)

5

Cagliari

Stromboli I.

Lipari Islands

CALABRIA

Catanzaro

Ionian Sea

6

Palermo

Sicily

Messina

Strait of Messina

Mt. Etna (volcano)

6

Strait of Sicily

Catania

Mediterranean Sea

Ragusa

Syracuse

7

Tunis

Pantelleria I. (Italy)

MALTA   Valletta

0   200 miles
0   300 kilometers

7

ALGERIA

TUNISIA

A **B** **C** **D** **E** **F** **G**

Did You Know?

- Europe's only active volcanoes are in Italy. Mount Etna is in Sicily, and Mount Vesuvius is near Naples.

- The Colosseum, in Rome, seated 50,000 people.

- According to legend, Rome was founded in 753 B.C. by the twin brothers Romulus and Remus.

- The Vatican Museums make up one of the world's largest museum complexes. The museums' 1,400 rooms are filled with antiquities and works of art.

- In 1508, Pope Julius II asked Michelangelo to paint the ceiling of the Vatican's Sistine Chapel. It took him four years to complete the project.

- The Swiss Guard is the world's smallest army. It consists of 100 men who have sworn allegiance to the Pope. The guards' colorful uniforms, left, have changed very little since the 16th century.

The Balkans

Busy City: **Split, Croatia, is a commercial center.**

The Balkan Peninsula is a mountainous area in Eastern Europe. Located between Western Europe and Asia are the nations known as the Balkan States. The western Balkan States include Albania, Bosnia and Herzegovina, Croatia, Macedonia, Serbia, Montenegro and Slovenia. Albanians are descendants of the Illyrians, whose civilization came before that of the Greeks. Split, Croatia, is the site of ancient Roman ruins, as is Butrint, Albania. Slovenia, a nation of mountains and lakes, has close ties to Germany, Austria and other Western European countries.

Because the Balkan Peninsula acts as a land bridge between east and west, it has great strategic value. As a result, it has been the site of frequent wars. Over many centuries, different portions of the Balkans were conquered by the Roman Empire, the Byzantine Empire and the Ottoman Empire. But the people of the region have always been fiercely independent. They are proud of their cultures and languages. During the 19th century, ethnic groups in the Balkans began to declare their independence and fight over territory. In 1912, the Balkan Wars began, and two years later, World War I engulfed the area. In the 1990s, much of the Balkans was again caught up in ethnic strife. Today, a fragile peace exists.

In 2006, Montenegro voted in favor of independence from Serbia and became a separate country.

Data Bank

Old and new modes of transportation in Albania

ALBANIA
AREA: 11,000 sq mi (28,748 sq km)
POPULATION: 3,581,655
CAPITAL: Tirana
LANGUAGES: Albanian (Tosk is the official dialect), Greek

BOSNIA AND HERZEGOVINA
AREA: 19,741 sq mi (51,129 sq km)
POPULATION: 4,498,976
CAPITAL: Sarajevo
LANGUAGES: Croatian, Serbian, Bosnian

CROATIA
AREA: 21,829 sq mi (56,542 sq km)
POPULATION: 4,494,749
CAPITAL: Zagreb
LANGUAGE: Croatian

MACEDONIA
AREA: 9,781 sq mi (25,333 sq km)
POPULATION: 2,071,210
CAPITAL: Skopje
LANGUAGES: Macedonian, Albanian, Turkish, Serbo-Croatian

MONTENEGRO
AREA: 5,415 sq mi (14,026 sq km)
POPULATION: 630,548
CAPITAL: Podgorica
LANGUAGES: Serbian, Bosnian, Albanian, Croatian

SERBIA
AREA: 34,116 sq mi (88,361 sq km)
POPULATION: 9,396,411
CAPITAL: Belgrade
LANGUAGES: Serbian, Romanian, Hungarian, Slovak, Ukrainian, Croatian

SLOVENIA
AREA: 7,827 sq mi (20,273 sq km)
POPULATION: 2,010,347
CAPITAL: Ljubljana
LANGUAGES: Slovenian, Serbo-Croatian

AUSTRIA

Budapest

Graz

HUNGARY

The Great Alföld

Grossglockner

Drau R.

Julian Alps

Maribor

Lake Balaton

Danube R.

Triglav Mtn.

Kras Plateau

Ljubljana

Zagorje Hills

SLOVENIA

Zagreb

Pécs

Timisoara

ROMANIA

Trieste

ISTRIA

Rijeka

Sisak

Sava R.

CROATIA

Drava R.

Osijek

VOJVODINA

Novi Sad

Venice

Pula

Banja Luka

Bosna R.

Brcko

Sava R.

Belgrade

Transylvanian Alps

Iron Gate Gorge

SAN MARINO

Zadar

Dinaric Alps

BOSNIA AND HERZEGOVINA

Tuzla

Drina R.

Valjevo

Kragujevac

Craiova

Danube R.

Zenica

Cacak

Ancona

Split

Brac I.

Sarajevo

SERBIA

Nis

Balkan Mtns.

Mostar

Bobotov K'uk

Morava R.

Sofia

Adriatic Sea

Apennines

Dubrovnik

MONTENEGRO

KOSOVO

Pristina

BULGARIA

Podgorica

North Albanian Alps

Pec

Lake Scutari

Mount Korab

Skopje

MACEDONIA

ITALY

Bari

Durres

Tirana

Lake Ohrid

Vardar R.

Bitola

Thessaloníki

Naples

Tyrrhenian Sea

Brindisi

ALBANIA

Lake Prespa

GREECE

Strait of Otranto

Vlore

Korce

Butrint

Pindus Mtns.

Corfu (Greece)

Ionian Sea

N W E S TFK

0   200 miles

0   300 kilometers

1 2 3 4 5 6 7

A B C D E F G

Did You Know?

- *Balkan* means "mountain" in Turkish.

- The ancient city of Butrint in southern Albania, reflects 3,000 years of history. It has Greek, Roman and Byzantine ruins.

- Bosnia and Herzegovina, Croatia, Macedonia, Serbia, Montenegro and Slovenia were all part of the larger nation of Yugoslavia. Yugoslavia broke into separate countries in 1991.

- The Balkan Peninsula is surrounded by the Adriatic, Black, Ionian and Aegean Seas.

- The rugged and beautiful Dinaric and Julian Alps in the Balkans are popular with skiers.

- Folk dancing and music are popular throughout the Balkan region. The music of Turkey has had a strong influence on the music of Bosnia and Herzegovina.

Southeastern Europe

An Ancient Treasure: The Acropolis in Athens, Greece

Surrounded on three sides by water, Greece is a land of sparkling beauty. Magnificent ruins are framed by deep blue skies and turquoise water. At the center of Greek life is the sea. Much of the country's early power and wealth came from shipping, trading and fishing. Today, the sea is still important to Greece's economy. Millions of people visit the country's sunny beaches and historic sites each year, making tourism Greece's top industry. Visitors especially love to cruise around the country's nearly 2,000 islands, most of which are uninhabited. Athens is the country's capital and largest city. Its most notable structure is the Acropolis, which was built some 2,000 years ago.

A Greek Orthodox church in Oia on the island of Santorini

Tourism is important for Greece's northeastern neighbors, Bulgaria and Romania. Black Sea resorts boast beautiful sandy beaches and draw many visitors from neighboring countries.

Bulgarian dancers in traditional dress.

Data Bank

BULGARIA
AREA: 48,822 sq mi (110,910 sq km)
POPULATION: 7,385,367
CAPITAL: Sofia
LANGUAGE: Bulgarian

GREECE
AREA: 50,942 sq mi (131,940 sq km)
POPULATION: 10,688,058
CAPITAL: Athens
LANGUAGES: Greek (official), English, French

ROMANIA
AREA: 91,700 sq mi (237,500 sq km)
POPULATION: 22,303,552
CAPITAL: Bucharest
LANGUAGES: Romanian (official), Hungarian, German

Did You Know?

Romania's Capital: Bucharest

● **Alexander the Great lived from 356 B.C. to 323 B.C. He made Greece a world power by conquering much of the known world.**

● **Bulgarian rose oil, used in fine perfumes around the world, is produced in the Kazanlak region of Bulgaria.**

● **Bucharest, Romania's capital, was once known as Little Paris for its wide boulevards and beautiful buildings.**

● **Transylvania, in Romania, is home to Count Dracula, the fictional character in Bram Stoker's classic tale. The Dracula legend is based on Vlad the Impaler, a Romanian leader who was known for his cruelty.**

N
W **TFK** E
S

HUNGARY

Budapest

Debrecen

Lake Balaton

The Great Alföld

Tisza R.

UKRAINE

Satu Mare

TRANSYLVANIA

Carpathian Mtns.

MOLDOVA

Iasi

Prut R.

Dniester R.

Chisinau

Cluj-Napoca

Bihor Mtns.

Tirgu Mures

ROMANIA

Siret R.

Arad

Mures R.

Timisoara

Transylvanian Alps

Moldoveanu

Brasov

Galati

Danube R.

CROATIA

Sava R.

Danube R.

Belgrade

Ploiesti

Olt R.

Bucharest

Mouths of the Danube

BOSNIA AND HERZEGOVINA

Iron Gate Gorge

Craiova

Danube R.

Ruse

Constanta

Sarajevo

SERBIA

Pleven

BULGARIA

Varna

Morova R.

Nis

Balkan Mtns.

MONTENEGRO

Dubrovnik

KOSOVO

Pristina

Sofia

Musala Peak

Plovdiv

Burgas

Black Sea

Podgorica

Rhodope Mtns.

Maritsa R.

Adriatic Sea

Tirana

Skopje

Vardar R.

Néstos R.

Bosporus

Istanbul

MACEDONIA

Struma R.

Alexandroúpolis

Sea of Marmara

ALBANIA

Thessaloníki

Thásos I.

Dardanelles

Site of ancient Troy

Pindus Mtns.

Aliákmon R.

GREECE

Mount Olympus

Límnos I.

Samothrace I.

ITALY

Corfu

Aegean Sea

Lárissa

Vólos

Northern Sporades

Skíros I.

Lesbos I.

TURKEY

Ionian Islands

Ionian Sea

Cephalonia I.

Mount Parnassus

Khalkis

Euboea I.

Chios I.

Izmir (Smyrna)

Pátrai

Athens

Sámos I.

Zante I.

Corinth

PELEPONNESE

Cyclades

Kalámata

Sparta

Náxos I.

Kos I.

Dodecanese Is.

Kithira I.

Thíra I.

Rhodes

Sea of Crete

Iráklion

Kárpathos I.

Crete

0   120 miles

0   180 kilometers

The Baltic States and Belarus

Medieval Treasure: Tallinn reflects Estonia's rich history.

During the early 1940s, the Soviet Union expanded its borders by invading the surrounding small nations. Estonia, Lithuania, Latvia and Belarus all fell to the armies of dictator Joseph Stalin. These ancient independent states became republics of the Soviet Union. Not until the early 1990s did they regain their independence. Today, each of these states is a sovereign nation with its own government, economy, language and history.

Estonia, Lithuania and Latvia are known as the Baltic States because they are located on the coast of the Baltic Sea. The Baltic Sea connects these nations to Scandinavia and northern Europe. Tallinn, Estonia's capital, is only 40 mi (64 km) from Helsinki, Finland. Since gaining their independence from the Soviet Union, the Baltic States have proudly reclaimed their historic languages and cultures. They have a rich legacy of music, dance, folklore and literature. The region is heavily forested and has a wide range of wildlife, including elk, deer and wild boar.

Belarus, just east of Lithuania, shares the Baltic States' flat landscape and cool climate. Unlike the Baltics, however, Belarus holds its Soviet past in high regard, and much of its culture is connected to that of Russia and the former Soviet Union. Minsk, the capital of Belarus, was largely rebuilt after World War II.

The Baltic States were invited to join NATO and the European Union in 2002. With these alliances, they will become important parts of the global economy. Belarus has continued to maintain its close ties with Russia.

The Latvian Freedom Monument in Riga, Latvia

Festival Fun: A Latvian girl dressed in traditional clothes

Data Bank

BELARUS
AREA: 80,154 sq mi (207,600 sq km)
POPULATION: 10,293,011
CAPITAL: Minsk
LANGUAGES: Belarusian, Russian

ESTONIA
AREA: 17,462 sq mi (45,226 sq km)
POPULATION: 1,324,333
CAPITAL: Tallinn
LANGUAGES: Estonian (official), Russian, Ukrainian, Finnish

LATVIA
AREA: 24,938 sq mi (64,589 sq km)
POPULATION: 2,274,735
CAPITAL: Riga
LANGUAGES: Latvian (official), Lithuanian, Russian

LITHUANIA
AREA: 25,174 sq mi (65,200 sq km)
POPULATION: 3,585,906
CAPITAL: Vilnius
LANGUAGES: Lithuanian (official), Polish, Russian

Gulf of Bothnia

FINLAND

SWEDEN

Lake Ladoga

Helsinki

Gulf of Finland

St. Petersburg

Stockholm

Tallinn

Narva

N

TFK

W — **E**

S

Hiiumaa I.

E S T O N I A

Narva Reservoir

Novgorod

Volkhov R.

Saaremaa I.

Lake Peipus

Lake Ilmen

Parnu

Tartu

Lake Pskov

Point Kolka

Gulf of Riga

Gotland

LIVONIA

Pskov

R U S S I A

Velikaya R.

Riga

LATVIA

Valdai Hills

Liepaja

Kurzeme Upland

Daugava R.

Mount Gaizins

Baltic Sea

Jelgava

Western Düna R.

Volga R.

COURLAND

Daugavpils

Klaipeda

Siaulai

Dnieper R.

KALININGRAD OBLAST (RUSSIA)

LITHUANIA

Polatsk

Polatsk Lowland

Polatsk

Gulf of Gdansk

Nemen R.

Neris R.

Vitsyebsk

Smolensk

Kaliningrad

Kaunas

Smolensk-Moscow Upland

Gdansk

Vilnius

Mahilyow

Alytus

Dnieper R.

MASURIA

Dzerzhinskaya Mountain

Berezina R.

Nemen R.

Minsk

Belorussian Ridge

Hrodna

Sozh R.

Vistula R.

P O L A N D

B E L A R U S

Bug R.

Babruysk

Warsaw

Homyel

Brest

Pinsk

Pripyat R.

Polesye Marshes

0   150 miles

Pripyat Marshes

U K R A I N E

0   200 kilometers

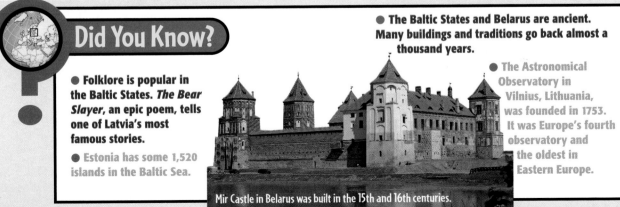

Did You Know?

● **Folklore is popular in the Baltic States.** *The Bear Slayer*, an epic poem, tells one of Latvia's most famous stories.

● **Estonia has some 1,520 islands in the Baltic Sea.**

● **The Astronomical Observatory in Vilnius, Lithuania, was founded in 1753. It was Europe's fourth observatory and the oldest in Eastern Europe.**

Mir Castle in Belarus was built in the 15th and 16th centuries.

71

Ukraine, Moldova and the Caucasus Republics

Eggs-traordinary: Ukrainian Easter eggs are works of art.

Ukraine, located in northern Europe, stretches across the top of the Black Sea. Its gently rolling countryside, called steppes, is rich in minerals, history and culture. The country has two mountain regions: the Crimean Mountains in the south and the Carpathians in the west. Because of its fertile black soil, Ukraine is sometimes called "the breadbasket of Europe."

The largest country entirely within Europe, Ukraine became part of the Soviet Union in 1922. Under Soviet rule, much of Ukraine's culture disappeared. Its famous painted Easter eggs (*pysanky*), fast-paced folk music, language and religious art were repressed because they were considered too nationalistic. Since 1991, when Ukraine declared its independence from the Soviet Union, many of its customs and art forms have been revived.

Parade in Chisinau, Moldova

Armenia, Azerbaijan, Georgia and Moldova also broke away from the Soviet Union. The small republic of Moldova lies to the west of Ukraine. The Caucasus Republics—Armenia, Azerbaijan and Georgia—are considered part of Asia. Beautiful mountain scenery can be found throughout the region. Nearly half of Azerbaijan is covered by mountains. Georgia, which sits on the Black Sea, enjoys a pleasant climate.

Data Bank

ARMENIA
AREA: 11,500 sq mi (29,800 sq km)
POPULATION: 2,976,372
CAPITAL: Yerevan
LANGUAGES: Armenian, Russian

AZERBAIJAN
AREA: 33,400 sq mi (86,000 sq km)
POPULATION: 7,961,619
CAPITAL: Baku
LANGUAGES: Azerbaijani (Azeri), Russian, Armenian

GEORGIA
AREA: 26,911 sq mi (69,700 sq km)
POPULATION: 4,661,473
CAPITAL: Tbilisi
LANGUAGES: Georgian (official), Russian, Armenian, Azeri

MOLDOVA
AREA: 13,067 sq mi (33,843 sq km)
POPULATION: 4,466,706
CAPITAL: Chisinau
LANGUAGES: Moldovan (official), Russian, Gagauz

UKRAINE
AREA: 233,088 sq mi (603,700 sq km)
POPULATION: 46,710,816
CAPITAL: Kiev
LANGUAGES: Ukrainian, Russian, Romanian, Polish, Hungarian

The Monastery Caves, in Kiev, U

Central Russian Upland

RUSSIA

BELARUS

Dnieper R.

Pripyat R.

Kursk

Chernigov

Kiev Reservoir

ytomyr

Kiev

Voronezh

Saratov

Volga R.

Yergeni Hills

ieper Upland

Vinnytsya

Kharkov

Poltava

Dnieper Lowland

Don R.

KAZAKHSTAN

Ural R.

Southern Bug R.

Donets Hills

Donets Basin

Volgograd

UKRAINE

Dnieper R.

Dnipropetrovsk

Donets R.

Donetsk

Tsimlyansk Reservoir

Volga R.

OVA

Zaporizhzhya

Kokhovka Reservoir

Mariupol

Rostov-na-Donu

Astrakhan

isinau

Odessa

Sea of Azov

Kuban Lowland

CRIMEA

Krasnodar

Stavropol

Stavropol Plateau

Caspian Sea

ube R.

Sevastopol

Crimean Mtns.

Kirch Strait

Kuban R.

onstanta

Yalta

Kuma R.

Mt. Elbrus

Grozny

Black Sea

Sukhumi

Caucasus Mtns.

Quba

Kutaisi

Bosporus

Poti

GEORGIA

Tbilisi

AZERBAIJAN

Baku

anbul

Samsun

Pontic Mtns.

ARMENIA

Ganca

Kura R.

Ankara

Mt. Aragats

Yerevan

LakeSevan

Araks R.

TURKEY

Araks R.

Mt. Ararat

Talish Mtns.

Lake Tuz

Kayseri

Lake Van

AZERBAIJAN

Lake Urmia

IRAN

Anatolian Plateau

0   300 miles

0   400 kilometers

Western Russia

Winter Palace Square in Saint Petersburg

Russia is the world's largest country. It spans two continents—Europe in the west and Asia in the east—and 11 time zones! Stretching across 6.6 million sq mi (17 million sq km), it reaches from the Baltic Sea in the west to the Pacific Ocean in the east. Between Russia's coasts lie historic cities, rugged mountain ranges and, in Siberia, some of the coldest places on earth.

At the heart of Russia is Moscow, the nation's capital and largest city. More than 850 years old, the city centers around the imposing Kremlin, a walled fortress that includes elaborate cathedrals, onion-domed churches and government buildings.

Saint Petersburg is Russia's second-largest—and perhaps most European—city. It has been called the "Venice of the North" for its elegant boulevards, lyrical bridges and palace-lined waterways. Saint Petersburg was the Russian capital until 1918. Today, it is still a major cultural and intellectual center.

Changing of the Guard, Red Square

Did You Know?

● Moscow's Red Square—the site of Saint Basil's Cathedral and Lenin's Mausoleum—was not named for communism or the red bricks of the Kremlin. The word for red also means beautiful in Russian.

● The opulent Hermitage, located in Saint Petersburg, is one of the world's largest museums. Visitors can view some 3 million works of art.

Saint Basil's cathedral

● The Trans-Siberian Railroad is the longest in the world, chugging 5,785 mi (9,310 km) from Moscow to Vladivostok, a distance equal to a quarter of the way around the globe.

● Moscow has more subway riders than any other city, transporting 3.2 billion people each year.

Data Bank

RUSSIA
AREA: 6,592,735 sq mi (17,075,200 sq km)
POPULATION: 142,893,540
CAPITAL: Moscow
LANGUAGES: Russian, others

Norwegian Sea

NORWAY

L A P L A N D

Barents Sea

Novaya Zemlya Is.

Yamal Peninsula

Murmansk

Kola Peninsula

Naryan-Mar

Arctic Circle

Salekhard

SWEDEN

FINLAND

Mount Narodnaya

White Sea

Timan Ridge

Pechora R.

Ob R.

Archangelsk

Gulf of Bothnia

Northern Dvina R.

R U S S I A

U r a l

Lake Onega

Serov

Lake Ladoga

Upper Kama Upland

Kirov

Perm

Yekaterinburg

M t n s.

Helsinki

Stockholm

Tallinn

St. Petersburg

Valdai Hills

Rybinsk Reservoir

Yaroslavl

Chelyabinsk

ESTONIA

Baltic Sea

Kama R.

R u s s i a n

P l a i n

Yamantau

LATVIA

Riga

Volga R.

Kazan

Kaliningrad

LITHUANIA

Western Dvina R.

Moscow

Nizhniy Novgorod

Ufa

Magnitogorsk

Vilnius

Minsk

POLAND

BELARUS

Smolensk

Central Russian Upland

Oka-Don Plain

Samara

Warsaw

Ural R.

Orsk

Kursk

Saratov

KAZAKHSTAN

UKRAINE

Kiev

Don R.

Volga R.

Ust Urt Plateau

Kharkov

MOLDOVA

Volgograd

Chisinau

Dnieper R.

ROMANIA

Bucharest

Sea of Azov

Rostov-na-Donu

Astrakhan

CRIMEA

Kuban Lowland

Stravrapol Plateau

Caspian Sea

Danube R.

BULGARIA

Black Sea

Sochi

Mt. Elbrus

Grozny

C a u c a s u s   M t n s.

TURKMENISTAN

Istanbul

GEORGIA

Tbilisi

TURKEY

ARMENIA

Yerevan

AZERBAIJAN

Baku

0   300 miles

0   450 kilometers

Asia

Peak Season: Ama Dablam in the Himalayas

Asia is the world's largest continent. It includes one third of the land on earth. Asia stretches all the way from the Arctic Circle in the north to the Indian Ocean in the Southern Hemisphere. To the east are the Mediterranean Sea and Red Sea and to the west are the Ural Mountains. Because the continents of Asia and Europe meet at the Ural Mountains, many geographers consider Asia and Europe to be one enormous land mass called Eurasia.

Asia's terrain is vast and varied. It includes lakes and deserts; rain forests and glaciers; wide, flat plateaus and the highest mountain range on earth. The Middle East, which lies just east of Europe and north of Africa, is the home of one of earth's oldest civilizations. Most of the Middle East is flat and dry, though some areas are green and lush. Central Asia includes nations such as Uzbekistan and Turkmenistan, which were part of a large country called the Soviet Union until 1991. East Asia includes China, the most populous nation in the world. Southeast Asia is home to dense rain forests and jungles in countries such as Singapore, Vietnam and Thailand. Southern Asia, including Nepal, India and Pakistan, is the location of Mount Everest, the world's tallest mountain.

Asia is home to about 3.4 billion people—three-fifths of the world's population. Most of these people live clustered in southern and Southeast Asia. Others parts of the continent, such as Mongolia and Siberia, are sparsely inhabited. Some Asian nations, including Cambodia and Afghanistan, are among the poorest in the world. Others, such as Saudi Arabia, Japan and Singapore, are among the wealthiest and most modern.

Continent Facts

NUMBER OF COUNTRIES: 44 countries including—Afghanistan, Armenia, Azerbaijan, Bahrain, Bangladesh, Bhutan, Brunei, Burma (Myanmar), Cambodia, China, Cyprus, East Timor, Georgia, India, Indonesia, Iran, Iraq, Israel, Japan, Jordan, Kazakhstan, Kuwait, Kyrgyzstan, Laos, Lebanon, Malaysia, Maldives, Mongolia, Nepal, North Korea, Oman, Pakistan, Philippines, Qatar, Russia, Saudi Arabia, Singapore, South Korea, Sri Lanka, Syria, Taiwan (not recognized internationally as a free and independent nation; it is instead considered to be part of China), Tajikistan, Thailand, Turkey, Turkmenistan, United Arab Emirates, Uzbekistan, Vietnam, Yemen

AREA: 7,212,000 sq mi (44,579,000 sq km)

LONGEST RIVER: The Yangtze is the longest river in Asia and the fourth longest river in the world. It flows for 3,400 mi (5,470 km).

LONGEST MOUNTAIN RANGE: The Himalayas are more than 1,550 mi (2,500 km) long.

HIGHEST PEAK: The world's tallest mountain is Mount Everest in Nepal, at 29,035 ft (8,850 m).

Buddha Statue, Chiang Mai, Thailand

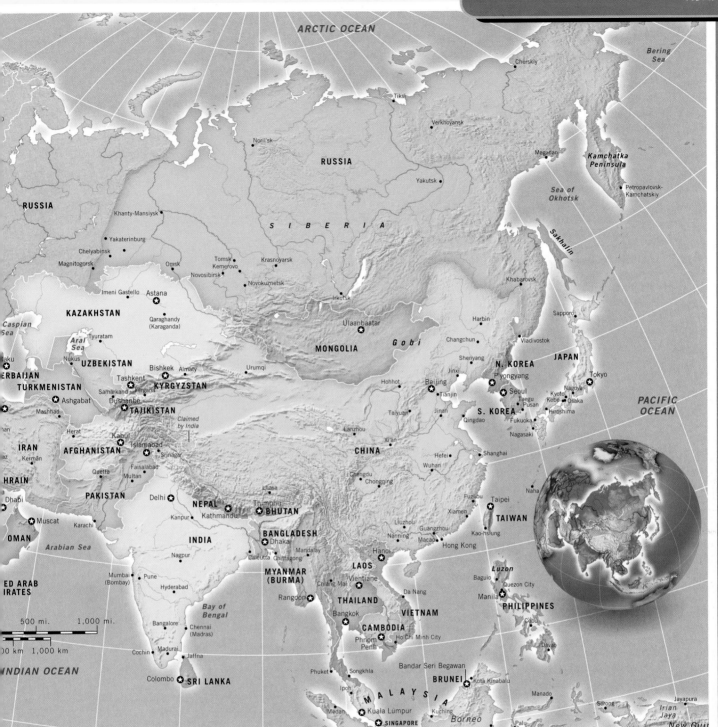

ARCTIC OCEAN

Bering Sea

Cherskiy

Tiksi

Verkhoyansk

Noril'sk

RUSSIA

Magadan

Kamchatka Peninsula

Yakutsk

Petropavlovsk-Kamchatskiy

Sea of Okhotsk

RUSSIA

Khanty-Mansiysk

S I B E R I A

Sakhalin

Yakaterinburg

Chelyabinsk

Magnitogorsk

Omsk

Tomsk

Kemerovo

Krasnoyarsk

Novosibirsk

Novokuznetsk

Khabarovsk

Irkutsk

Imeni Gastello

Astana

Sapporo

Caspian Sea

KAZAKHSTAN

Qaraghandy (Karaganda)

Ulaanbaatar

Harbin

Vladivostok

Aral Sea

Tyuratam

MONGOLIA

Gobi

Changchun

JAPAN

aku

Nukus

UZBEKISTAN

Bishkek Almaty

Urumqi

Shenyang

N. KOREA

RBAIJAN

Tashkent

KYRGYZSTAN

Hohhot

Jinxi

P'yongyang

Tokyo

TURKMENISTAN

Samarkand Fergana

Beijing

Seoul

Kyoto Nagoya

Ashgabat

Dushanbe

Tianjin

Kobe Osaka

Mashhad

TAJIKISTAN

Taiyuan

Jinan

S. KOREA

Pusan

Hiroshima

Herat

Kabul

Claimed by India

Lanzhou

Qingdao

Fukuoka

IRAN

Islamabad

Xi'an

Nagasaki

Kermān

AFGHANISTAN

Srinagar

CHINA

Hefei

Shanghai

Faisalabad

Chengdu

Wuhan

Quetta

Multan

Chongqing

PACIFIC OCEAN

HRAIN

PAKISTAN

Delhi

NEPAL

Lhasa

Naha

Dhabi

Kanpur

Thimphu

Kathmandu

BHUTAN

Fuzhou

Taipei

Muscat

Karachi

Xiamen

OMAN

INDIA

BANGLADESH

Lluzhou

Guangzhou

TAIWAN

Kao-hsiung

Arabian Sea

Nagpur

Dhaka

Mandalay

Nanning

Macao

Luzon

ED ARAB IRATES

Mumbai (Bombay)

Pune

Hyderabad

Calcutta Chittagong

LAOS

Hanoi

Hong Kong

Baguio

Quezon City

MYANMAR (BURMA)

Chiang Mai

Vientiane

Manila

500 mi.

1,000 mi.

Bangalore

Chennai (Madras)

Bay of Bengal

Rangoon

THAILAND

Da Nang

PHILIPPINES

00 km 1,000 km

Cochin

Madurai

Jaffna

Bangkok

VIETNAM

Cebu

CAMBODIA

NDIAN OCEAN

Colombo

SRI LANKA

Phnom Penh

Ho Chi Minh City

Davao

Phuket

Songkhla

Bandar Seri Begawan

Ipoh

BRUNEI

Kota Kinabalu

Manado

Jayapura

Medan

Kuala Lumpur

Kuching

Sorong

Irian Jaya

M A L A Y S I A

SINGAPORE

Borneo

Palu

New Gui

Eastern Russia

A Russian Orthodox church in Novosibirsk

East of the Ural Mountains lies Eastern Russia, an enormous territory that stretches more than 5 million sq mi (13 million sq km). Commonly called Siberia, the region covers the entire northern part of Asia. It makes up 75% of Russia, the largest country in the world, although fewer than 25% of Russia's people live there. Siberia alone is bigger than all of Canada.

A village at the foot of the Altai Mountains in Siberia, Russia

Parts of Siberia can be forbiddingly cold. Two-thirds of the region is covered by permafrost, ground that is frozen year-round. The town of Verkhoyansk, in northeastern Russia, sits in the coldest part of the Northern Hemisphere. Though the average January temperature there is −58°F (−50°C), the temperature has dropped as low as −90°F (−68°C)! Most of Eastern Russia's population lives in the southern and western parts of the region, where the temperatures are milder. Novosibirsk, a chief city in Siberia and the third-largest city in Russia, has an average temperature of 3°F (−16°C) in winter and about 68°F (20°C) in summer.

Though Siberia has few people, it has tremendous natural resources and wildlife. Siberia is Russia's leading producer of gold and diamonds and is rich in coal, oil and gas. Eastern Russia is also the home of the only viable population of wild Siberian tigers.

Endangered: There are fewer than 500 Siberian tigers left in the wild.

Novaya Zemlya Is.

Kar

Mar

B

Ural Mtns.

Salekhard

West Siberian Plain

Khanty-Mansiysk
Surgut
Ob R.
Nizhnevartovsk
Vasyugan'y Swamp

Kurgan
Irtysh R.

Omsk
Tomsk
Astana
Novosibirsk

The Steppes

KAZAKHSTAN

Kazakh Uplands
Irtysh R.
Ob R.
Lake Balkhash

Almaty

Tian Mtns.
Urumqi

Taklimakan Desert

CHINA

A   B

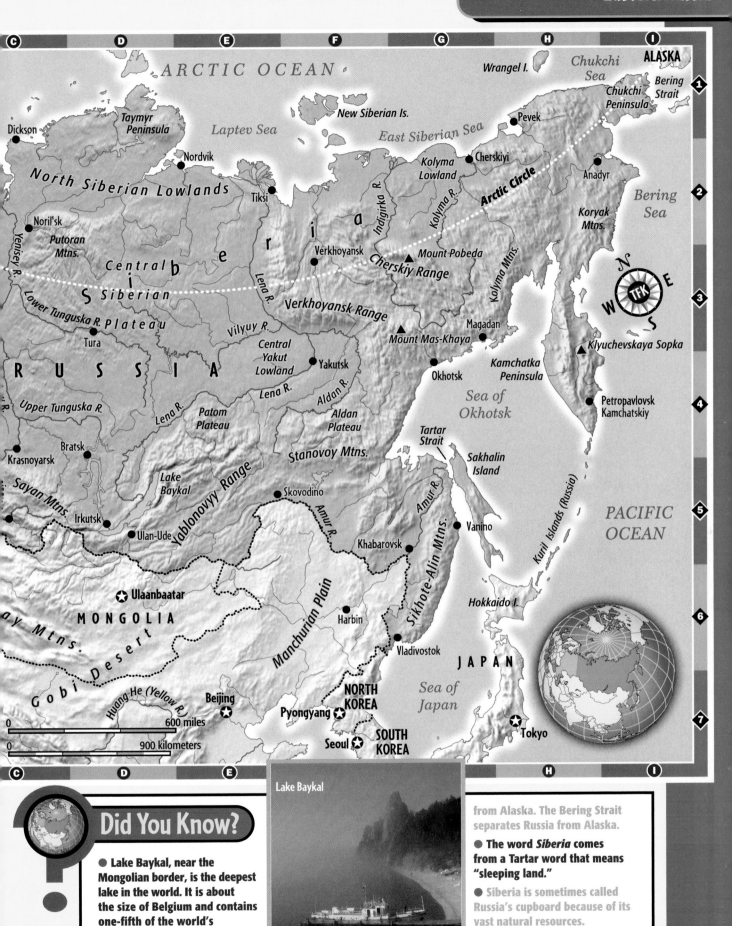

ARCTIC OCEAN

ALASKA

Wrangel I.

Chukchi Sea

Chukchi Peninsula

Bering Strait

Dickson

Taymyr Peninsula

New Siberian Is.

Laptev Sea

East Siberian Sea

Pevek

Nordvik

North Siberian Lowlands

Tiksi

Kolyma Lowland

Cherskiy

Anadyr

Bering Sea

Noril'sk

Putoran Mtns.

Indigirka R.

Kolyma R.

Arctic Circle

Koryak Mtns.

Yenisey R.

Central

S i b e r i a

Verkhoyansk

Mount Pobeda

Cherskiy Range

Kolyma Mtns.

N

Lower Tunguska R.

Siberian Plateau

Lena R.

Verkhoyansk Range

TFK

W   E

S

Tura

Vilyuy R.

Central Yakut Lowland

Mount Mas-Khaya

Magadan

Klyuchevskaya Sopka

Upper Tunguska R.

R U S S I A

Lena R.

Yakutsk

Lena R.

Aldan R.

Okhotsk

Kamchatka Peninsula

Petropavlovsk Kamchatskiy

Patom Plateau

Aldan Plateau

Sea of Okhotsk

Bratsk

Stanovoy Mtns.

Tartar Strait

Sakhalin Island

Krasnoyarsk

Sayan Mtns.

Lake Baykal

Yablonovyy Range

Skovodino

Amur R.

Amur R.

Vanino

Kuril Islands (Russia)

PACIFIC OCEAN

Irkutsk

Ulan-Ude

Khabarovsk

Sikhote-Alin Mtns.

Ulaanbaatar

M O N G O L I A

Manchurian Plain

Harbin

Hokkaido I.

ay Mtns.

Gobi Desert

Vladivostok

J A P A N

Huang He (Yellow R.)

Beijing

NORTH KOREA

Sea of Japan

0   600 miles

Pyongyang

Tokyo

0   900 kilometers

Seoul

SOUTH KOREA

Did You Know?

● Lake Baykal, near the Mongolian border, is the deepest lake in the world. It is about the size of Belgium and contains one-fifth of the world's fresh water.

● The tip of northeastern Russia is just 50 mi (80.5 km)

from Alaska. The Bering Strait separates Russia from Alaska.

● The word *Siberia* comes from a Tartar word that means "sleeping land."

● Siberia is sometimes called Russia's cupboard because of its vast natural resources.

● In some parts of Eastern Russia, the permafrost is almost 1 mi (1.6 km) deep!

Turkey and Cyprus

Turkey, a nation about the size of the state of Texas, straddles the border between Europe and Asia. On its western border sit Greece and Bulgaria; to the east and south are Syria, Iraq, Iran, Azerbaijan, Armenia and Georgia. Turkey's unique location means that it is both European and Asian. For more than 4,000 years, it has served as a bridge between the two continents and many different civilizations. Its art, architecture and customs reflect its complicated past.

Turkish Delight: A woman buys melons at a market

Up until 1923, Turkey was a Muslim territory under the Ottoman Empire. It was a preindustrial region, with few ties to the modern world. Then Kemal Atatürk, a Turkish soldier who had led a revolution to overthrow the Ottomans, became the leader of the Turkish nation. Atatürk changed many aspects of Turkish culture, including its alphabet, clothing styles, calendar and relationship to the West.

Cyprus, an island off the coast of Turkey and Greece, has been fought over for centuries. In 1960, it became an independent nation whose government included both Turks and Greeks. Tension between the two nationalities grew until 1974, when conflict split the island into two parts. The Greek-led nation of Cyprus, not the Turkish Republic of Northern Cyprus, is considered to be the official government.

Turkey and Cyprus have a warm, dry climate and rely on farming for income, although both countries are becoming more industrialized.

 Data Bank

CYPRUS
AREA: 3,572 sq mi (9,250 sq km)
POPULATION: 784,301
CAPITAL: Nicosia
LANGUAGES: Greek, Turkish, English

TURKEY
AREA: 301,381 sq mi (780,580 sq km)
POPULATION: 70,413,958
CAPITAL: Ankara
LANGUAGES: Turkish (official), Kurdish, Arabic, Armenian, Greek

The Blue Mosque in Istanbul, Turkey

80

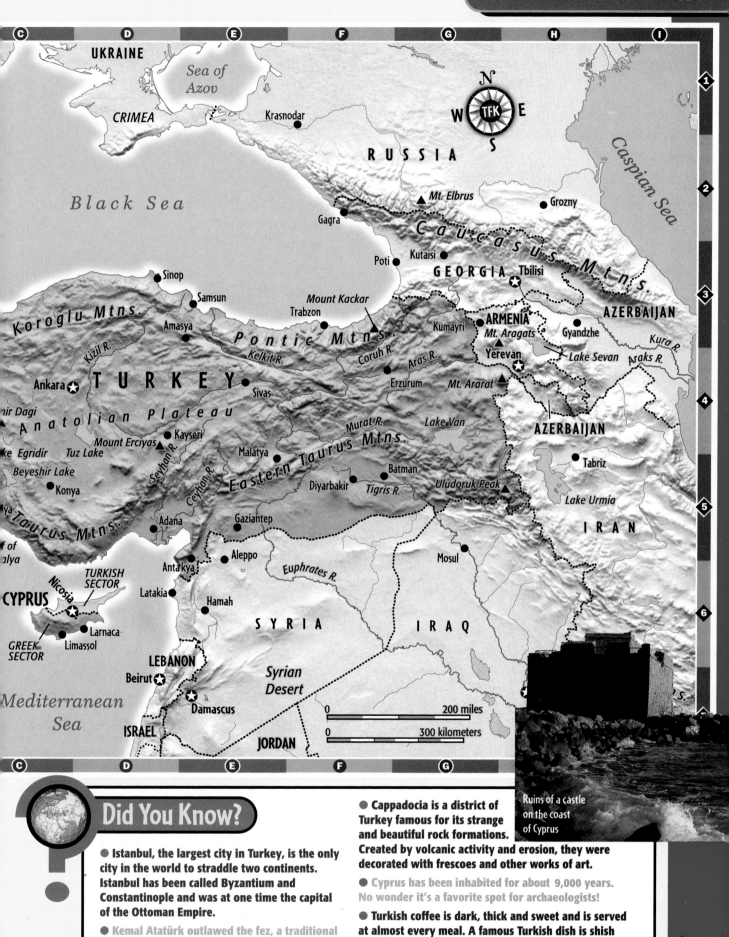

UKRAINE

Sea of Azov

CRIMEA

Krasnodar

RUSSIA

Black Sea

Mt. Elbrus

Grozny

Gagra

Caucasus Mtns.

Poti   Kutaisi

GEORGIA   Tbilisi

AZERBAIJAN

Sinop

Samsun

Mount Kackar

Koroglu Mtns.

Amasya

Trabzon

Pontic Mtns.

Kumayri

ARMENIA

Mt. Aragats

Gyandzhe

Kura R.

Kizil R.

Kelkit R.

Coruh R.

Yerevan

Lake Sevan

Araks R.

Ankara

T U R K E Y

Sivas

Aras R.

Erzurum

Mt. Ararat

AZERBAIJAN

ir Dagi

Anatolian Plateau

Lake Van

ke Egridir   Tuz Lake

Mount Erciyas   Kayseri

Seyhan R.

Murat R.

Tabriz

Beyeshir Lake

Malatya

Eastern Taurus Mtns.

Batman

Uludoruk Peak

Lake Urmia

Konya

Ceyhan R.

Diyarbakir

Tigris R.

I R A N

ya

Taurus Mtns.

Adana

Gaziantep

Antakya

Aleppo

Mosul

TURKISH SECTOR

Latakia

Euphrates R.

CYPRUS   Nicosia

Hamah

S Y R I A

I R A Q

Larnaca

GREEK SECTOR

Limassol

LEBANON

Beirut

Syrian Desert

Mediterranean Sea

Damascus

ISRAEL

JORDAN

0   200 miles

0   300 kilometers

Ruins of a castle on the coast of Cyprus

Did You Know?

● Istanbul, the largest city in Turkey, is the only city in the world to straddle two continents. Istanbul has been called Byzantium and Constantinople and was at one time the capital of the Ottoman Empire.

● Kemal Atatürk outlawed the fez, a traditional Turkish hat, because he thought it made Turks look too old-fashioned.

● Cappadocia is a district of Turkey famous for its strange and beautiful rock formations. Created by volcanic activity and erosion, they were decorated with frescoes and other works of art.

● Cyprus has been inhabited for about 9,000 years. No wonder it's a favorite spot for archaeologists!

● Turkish coffee is dark, thick and sweet and is served at almost every meal. A famous Turkish dish is shish kebob—meat or seafood and vegetables cut into small chunks, threaded onto a skewer and grilled.

Israel, Lebanon, Jordan and Syria

City of Gold: A view of old Jerusalem

Israel, Jordan, Lebanon and Syria are Middle Eastern lands of ancient cultures and archaeological treasures. Stretching from the banks of the Tigris River to the Gulf of Aqaba, the region has long been a crossroads of conquerors and Crusaders. Because the land is sacred to Judaism, Christianity and Islam, it has also been at the center of centuries-old religious conflicts and political disputes.

Many of the world's holiest sites are found in Israel. Jews pray at the 2,000-year-old Western Wall in Jerusalem. Muslims pray at the golden Dome of the Rock mosque. Christians pray at the Church of the Holy Sepulchre, site of the tomb of Jesus.

The kingdom of Jordan is also known for its religious and archaeological sites. Petra, the best-known of them, is an ancient city of elaborate temples and tombs carved completely from sandstone. Two thousand years ago, the city was a crossroads for the spice trade. Syria, which is to the north of Jordan, has one of the oldest recorded histories in the world. The country's capital, Damascus, has been inhabited since prehistoric times! Lebanon lies between Israel and Syria. From 1975 to 1990, a civil war raged in Lebanon, and the country is still recovering from it.

Syrian Soda:
A man in Damascus sells soft drinks.

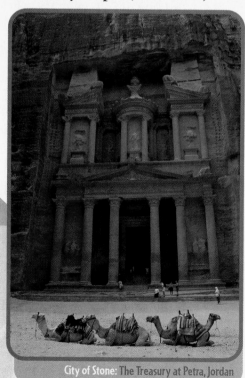

City of Stone: The Treasury at Petra, Jordan

Data Bank

ISRAEL
AREA: 8,020 sq mi (20,770 sq km)
POPULATION: 6,352,117
CAPITAL: Jerusalem
LANGUAGES: Hebrew, Arabic (both official), English

JORDAN
AREA: 35,637 sq mi ((92,300 sq km)
POPULATION: 5,906,760
CAPITAL: Amman
LANGUAGES: Arabic (official), English

LEBANON
AREA: 4,015 sq mi (10,400 sq km)
POPULATION: 3,874,050
CAPITAL: Beirut
LANGUAGES: Arabic (official), French, English, Armenian

SYRIA
AREA: 71,498 sq mi (185,180 sq km)
POPULATION: 18,881,361
CAPITAL: Damascus
LANGUAGES: Arabic (official), French, English

TURKEY

SYRIA

LEBANON

ISRAEL

JORDAN

IRAQ

SAUDI ARABIA

EGYPT

CYPRUS

Taurus Mtns.

Mediterranean Sea

Seyhan R.
Ceyhan R.
Euphrates R.
Tigris R.
Euphrates R.
Khabur R.
Wadi Hauran
Euphrates R.

Adana
Antakya
Aleppo
al-Qamishi
al-Hasakah
Lake al-Assad
ar Raqqah
Dayr az-Zawr

Latakia
Orontes R.
Hamah
Abu Rujmayn Mtns.
Tartus
Homs
Tadmur
Tripoli

Lebanon Mtns.
▲ Qurnat as-Sawda
Juniyah
Beirut ✪
Bekaa Valley
Damascus ✪
▲ Mt. Hermon
Tyre
Golan Heights
Acre
Lake Tiberias (Sea of Galilee)
Haifa
▲ Mount ad Duruz

Syrian Desert

Jebel Aneiza ▲

Tel Aviv-Jaffa
West Bank
Irbid
az-Zarqa
Jerusalem ✪
Amman ✪
Gaza Strip
Hebron
Madaba
Beersheba
Dead Sea
Port Said

Negev
Araba R.
Great Rift Valley
Esh Shera
Petra
Ma'an
el Jafr Depression

an-Nafud Desert

Suez Canal
EGYPT
Suez
Sinai Peninsula

Elat
Aqaba
▲ Mount Ramm

Gulf of Suez
Gulf of Aqaba

Jordan R.

Mt. Olympus ▲
Nicosia ✪
TURKISH SECTOR
Larnaca
Limassol
GREEK SECTOR

0 — 150 miles
0 — 200 kilometers

TFK

A swimmer in the Dead Sea

Did You Know?

● The ancient walled city of Jerusalem is divided into quarters: Jewish, Christian, Muslim and Armenian.

● The cedar tree is the national symbol of Lebanon. In biblical times, cedar trees covered the countryside.

● The city of Petra takes its name from a Greek word meaning rock.

● Beirut, the Lebanese capital, was once known as "the Paris of the Middle East."

● The Dead Sea, located between Israel and Jordan, is so salty, bathers float easily on top of the water!

The Arabian Peninsula

Windblown desert sands cover much of the Arabian Peninsula. The area's climate is generally hot and dry, and the vegetation is sparse. The Arabian Desert, which takes up a large part of Saudi Arabia, Kuwait, Qatar, the United Arab Emirates and Oman, is the largest subtropical desert in the world. Only the Sahara Desert is larger.

Pilgrimage: Muslims gather at the Great Mosque in Mecca, Saudi Arabia.

Beneath the desert sands lies a treasure—oil. The countries in this region are highly dependent on the petroleum industry. It has made many of them rich. Saudi Arabia, the largest country in the region, has one-third of the world's known oil reserves. Oil has been both a blessing and a curse for Kuwait. In 1990, in a bid to gain control of Kuwait's lucrative oil fields, Iraq invaded its tiny neighbor. The United States and its allies intervened, and in January 1991, they used bombs and ground forces to set Kuwait free. In 2003, the U.S. went to war against Iraq again. Iraq's leader, Saddam Hussein, was executed for crimes against humanity in 2006.

At the tip of the Arabian Peninsula are Yemen and Oman. Although Yemen does not have the oil riches of its neighbors, its location—at the southern entrance to the Red Sea—is strategic. Qatar, Bahrain and the United Arab Emirates lie on the Persian Gulf, along the west coast of Saudi Arabia. Bahrain is made up of a group of small islands, and the United Arab Emirates is a union of seven kingdoms.

Data Bank

BAHRAIN
AREA: 257 sq mi (665 sq km)
POPULATION: 698,585
CAPITAL: Manama
LANGUAGES: Arabic, English, Farsi, Urdu

IRAQ
AREA: 168,753 sq mi (437,072 sq km)
POPULATION: 26,783,383
CAPITAL: Baghdad
LANGUAGES: Arabic, Kurdish, Assyrian, Armenian

KUWAIT
AREA: 6,880 sq mi (17,820 sq km)
POPULATION: 2,418,393
CAPITAL: Kuwait
LANGUAGES: Arabic (official), English

OMAN
AREA: 82,030 sq mi (212,460 sq km)
POPULATION: 3,102,229
CAPITAL: Muscat
LANGUAGES: Arabic (official), English, Indian languages

QATAR
AREA: 4,416 sq mi (11,437 sq km)
POPULATION: 885,359
CAPITAL: Doha
LANGUAGES: Arabic (official), English

SAUDI ARABIA
AREA: 756,981 sq mi (1,960,582 sq km)
POPULATION: 27,019,731
CAPITAL: Riyadh
LANGUAGE: Arabic

UNITED ARAB EMIRATES
AREA: 32,000 sq mi (82,880 sq km)
POPULATION: 2,602,713
CAPITAL: Abu Dhabi
LANGUAGES: Arabic (official), Persian, English, Hindi, Urdu

YEMEN
AREA: 203,848 sq mi (527,970 sq km)
POPULATION: 21,456,188
CAPITAL: Sanaa
LANGUAGE: Arabic

Gleaming Skyline: Dubai, in the United Arab Emirates

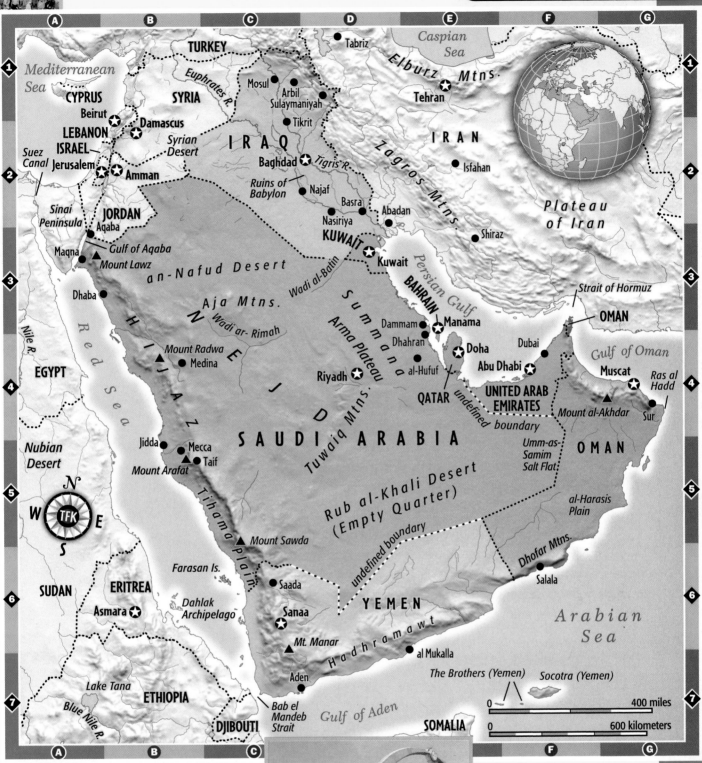

A B C D E F G

1 Mediterranean Sea

TURKEY

Tabriz

Caspian Sea

CYPRUS

Euphrates R.

SYRIA

Mosul

Arbil
Sulaymaniyah

Elburz Mtns.

Tehran

IRAN

2 Beirut

LEBANON

Damascus

Syrian Desert

IRAQ

Tikrit

Baghdad

Tigris R.

Zagros Mtns.

Isfahan

Suez Canal

ISRAEL

Jerusalem

Amman

Ruins of Babylon

Najaf

Basra

Nasiriya

Abadan

Shiraz

Plateau of Iran

JORDAN

Aqaba

KUWAIT

Kuwait

Persian Gulf

3 Sinai Peninsula

Magna

Gulf of Aqaba

Mount Lawz

an-Nafud Desert

Wadi al-Batin

Strait of Hormuz

BAHRAIN

Dhaba

Aja Mtns.

Wadi ar- Rimah

Summan

Dammam

Manama

OMAN

N E J D

Arma Plateau

Dhahran

Doha

Dubai

Gulf of Oman

Red Sea

H I J A Z

Mount Radwa

Medina

Riyadh

al-Hufuf

Abu Dhabi

UNITED ARAB EMIRATES

Muscat

Ras al Hadd

4 EGYPT

QATAR

undefined boundary

Mount al-Akhdar

Sur

Nubian Desert

Jidda

Mecca

Taif

SAUDI ARABIA

Tuwaiq Mtns.

Umm-as-Samim Salt Flat

OMAN

Mount Arafat

5 N W E S TFK

Rub al-Khali Desert (Empty Quarter)

al-Harasis Plain

undefined boundary

Dhofar Mtns.

6 SUDAN

ERITREA

Asmara

Tihama Plain

Mount Sawda

Farasan Is.

Dahlak Archipelago

Saada

Sanaa

YEMEN

Salala

Arabian Sea

Mt. Manar

Hadhramawt

al Mukalla

7 Lake Tana

Blue Nile R.

ETHIOPIA

DJIBOUTI

Aden

Bab el Mandeb Strait

Gulf of Aden

SOMALIA

The Brothers (Yemen)

Socotra (Yemen)

0 400 miles

0 600 kilometers

A B C F G

Nile R.

Did You Know?

The Arch of Swords in Doha, Qatar

● In ancient times, Iraq was called Mesopotamia, which means "land between the rivers" in Greek. Much of the country is made up of the fertile plains that lie between the Tigris and Euphrates Rivers.

● Islam's holiest cities, Mecca and Medina, are located in Saudi Arabia.

● Mecca is the birthplace of the Prophet Muhammad.

● The Rub al-Khali desert, located in Saudi Arabia, is the biggest expanse of unbroken sand in the world. Its name means "empty quarter."

● Four countries—Saudi Arabia, Iraq, Iran and Russia—control almost 70% of the world's oil reserves.

85

Central Asia

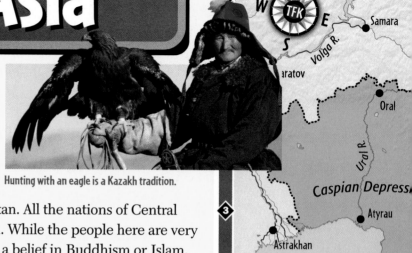

Central Asia, which includes the nations of Kazakhstan, Turkmenistan, Uzbekistan, Tajikistan and Kyrgyzstan, stretches from Russia and the Ural Mountains all the way to China. To the south, Central Asia borders Iran and Afghanistan. All the nations of Central Asia were once part of the Soviet Union. While the people here are very different from one another, many share a belief in Buddhism or Islam. Many are also nomads, traveling from place to place. The yurt, which is similar to a tent, is the traditional dwelling of these nomadic people.

Hunting with an eagle is a Kazakh tradition.

Kazakhstan is the largest Central Asian nation. To the west are the Ural Mountains and their foothills. The remainder of the country includes deserts and vast plains called steppes. Kazakhstan is the most modernized of the Central Asian nations. Turkmenistan, the second-largest nation in the region, is almost entirely covered by dry, grassy steppes and the huge Kara-Kum Desert. Uzbekistan, like neighboring Turkmenistan, is largely desert and steppes.

The Pamir Mountains in Tajikistan are among the highest in the world. Two Central Asian mountain systems, the Tian Shan and the Pamirs, meet in Kyrgyzstan. As a result, it is a nation of peaks and valleys. Since Kyrgyzstan gained its independence in 1991, its economy has grown. Today, it is a major exporter of energy to other Central Asian nations.

Data Bank

KAZAKHSTAN
AREA: 1,049,150 sq mi (2,717,300 sq km)
POPULATION: 15,233,244
CAPITAL: Astana
LANGUAGES: Russian (official), Kazakh

KYRGYZSTAN
AREA: 76,641 sq mi (198,500 sq km)
POPULATION: 5,213,898
CAPITAL: Bishkek
LANGUAGES: Kyrgyz, Russian (both official)

TAJIKISTAN
AREA: 55,251 sq mi (143,100 sq km)
POPULATION: 7,320,815
CAPITAL: Dushanbe
LANGUAGES: Tajik (official), Russian

TURKMENISTAN
AREA: 188,455 sq mi (488,100 sq km)
POPULATION: 5,042,920
CAPITAL: Ashgabat
LANGUAGES: Turkmen, Russian, Uzbek, others

UZBEKISTAN
AREA: 172,740 sq mi (447,400 sq km)
POPULATION: 27,307,134
CAPITAL: Tashkent
LANGUAGES: Uzbek, Russian, Tajik, others

Life in a Yurt: Views of the inside and outside of a nomadic home

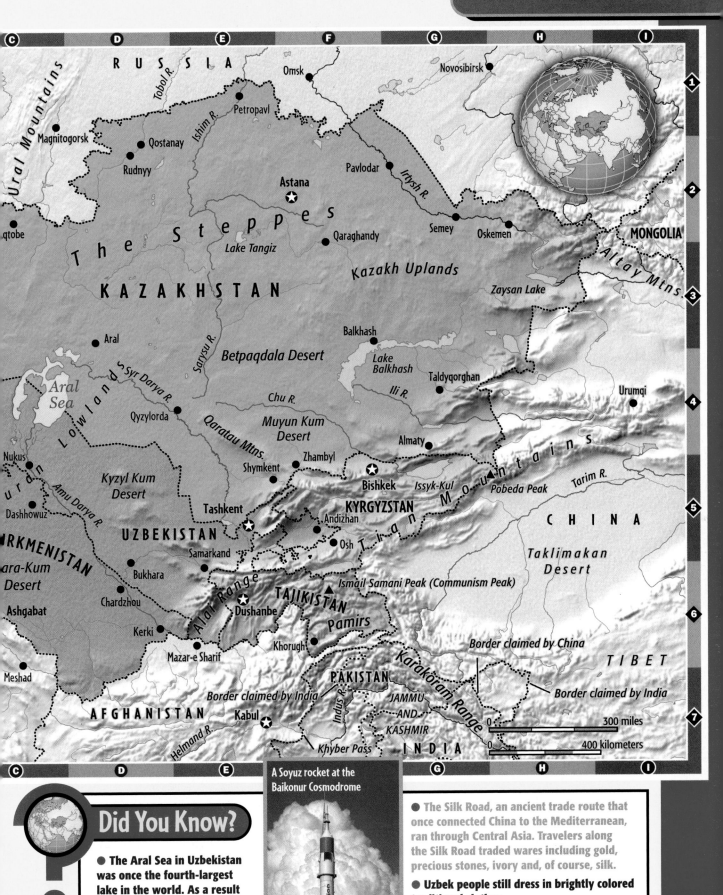

C D E F G H I

RUSSIA

1

Omsk   Novosibirsk

Ural Mountains

Tobol R.

Magnitogorsk   Petropavl

Qostanay   Ishim R.

Rudnyy   Pavlodar

Astana   Irtysh R.   2

qtobe   Semey   Oskemen   MONGOLIA

The Steppes   Altay Mtns.

Qaraghandy

Lake Tangiz   Kazakh Uplands

KAZAKHSTAN   Zaysan Lake   3

Aral   Balkhash

Sarysu R.   Lake
Balkhash   Taldyqorghan

Aral   Betpaqdala Desert   Urumqi   4

Sea   Syr Darya R.   Ili R.

Qyzylorda   Chu R.

Qaratau Mtns.   Muyun Kum
Desert

Nukus   Almaty

Kyzyl Kum   Shymkent   Zhambyl

Desert   CHINA

Tashkent   Bishkek   Issyk-Kul   Pobeda Peak   Tarim R.   5

Amu Darya R.   KYRGYZSTAN   Tian Mountains

Dashhowuz   Andizhan   Taklimakan
Desert

RKMENISTAN   UZBEKISTAN   Samarkand   Osh

ara-Kum   Bukhara   Ismail Samani Peak (Communism Peak)

Desert   Alai Range   TAJIKISTAN

Chardzhou   Dushanbe   Pamirs   6

Ashgabat

Kerki   Khorugh   Karakoram Range   Border claimed by China

Mazar-e Sharif   TIBET

Meshad   PAKISTAN   Border claimed by India

Border claimed by India   JAMMU

AFGHANISTAN   Kabul   AND   0   300 miles   7

Helmand R.   Indus R.   KASHMIR

Khyber Pass   INDIA   0   400 kilometers

C D E F G H I

Did You Know?

● The Aral Sea in Uzbekistan
was once the fourth-largest
lake in the world. As a result
of misuse, the lake has
almost completely dried up,
destroying the area's fishing
industry and damaging its
natural environment.

● The Silk Road, an ancient trade route that
once connected China to the Mediterranean,
ran through Central Asia. Travelers along
the Silk Road traded wares including gold,
precious stones, ivory and, of course, silk.

● Uzbek people still dress in brightly colored
traditional clothes.

● The Soviet Union's rocketry program
was based at the Baikonur Cosmodrome in
Star City, Kazakhstan, the site for Russia's
space-shuttle program.

Afghanistan, Iran and Pakistan

ore than 2,000 years ago, the region now called Iran was the center of the Persian Empire. In 518 B.C., Darius I built an immense palace complex called Persepolis. Today, its ruins are an important archaeological site.

Landmark from Long Ago: Persepolis in Iran

Rugged landscapes mark this part of the world. Much of Iran, Afghanistan and Pakistan is covered by deserts or mountains, although Pakistan also has rich wetlands. An 800-mi (1,287-km) desert covers a large portion of Iran. The Hindu Kush, the world's second-highest mountain range, reaches across landlocked Afghanistan into Pakistan. Iran, which lies west of Afghanistan and Pakistan, has a coast on the Caspian Sea to the north and on the Persian Gulf and Arabian Sea to the south. Pakistan, too, has a coast on the Arabian Sea.

All three countries are lands of diverse ethnic and religious groups. The different cultures and beliefs have often been a source of tension. The region has struggled with civil unrest and acts of violence. In 2001, the United States went to war with Afghanistan's Taliban government in an effort to combat terrorism. Since then, the Afghan people have made strides toward a democratic, more inclusive system of government. The new government lifted a ban on education for girls age ten and older.

Data Bank

AFGHANISTAN
AREA: 249,999 sq mi (647,500 sq km)
POPULATION: 31,056,997
CAPITAL: Kabul
LANGUAGES: Pashtu, Afghan Persian (Dari), other Turkic languages

IRAN
AREA: 636,293 sq mi (1,648,000 sq km)
POPULATION: 68,688,433
CAPITAL: Tehran
LANGUAGES: Persian, Turkic, Kurdish

PAKISTAN
AREA: 310,400 sq mi (803,940 sq km)
POPULATION: 165,803,560
CAPITAL: Islamabad
LANGUAGES: Urdu (official), Punjabi, Sindhi, Siraiki, Pashtu, others

A Kashmir refugee camp set up after an earthquake destroyed millions of homes in 2005

RUSSIA
GEORGIA
ARMENIA
Yerevan
TURKEY
AZERBAIJAN
AZERBAIJAN
Tabriz
Ardabil
Sabalan (volcano)
Lake Urmia
Qezel Ow
Rash
Baghdad
Hamadan
Tigris R.
Zagro
Euphrates R.
Korun R.
IRAQ
Abadan
KUWAIT
Kuwait
SAUDI ARABIA
Persian Gulf
Manama
BAHRAIN
QAT

C | **D** | **E** | **F** | **G** | **H** | **I**

KAZAKHSTAN

KAZAKHSTAN

⭐ Bishkek

UZBEKISTAN

KYRGYZSTAN

Dashhowuz

Amu Darya R.

TURKMENISTAN

⭐ Tashkent

Samarkand

CHINA

Caspian Sea

Kara-Kum Desert

Bukhara

Dushanbe

▲ Ismail Samani Peak

Damavand (volcano)

Ashgabat ⭐

Atrek R.

Kerki

TAJIKISTAN

Boundary claimed by India

Elburz Mtns.

Meshad ●

Mazar-e Sharif ●

Baghlan

Hindu Kush Mtns

Tirich Mir ▲

Karakoram Range

K2

ehran

Paropamisus Range

Kunduz R.

Nanga Parbat

Great Salt Desert

Hari R.

Kabul ⭐

Khyber Pass

▲ JAMMU

Indus R.

AND

ahan

Plateau of Iran

Herat ●

AFGHANISTAN

▲ Mt. Fuladi

Islamabad ●

Srinagar ●

Himalayas

IRAN

Dasht-e-Lut

Mt. Sangan ▲

Peshawar ●

KASHMIR

Yazd ●

Farah R.

Rawalpindi

Boundary claimed by Pakistan

Kerman ●

Margow Desert

Helmand R.

Kandahar ●

Chenab R.

Faisalabad ●

Lahore ●

n s.

RIGESTAN

Multan ●

Amritsar ●

● Shiraz

Zahedan ●

Quetta ●

Kuh-e Laleh Zar ▲

Bam ●

BALUCHISTAN

Brahui Range

PAKISTAN

INDIA

Kuh-e Taftan (volcano) ▲

Baluchistan Plateau

Indus R.

Thar Desert

Mehran R.

Nal R.

Sutlej R.

Bandar Abbas ●

Dadu ●

Strait of Hormuz

OMAN

Turbat ●

Great Indian Desert

Abu Dhabi ⭐

Gulf of Oman

Hyderabad ●

UNITED ARAB EMIRATES

Karachi ●

Ahmadabad ●

Muscat ⭐

Arabian Sea

0 _____ 400 miles

OMAN

0 _____ 600 kilometers

C | **D** | **E** | | **H** | **I**

Did You Know?

● Temperatures in Afghanistan can change rapidly during the course of a single day. It's not unusual for the temperature to go from 32°F at dawn to 90°F by noon.

● Alexander the Great conquered Persepolis in 330 B.C. He carried away the palace's treasures on 20,000 mules and 5,000 camels.

Fruit vendor in Iran

● In 1947, India and Pakistan were partitioned along religious lines. Pakistan is predominantly Muslim, and India is mostly Hindu.

● Both India and Pakistan claim to own the Kashmir region, which separates the two countries.

● K2, the second-highest mountain in the world, is located in Pakistan. The country boasts 13 of the world's 30 tallest peaks.

Indian Subcontinent

The Taj Mahal, in Agra, India, is one of the world's most magnificent buildings.

Chattering monkeys, brightly painted elephants, high-tech computer whizzes and glamorous movie stars are all found in India. The world's seventh-largest country is a vast and diverse land. From snowcapped mountains to leafy jungles and bustling cities, India offers a wealth of sights, smells and sounds. India, which is predominantly Hindu, has on its northeast border the small, Muslim country of Bangladesh.

The Himalayas, the world's tallest mountains, form India's northern border. Nestled at the foot of the mountains' mammoth peaks are the tiny Buddhist kingdoms of Nepal and Bhutan. Despite their rugged setting, the two countries have much to offer. More than 9,500 species of birds can be found in Nepal. The majority of the people in Nepal and Bhutan work in the fields, raising crops or tending livestock. Tourism is an important industry. Nepal's Sherpas are famous for guiding mountain climbers up the steep slopes of Mount Everest and other forbidding peaks.

To India's south, in the Indian Ocean, sits the pearl-shaped island nation of Sri Lanka. Although ethnic conflict has festered in the country for years, Sri Lanka's natural beauty beckons visitors. Sri Lanka is known for its lovely beaches, exotic wildlife and large tea plantations.

Data Bank

A baby elephant taking a bath at the Pinnawala elephant orphanage in Sri Lanka

BANGLADESH
AREA: 55,598 sq mi (144,000 sq km)
POPULATION: 147,365,352
CAPITAL: Dhaka
LANGUAGES: Bangla (official), English

BHUTAN
AREA: 18,147 sq mi (47,000 sq km)
POPULATION: 2,279,723
CAPITAL: Thimphu
LANGAGES: Dzongkha (official), Tibetan and Nepalese dialects

INDIA
AREA: 1,269,338 sq mi (3,287,590 sq km)
POPULATION: 1,095,351,995
CAPITAL: New Delhi
LANGUAGES: Hindi (official), English, native languages

NEPAL
AREA: 54,363 sq mi (140,800 sq km)
POPULATION: 28,287,147
CAPTIAL: Kathmandu
LANGUAGES: Nepali (official), English

SRI LANKA
AREA: 23,332 sq mi (65,610 sq km)
POPULATION: 20,222,240
CAPITAL: Colombo
LANGUAGES: Sinhala (official), Tamil, English

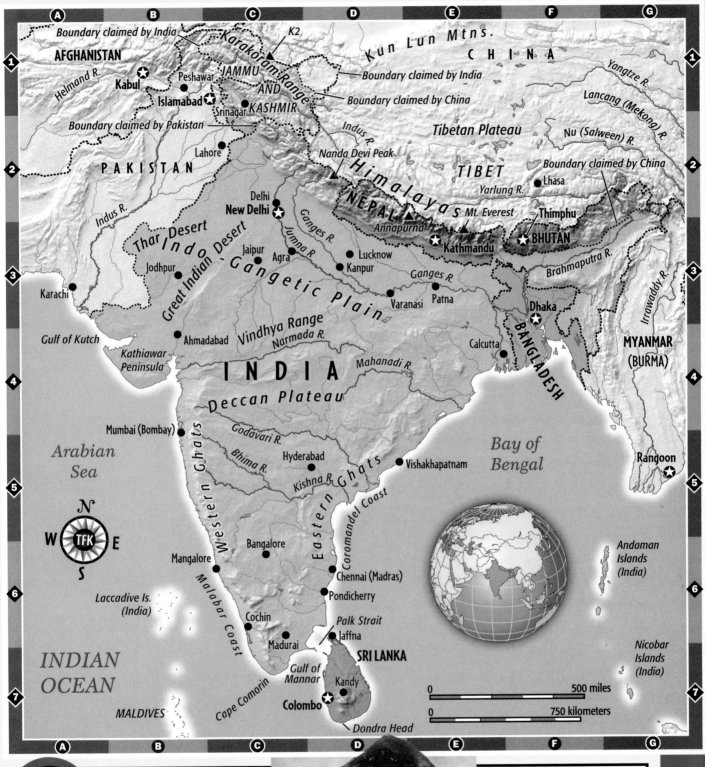

A · B · C · D · E · F · G

Boundary claimed by India

AFGHANISTAN

Karakoram Range

K2

Kun Lun Mtns.

C H I N A

Helmand R.

Kabul

Peshawar

JAMMU

AND

Boundary claimed by India

Yangtze R.

Islamabad

Srinagar

KASHMIR

Boundary claimed by China

Tibetan Plateau

Lancang (Mekong) R.

Boundary claimed by Pakistan

Indus R.

Nu (Salween) R.

Lahore

Nanda Devi Peak

H i m a l a y a s

T I B E T

Boundary claimed by China

PAKISTAN

NEPAL

Mt. Everest

Lhasa

Yarlung R.

Indus R.

Delhi

Annapurna

Thimphu

New Delhi

Ganges R.

Kathmandu

BHUTAN

Thar Desert

Jumna R.

Lucknow

Brahmaputra R.

Great Indian Desert

Jaipur

Agra

Kanpur

Ganges R.

Irrawaddy R.

Jodhpur

I n d o - G a n g e t i c P l a i n

Varanasi

Patna

Karachi

Dhaka

Gulf of Kutch

Ahmadabad

Vindhya Range

Narmada R.

Calcutta

BANGLADESH

MYANMAR

(BURMA)

Kathiawar

Peninsula

I N D I A

Mahanadi R.

Deccan Plateau

Arabian

Sea

Mumbai (Bombay)

Godavari R.

Bhima R.

Hyderabad

Bay of

Bengal

Rangoon

Kishna R.

Vishakhapatnam

W
N
E
S

TFK

Bangalore

Eastern Ghats

Andaman

Islands

(India)

Mangalore

Western Ghats

Chennai (Madras)

6

Laccadive Is.

(India)

Pondicherry

Malabar Coast

Cochin

Palk Strait

Nicobar

Islands

(India)

INDIAN

OCEAN

Madurai

Jaffna

Coromandel Coast

SRI LANKA

MALDIVES

Gulf of

Mannar

Kandy

0   500 miles

0   750 kilometers

Cape Comorin

Colombo

Dondra Head

A · B · C · D · E · F · G

Did You Know?

● The people of Bhutan call their land Druk Yul meaning "land of the thunder dragon."

● Mount Everest is named after Sir George Everest, the British surveyor-general of India, who was the first to record the mountain's height and location.

● Emperor Shah Jahan built the Taj Mahal in memory of his second wife, Mumtaz Mahal. It took more than 20 years to build the monument.

● India is the world's largest democracy. In the past 10,000 years, it has never invaded another country.

● Until 1972, Sri Lanka was known as Ceylon.

91

China, Mongolia and Taiwan

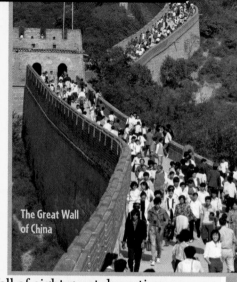

The Great Wall of China

China is a country of giant land mass and giant population. It has more people than any country. One in every five people on the planet is Chinese. The country's varied landscapes include towering mountains, barren deserts and lush valleys. China is also a land of busy cities and gleaming skyscrapers.

Through 2,200 years of recorded history, the Chinese have developed rich traditions in food, festivals, art and medicine. China has seen the rise and fall of eight great dynasties, or ruling families. In 1949, the country embraced a form of government called communism. China insists that the island of Taiwan is not a separate country but belongs to the mainland.

The Gobi Desert, a huge expanse of rocks and dry grasslands, extends north from China into Mongolia. The landlocked nation, which gained its independence from China in 1921, is a place of harsh winters and little vegetation. It is one of Asia's most sparsely populated countries.

Data Bank

CHINA
AREA: 3,705,386 sq mi (9,596,960 sq km)
POPULATION: 1,313,973,713
CAPITAL: Beijing
LANGUAGES: Chinese (Mandarin), local dialects

MONGOLIA
AREA: 604,250 sq mi (1,565,000 sq km)
POPULATION: 2,832,224
CAPITAL: Ulaanbaatar
LANGUAGES: Khalkha Mongol, Turkic, Russian

TAIWAN
AREA: 13,892 sq mi (35,980 sq km)
POPULATION: 23,036,087
CAPITAL: Taipei
LANGUAGES: Chinese (Mandarin), Taiwanese, Hakka dialects

Hong Kong's sparkling skyline

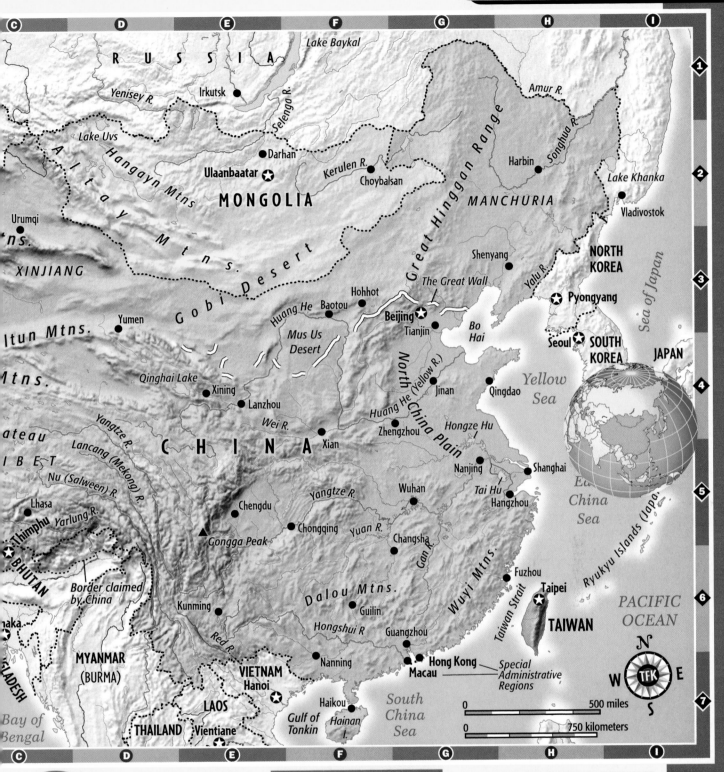

RUSSIA

Lake Baykal

Yenisey R.
Irkutsk
Selenga R.
Lake Uvs
Hangayn Mtns.
Darhan
Amur R.
Ulaanbaatar
Kerulen R.
Choybalsan
Harbin
Songhua R.
MONGOLIA
MANCHURIA
Lake Khanka

Urumqi
Altay Mtns.
Vladivostok

XINJIANG
Gobi Desert
Great Hinggan Range
Shenyang
NORTH KOREA
Sea of Japan

Itun Mtns.
Yumen
Mus Us Desert
Hohhot
Baotou
Huang He
The Great Wall
Beijing
Yalu R.
Pyongyang

Mtns.
Tianjin
Bo Hai
Seoul
SOUTH KOREA
JAPAN

Qinghai Lake
Xining
Wei R.
North China Plain
Huang He (Yellow R.)
Jinan
Qingdao
Yellow Sea

ateau
Lanzhou
CHINA
Xian
Zhengzhou
Hongze Hu

TIBET
Yangtze R.
Lancang (Mekong) R.
Nu (Salween) R.
Nanjing
Shanghai

Lhasa
Yarlung R.
Chengdu
Yangtze R.
Wuhan
Tai Hu
Hangzhou
East China Sea

Thimphu
BHUTAN
Gongga Peak
Chongqing
Yuan R.
Changsha
Gan R.

Border claimed by China
Kunming
Dalou Mtns.
Guilin
Wuyi Mtns.
Fuzhou
Taipei
PACIFIC OCEAN

naka
Hongshui R.
Guangzhou
Taiwan Strait
TAIWAN
Ryukyu Islands (Japan)

MYANMAR (BURMA)
Red R.
Nanning
Hong Kong
Macau
Special Administrative Regions

BANGLADESH
VIETNAM
Hanoi
Haikou
South China Sea

LAOS
Gulf of Tonkin
Hainan I.

Bay of Bengal
THAILAND
Vientiane

N W E S
TFK

0   500 miles
0   750 kilometers

Did You Know?

● The Great Wall is about 4,000 mi (6,437 km) long. It is so big that astronauts have seen it from space!

● The Grand Canal is the longest and oldest man-made river in the world. Parts of the canal were built almost 2,500 years ago.

Chinese women harvesting rice

● The Chinese invented paper, ink, the compass and silk.

● Shanghai, China's biggest city, is home to 17 million people.

● In 1997, the former British colony of Hong Kong became part of China.

● Almost 100 endangered species are in China, including the giant panda, the South China tiger and the crowned crane.

● *Gobi* means "waterless place" in Mongolian.

Japan, North Korea and South Korea

Off the southeast coast of Asia, in the North Pacific Ocean, lie the islands of Japan. The country is made up of four main islands and 3,900 smaller islands. Its location in the Ring of Fire makes Japan a hot spot for volcanoes and earthquakes. Most of the country is made up of volcanic mountains.

Japan has been inhabited for over 10,000 years and has a tradition of fine arts. For centuries, artists have painted beautiful portraits and scenes on silks and ceramics. In homes and parks, exquisite gardens feature delicately pruned plants. Japan is also an economic superpower. Tokyo, Japan's capital and largest city, is one of the most important business centers in the world.

Not far to Japan's north, the Korean Peninsula juts off the mainland of Asia. Through war and peace, Japan and Korea have been closely linked. In 1904, the Japanese invaded Korea and, in 1910, made Korea a Japanese territory. In 1945, following World War II, the Allies separated Japan and Korea and split the Korean Peninsula into two separate nations. Today, though sharing a common heritage, North and South Korea remain two distinct and very different countries.

Japan has had a strong influence on the culture of Korea. So, too, has China, which borders North Korea. Yet, the peninsula retains its own language, traditions and cuisine.

Torii gates are found throughout Japan and are symbols of prosperity

Data Bank

JAPAN
AREA: 145,882 sq mi (377,835 sq km)
POPULATION: 127,463,611
CAPITAL: Tokyo
LANGUAGE: Japanese

NORTH KOREA
AREA: 46,540 sq mi (120,540 sq km)
POPULATION: 23,113,019
CAPITAL: Pyongyang
LANGUAGE: Korean

SOUTH KOREA
AREA: 38,023 sq mi (98,480 sq km)
POPULATION: 48,846,823
CAPITAL: Seoul
LANGUAGE: Korean

Serene Scene: Matsushima Bay, Japan

A1 · B1 · C1 · D1 · E1 · F1 · G1

Harbin

Songhua R.

CHINA

Tartar Strait

Point Soya —

Sakhalin I. (Russia)

Sea of Okhotsk

Kuril Is.

RUSSIA

Sikhote-Alin Range

Jilin

Vladivostok

Otaru

Asahi Dake ▲

Hokkaido

Sapporo

(occupied by Russia, claimed by Japan)

Liao R.

Peter the Great Bay

Tsugaru Strait

Fushun

Mount Paektu ▲

▲ Chongjin

Kwanmo Peak

Aomori

Dandong

Yalu R.

NORTH KOREA

Kitakami R.

Taedong R.

E. Korea Bay

Akita

Korea Bay

Wonsan

Sea of Japan

Sado

Honshu

Sendai

Pyongyang ★

Taebaek Mtns.

Tok Is. (occupied by South Korea, claimed by Japan)

Noto Peninsula

Niigata

Han R.

Japanese Alps

Shinano R.

Seoul ★

SOUTH KOREA

Oki Is.

J A P A N

Taejon

Mt. Fuji ▲

★ Tokyo

Yokohama

Yellow Sea

Matsue

L. Biwa

Nagoya

Taegu

Korea Strait

Kobe

Kyoto

Kwangju

Pusan

Osaka

PACIFIC OCEAN

Tsushima Is.

Hiroshima

Tsushima Strait

Kitakyushu

Inland Sea

Shikoku

Cheju I.

Kyushu

Kochi

Kii Peninsula

Izu Islands

Goto Is.

Kagoshima

Osumi Strait

East China Sea

Yaku-Shima

Tanega-Shima

Ryukyu Islands

Bonin Is. (Japan)

0 —— 400 miles

0 —— 600 kilometers

Okinawa

A7 · B7 · C7 · D7 · E7 · F7 · G7

Did You Know?

Celebrating Buddha's birthday in Seoul, Korea

- At 12,388 ft (3,776 m), Mount Fuji is Japan's tallest mountain. It is a volcano that last erupted in 1707.
- According to legend, Japan's islands were formed from the tears of a goddess.
- Of the world's 720,000 working robots, 410,000 can be found in Japan.

- Japan has the highest percentage of daily newspaper readers in any country: 86%.
- The people of Korea come from huge clans. Throughout Korea, there are only about a dozen last names.
- Ch'usok, an important harvest festival in Korea, is also a time for families to gather to honor their ancestors.
- A demilitarized zone 4 mi (6.4 km) wide splits the Korean Peninsula at the 38th parallel, or line of latitude.

Southeast Asia

Southeast Asia is a tropical peninsula covered by thick forests, mighty rivers, fertile plains and tall mountains. For most of its residents, farming is a way of life. Rice is the region's most important crop. It is grown in flooded rice paddies on the plains and on stairlike green terraces on mountain slopes. In the region's cities, exotic sights and smells are everywhere. Bangkok, Thailand, is a teeming commercial center, a mixture of modern skyscrapers and bicycle taxis, ancient temples and brightly colored floating markets.

For sale: Fruits and vegetables in one of Bangkok's floating markets

For many older Americans, Vietnam brings to mind images of war. But the country is also a land of spectacular scenery. From the Red River Delta in the north to the Mekong Delta in the south, Vietnam is a patchwork of rushing rivers, sandy coastlines and brilliant green paddy fields.

Boy monks in Burma

Vietnam, Cambodia and Laos have historic ties to France. Myanmar, previously called Burma, was once controlled by Britain. Of the countries in this region, only Thailand was never a European colony. In recent years, Southeast Asia has been plagued by wars and civil unrest. Today, these small countries are slowly rebuilding and reopening to tourists and foreign companies.

Did You Know?

● Most of Laos is covered by forest. The country's nickname is the Land of One Million Elephants.

● Myanmar is known for its deep red rubies, which are mined in the north of the country.

● The world's smallest mammal is the bumblebee bat, found in Thailand.

● Cambodia's Angkor Wat, built in the 12th century, is the world's largest religious structure.

Data Bank

CAMBODIA
AREA: 69,900 sq mi (181,040 sq km)
POPULATION: 13,881,427
CAPITAL: Phnom Penh
LANGUAGES: Khmer (official), French, English

LAOS
AREA: 91,429 sq mi (236,800 sq km)
POPULATION: 6,368,481
CAPITAL: Vientiane
LANGUAGES: Lao (official), French, English, ethnic languages

MYANMAR (BURMA)
AREA: 261,969 sq mi (678,500 sq km)
POPULATION: 47,382,633
CAPITAL: Rangoon
LANGUAGES: Burmese, minority languages

THAILAND
AREA: 198,455 sq mi (514,000 sq km)
POPULATION: 64,631,595
CAPITAL: Bangkok
LANGUAGES: Thai, English

VIETNAM
AREA: 127,243 sq mi (329,560 sq km)
POPULATION: 84,402,966
CAPITAL: Hanoi
LANGUAGES: Vietnamese (official), English, French, Chinese, Khmer, others

Angkor Wat

BHUTAN

Brahmaputra R.

INDIA

Naga Hills

BANGLADESH

Chin Hills

Border claimed by China

Mount Hkakabo ▲

Yangtze R.

CHINA

Kunming

Guilin

N
W TFK E
S

Hongshui R.

Guangzhou

MYANMAR
(BURMA)

Irrawaddy R.

Nu R. (Salween)

Lancang R. (Mekong)

Red R.

Nanning

Macau

Hong Kong

Sittwe

Mandalay

Shan Plateau

Salween R.

Sittang R.

LAOS

Louangphrabang

Fan Si Pan ▲

VIETNAM

Hanoi

Haiphong

Bay of
Bengal

Doi Inthanon ▲

Chiang Mai

Plain of Jars

Vientiane

Ping R.

Nan R.

Vinh

Annamese Cordillera

Gulf of Tonkin

Hainan I.

South
China
Sea

Rangoon

Mouths of the Irrawaddy

Mekong R.

Udon Thani

Khorat Plateau

THAILAND

Ubon

Kong R.

Hue

Da Nang

Andaman Sea

Mergui
Archipelago

Bangkok

Angkor Wat

Tonle Sap

CAMBODIA

Phnom Penh

Nha Trang

Cam Ranh

Andaman
Is. (India)

Gulf of
Thailand

Phu Quoc I.

Ho Chi Minh City

Mouths of the Mekong

Nicobar
Is. (India)

Isthmus
of Kra

Pte. de Ca Mau

INDIAN
OCEAN

Phuket

Songkhla

Kota Baharu

South
China
Sea

George Town

Ipoh

MALAYSIA

Malay
Peninsula

Strait of Malacca

Kuala
Lumpur

MALAYSIA

Sumatra I.

SINGAPORE

0   400 miles
0   600 kilometers

I N D O N E S I A

Maritime Southeast Asia

Island Nation: Singapore's stunning skyline

The sea is a major part of this region's geography. Indonesia is the world's largest archipelago, or group of islands. It is made up of about 17,000 islands, with people living on 6,000 of them. The Philippines is made up of more than 7,000 islands. Since the end of World War II, many newly independent nations have emerged in the region. Brunei, Malaysia and Singapore used to be part of the British Empire. The Philippines was ruled by Spain until 1898 when it became a U.S. possession. The nation gained its independence in 1946. Indonesia was once part of the Netherlands. East Timor did not come into existence until 2002.

Much of the region is rain forest, and wildlife is abundant. Malaysia is divided into two areas, one on the Malay Peninsula and the other on the island of Borneo, where elephants, tigers, orangutans and rare Sumatran rhinoceroses can be found. The small nation of Brunei is also located on Borneo. Brunei is made up of two separate areas surrounded by Malaysia and the South China Sea.

Off the tip of the Malay Peninsula lies Singapore. The modern island nation, which gained independence from Malaysia in 1965, boasts one of Asia's best public-transportation systems.

Data Bank

BRUNEI
AREA: 2,228 sq mi (5,770 sq km)
POPULATION: 379,444
CAPITAL: Bandar Seri Begawan
LANGUAGES: Malay (official), English, Chinese

EAST TIMOR
AREA: 5,814 sq mi (15,007 sq km)
POPULATION: 1,062,777
CAPITAL: Dili
LANGUAGES: Tetum, Portuguese (both official), Indonesian, English

INDONESIA
AREA: 741,096 sq mi (1,919,440 sq km)
POPULATION: 245,452,739
CAPITAL: Jakarta
LANGUAGES: Bahasa Indonesian, English, Dutch, local dialects

MALAYSIA
AREA: 127,316 sq mi (329,750 sq km)
POPULATION: 24,385,858
CAPITAL: Kuala Lumpur
LANGUAGES: Bahasa Melayu (official), English, Chinese, Tamil, Telugu, Malayalam

PHILIPPINES
AREA: 115,830 sq mi (300,000 sq km)
POPULATION: 89,468,677
CAPITAL: Manila
LANGUAGES: Filipino, English (both official), Tagalog, other native languages

SINGAPORE
AREA: 267 sq mi (692 sq km)
POPULATION: 4,492,150
CAPITAL: Singapore
LANGUAGES: Malay, Chinese, Tamil, English (all official)

A dancer on the Indonesian island of Bali

Map labels: THAILAND · Bangkok · CAMB · Phnom · Gulf of Thailand · Nicobar Is. (India) · Phuket · Malay Peninsula · George Town · Mt. T · Medan · Ipoh · Mt. Leuser · Kuala Lumpur · Strait of Malacca · Nias I. · Sumatra · Padang · Mt. Kerinci · Mentawai Is. · Barisan · Palen · Krakatoa (volcan · Sunda St · LA · B

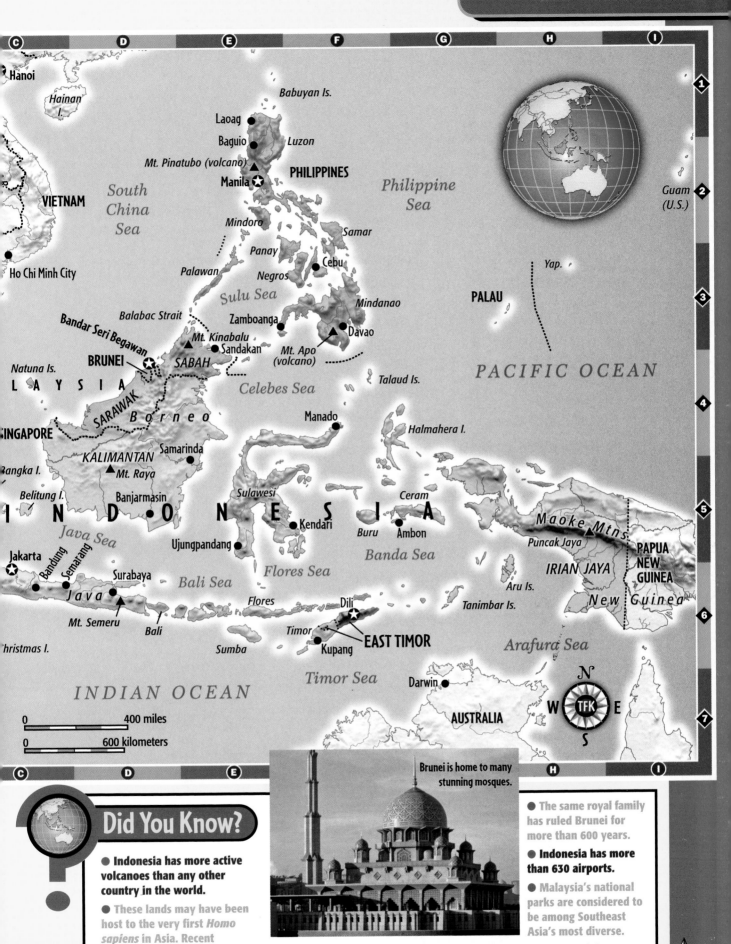

Hanoi

Hainan I.

VIETNAM

South China Sea

Ho Chi Minh City

Babuyan Is.

Laoag

Baguio — Luzon

Mt. Pinatubo (volcano)

Manila

PHILIPPINES

Philippine Sea

Mindoro

Panay — Samar

Palawan — Negros

Cebu

Sulu Sea

Mindanao

Balabac Strait

Zamboanga

Bandar Seri Begawan

Mt. Kinabalu — Sandakan

Mt. Apo (volcano)

BRUNEI — **SABAH**

Natuna Is.

L A Y S I A

SARAWAK — Borneo

SINGAPORE

Bangka I.

KALIMANTAN — Samarinda

Mt. Raya

Belitung I.

Banjarmasin

I N D O N E S I A

Java Sea

Jakarta — Bandung — Semarang — Surabaya

Christmas I.

Java

Mt. Semeru

Bali

Sumba

Sumba

Talaud Is.

Celebes Sea

Manado

Halmahera I.

Sulawesi

Ceram

Kendari

Buru — Ambon

Flores Sea

Bali Sea

Flores

Timor

Kupang

EAST TIMOR

Dili

Banda Sea

Aru Is.

Tanimbar Is.

PACIFIC OCEAN

Yap.

PALAU

Guam (U.S.)

Maoke Mtns.

Puncak Jaya

IRIAN JAYA

PAPUA NEW GUINEA

New Guinea

Arafura Sea

Darwin

AUSTRALIA

Timor Sea

INDIAN OCEAN

Ujungpandang

0 — 400 miles

0 — 600 kilometers

N W TFK E S

C D E F G H I

1 2 3 4 5 6 7

Brunei is home to many stunning mosques.

Did You Know?

- Indonesia has more active volcanoes than any other country in the world.
- These lands may have been host to the very first *Homo sapiens* in Asia. Recent discoveries show that humans lived in this region as far back as 40,000 years ago.

- The same royal family has ruled Brunei for more than 600 years.
- Indonesia has more than 630 airports.
- Malaysia's national parks are considered to be among Southeast Asia's most diverse.
- Training songbirds has become one of the most popular hobbies in Singapore.

Africa

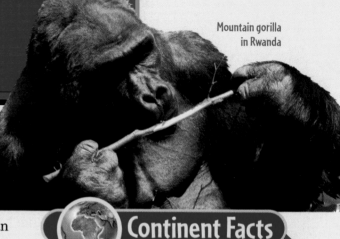
Mountain gorilla in Rwanda

The world's second-largest continent, Africa, is surrounded by water. To the west of Africa lies the Atlantic Ocean; to the east is the Indian Ocean; to the north is the Mediterranean Sea; and to the northeast is the Red Sea. Many islands and island chains, including Madagascar and the Seychelle Islands, are considered part of the African continent.

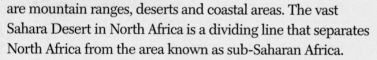
The Sahara is the biggest desert in the world.

The central part of Africa is one big, flat plain. There, lying across the warm equator, are Africa's famous rain forests and savannas, or grasslands. Far to the continent's north and south are mountain ranges, deserts and coastal areas. The vast Sahara Desert in North Africa is a dividing line that separates North Africa from the area known as sub-Saharan Africa.

Africa is known for its wide range of amazing wildlife. Though the continent has suffered from environmental damage, it is still home to many creatures. There are camels in the north, penguins in the south, gorillas in the forests and lions and giraffes in the savannas. The island of Madagascar, which separated from the African mainland millions of years ago, is home to many unique species of mammals and amphibians. There are fewer than a billion people in Africa, but they speak more than 2,000 different languages and live in 53 different nations. The African population is growing quickly, and the continent is home to some of the biggest cities in the world. Most people live in rural areas.

Continent Facts

NUMBER OF COUNTRIES:
53 countries, including Algeria, Angola, Benin, Botswana, Burkina Faso, Burundi, Cameroon, Cape Verde, Central African Republic, Chad, Comoros, Congo (Democratic Republic of the), Congo (Republic of the), Côte d'Ivoire, Djibouti, Egypt, Equatorial Guinea, Eritrea, Ethiopia, Gabon, Gambia, Ghana, Guinea, Guinea-Bissau, Kenya, Lesotho, Liberia, Libya, Madagascar, Malawi, Mali, Mauritania, Mauritius, Morocco, Mozambique, Namibia, Niger, Nigeria, Rwanda, São Tomé and Príncipe, Senegal, Seychelles, Sierra Leone, Somalia, South Africa, Sudan, Swaziland, Tanzania, Togo, Tunisia, Uganda, Zambia, Zimbabwe

AREA: 11.7 million sq mi (30.3 million sq km)

LONGEST RIVER: The Nile, 4,241 mi (6,825 km)

LONGEST MOUNTAIN RANGE: Atlas Mountain Range in North Africa, about 400 mi (644 km)

HIGHEST PEAK: Mount Kilimanjaro, in Tanzania, 19,340 ft (5,895 m)

LARGEST LAKE: Victoria, 26,828 sq mi (69,485 sq km)

DEEPEST LAKE: Tanganyika, the second-deepest lake in the world, has a maximum depth of 4,710 ft (1,435 m).

Wow Zone!

● Victoria Falls, on the Zambezi River in Zimbabwe, is 355 ft (108 m) high and 5,500 ft (1,676 m) wide. It is twice as big as Niagara Falls.

● Lake Nyasa (also known as Lake Malawi), in east-central Africa, has more fish species in it than any other lake in the world.

● African elephants are the largest land animals in the world.

● The Goliath beetle, found in equatorial Africa, is the world's largest beetle. It can grow to be 5 in (13 cm) long.

A lion watches over the sava

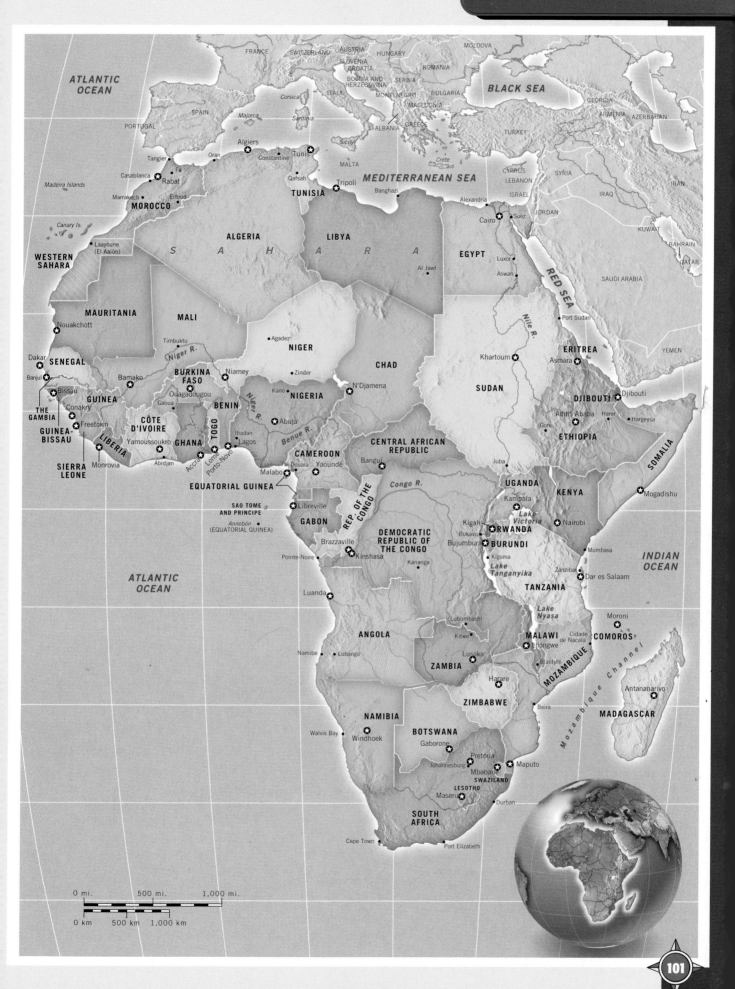

ATLANTIC
OCEAN

FRANCE SWITZERLAND AUSTRIA HUNGARY MOLDOVA
SLOVENIA ROMANIA
CROATIA
BOSNIA AND SERBIA BULGARIA **BLACK SEA**
HERZEGOVINA MONTENEGRO MACEDONIA GEORGIA
PORTUGAL SPAIN Corsica ITALY ALBANIA GREECE ARMENIA AZERBAIJAN
Majorca Sardinia TURKEY
Tangier Algiers Tunis Sicily **MEDITERRANEAN SEA** CYPRUS IRAN
Oran Constantine MALTA LEBANON SYRIA
Casablanca Fès Qafsah Tripoli Banghazi Alexandria ISRAEL IRAQ
Rabat JORDAN KUWAIT
Marrakech Erfoud Cairo Suez BAHRAIN
MOROCCO QATAR
Madeira Islands

S A H A R A
ALGERIA **LIBYA** **EGYPT** Luxor
SAUDI ARABIA
Canary Is. Laayoune Al Jawf Aswan
(El Aaiún)
WESTERN
SAHARA RED SEA
YEMEN
MAURITANIA Port Sudan
MALI Nile R.
Nouakchott Timbuktu Agadez **ERITREA**
Khartoum Asmara
Dakar **NIGER** **CHAD** **SUDAN** **DJIBOUTI** Djibouti
SENEGAL Bamako Niamey Zinder **NIGERIA** N'Djamena Addis Ababa Harer
Banjul **BURKINA** Kano Hargeysa
THE **FASO** Ouagadougou Abuja Gore **ETHIOPIA**
GAMBIA Bissau **GUINEA** Gaoua **BENIN** Ibadan Benue R. **CENTRAL AFRICAN** Juba **SOMALIA**
Conakry **CÔTE** **GHANA** Lagos **REPUBLIC**
GUINEA- Freetown **D'IVOIRE** **TOGO** Bangui **UGANDA** Mogadishu
BISSAU **LIBERIA** Yamoussoukro Lomé **CAMEROON** Kampala **KENYA**
SIERRA Accra Porto-Novo Douala Yaoundé Lake
LEONE Monrovia Abidjan **EQUATORIAL GUINEA** Malabo **REP. OF THE** Congo R. Victoria **RWANDA** Nairobi
SAO TOME Libreville **CONGO** Kigali Bukavu **INDIAN**
AND PRINCIPE **GABON** **DEMOCRATIC** **BURUNDI** Mombasa **OCEAN**
Annobón Brazzaville **REPUBLIC OF** Bujumbura
(EQUATORIAL GUINEA) Pointe-Noire Kinshasa **THE CONGO** Kigoma Zanzibar
Kananga Lake Dar es Salaam
Tanganyika
ATLANTIC Luanda **TANZANIA**
OCEAN Lubumbashi Lake
Nyasa Moroni
ANGOLA Kitwe Cidade **COMOROS**
Namibe Lubango **MALAWI** de Nacala
Lilongwe Mozambique Channel
ZAMBIA Lusaka Blantyre
Walvis Bay Harare Beira
NAMIBIA **ZIMBABWE** **MADAGASCAR** Antananarivo
Windhoek **BOTSWANA**
Gaborone Pretoria
Johannesburg Maputo
Mbabane
SWAZILAND
LESOTHO
Maseru Durban
SOUTH
AFRICA
Cape Town Port Elizabeth

0 mi. 500 mi. 1,000 mi.

0 km 500 km 1,000 km

101

Northeastern Africa

A sailboat on the White Nile in Sudan

Khartoum, the capital of Sudan, stands at the crossroads of the Blue Nile and the White Nile. The two rivers converge to form the Nile, the world's longest river. The life-giving Nile flows through Sudan and Egypt. The river's waters are precious to the area's people, who live and work near its banks. Nearly 95% of Egypt is desert.

Almost 5,000 years ago, Egypt had already established one of the world's most advanced civilizations. Ancient Egyptians mastered a new writing system, unique art forms and grand architecture. In neighboring Nubia, which today is part of Sudan, another great civilization flourished. There, archaeologists have found beautiful ceramic figurines and bowls that date from at least 8,000 B.C. That's 3,000 years older than any known Egyptian objects!

To the east of Sudan lie Eritrea and Ethiopia, which is sub-Saharan Africa's oldest country. In 1993, Ethiopia recognized Eritrea's independence. Until recently, both countries were involved in costly and destructive border clashes.

Harsh weather conditions and drought play important roles in the lives of the people of the region. Djibouti, which lies at the edge of the Red Sea, is mostly desert. Much of Somalia receives less than one quart (almost one liter) of rain a year.

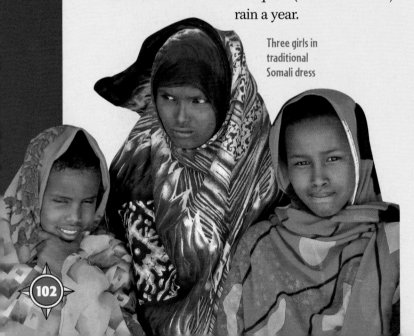

Three girls in traditional Somali dress

Data Bank

DJIBOUTI
AREA: 8,800 sq mi (23,000 sq km)
POPULATION: 486,530
CAPITAL: Djibouti
LANGUAGES: French, Arabic (both official), Somali, Afar

EGYPT
AREA: 386,660 sq mi (1,001,450 sq km)
POPULATION: 78,887,007
CAPITAL: Cairo
LANGUAGE: Arabic (official)

ERITREA
AREA: 46,842 sq mi (121,320 sq km)
POPULATION: 4,786,994
CAPITAL: Asmara
LANGUAGES: Afar, Amharic, Arabic, Tigre, Kunama, others

ETHIOPIA
AREA: 485,184 sq mi (1,256,634 sq km)
POPULATION: 74,777,981
CAPITAL: Addis Ababa
LANGUAGES: Amharic, Tigrinya, Oromigna, others

SOMALIA
AREA: 246,199 sq mi (637,659 sq km)
POPULATION: 8,863,338
CAPITAL: Mogadishu
LANGUAGES: Somali, Arabic, English, Italian

SUDAN
AREA: 967,493 sq mi (2,505,822 sq km)
POPULATION: 41,236,378
CAPITAL: Khartoum
LANGUAGES: Arabic, Nubian, Nilotic, Nilo-Hamitic, Sudanic languages, English

Benghazi
Mediterranean Sea
Suez Canal
ISRAEL
Alexandria
Cairo
Suez
Sinai
Peninsula
El Faiyum
Western
Desert
EGYPT
Nile R.
Gulf
of Suez
LIBYA
Luxor
Libyan Desert
Aswan
Lake Nasser
Kufra
Oasis
Uweinat Mtn.
Nubian Desert
Sahara
Nile R.
CHAD
Albara R.
Omdurman
Khartoum
SUDAN
Wad
Medani
Mount Marra
El Obeid
Kosti
Marra Mtns.
White Nile R.
Blue Nile R.
Lol R.
Malakal
Sudd
CENTRAL
AFRICAN
REPUBLIC
Wau
Badigeru
Swamp
Juba
Congo R.
DEMOCRATIC
REPUBLIC OF
THE CONGO
Equator
Kampala
UGANDA
Lake
Victoria

Baghdad
IRAQ
JORDAN
KUWAIT
IRAN
Persian Gulf
Abu Dhabi
Doha
BAHRAIN
QATAR
Riyadh
U.A.E.
SAUDI ARABIA
Mecca
OMAN
Red Sea
Port Sudan
YEMEN
ERITREA
Asmara
Sanaa
Ras Dashan
Bab el
Mandeb Strait
Gondar
Lake Tana
Socotra
(Yemen)
Raas
Caseyr
DJIBOUTI
Djibouti
Berbera
Gulf of Aden
Choke Mtns.
Dire Dawa
Ahmar Mtns.
Karkar
Mtns.
Addis Ababa
Harar
Eyl
Great Rift Valley
ETHIOPIA
Goba
Shebele R.
Ethiopian
Highlands
INDIAN
OCEAN
Lake Turkana
SOMALIA
KENYA
Mogadishu
Mount Kenya
Kismaayo
Nairobi

0   400 miles
0   600 kilometers

Did You Know?

● Egypt's Suez Canal, which links the Mediterranean Sea with the Red Sea, was opened in 1869.

● The Great Sphinx has a human head and a lion's body. It is 240 ft (73 m) long and 65 ft (20 m) high. For centuries, the monument was buried under sand.

● Ethiopia's royal family claims to be descended from the Queen of Sheba and King Solomon.

● Sudan, the largest country on the continent, became independent on December 15, 1955. Britain and Egypt had governed Sudan jointly for almost 60 years.

● Sudan has more pyramids than Egypt.

103

Northwestern Africa

Roman Ruins: The Leptis Magna theater, in Libya

High on the northwest shoulder of Africa sit the countries of Morocco, Algeria, Tunisia and Libya and the territory of Western Sahara. Since ancient times, conquerors—such as Vandals, Romans, Ottoman Turks and the French—have been drawn to the sparkling coast along the southern Mediterranean Sea. In modern times, the area retains Islamic and French influences.

The geography of Northwestern Africa is varied and dramatic. Along the fertile coast, crops of wheat, olives, figs and citrus fruits are grown, and the palm-fringed beaches of Morocco and Tunisia attract many tourists. Just south is a ribbon of mountains, called the Atlas, that stretches 1,200 mi (1,931 km) from Morocco across Algeria to Tunisia. And below this ridge is the great desert of the Sahara.

Tunisia, the small finger of land between Algeria and Libya, freed itself from French rule in 1956. Ruins of two great civilizations, the Phoenician and the Roman, can be viewed in Carthage, on the Tunisian coast. Other popular destinations for visitors to this region are the pink-walled city of Marrakech, in Morocco, and the Leptis Magna, in Libya, the site of impressive Roman ruins. The territory of Western Sahara, once held by Spain but now overseen by Morocco, has been the object of many conflicts.

Data Bank

ALGERIA
AREA: 919,586 sq mi (2,381,740 sq km)
POPULATION: 32,930,091
CAPITAL: Algiers
LANGUAGES: Arabic (official), French, Berber dialects

LIBYA
AREA: 679,358 sq mi (1,759,540 sq km)
POPULATION: 5,900,754
CAPITAL: Tripoli
LANGUAGES: Arabic, Italian, English

MOROCCO
AREA: 172,413 sq mi (446,550 sq km)
POPULATION: 33,241,259
CAPITAL: Rabat
LANGUAGES: Arabic (official), Berber dialects, French

TUNISIA
AREA: 63,170 sq mi (163,610 sq km)
POPULATION: 10,175,014
CAPITAL: Tunis
LANGUAGES: Arabic (official), French

Madeira Is. (Portugal)

ATLANTIC OCEAN

Canary Is. (Spain)
Santa Cruz de Tenerife

Tarfaya

el Aaiun

Smara

WESTERN SAHARA (occupied by Morocco)

Dakhla

Nouakchott

MAURITANIA

Senegal R.

Moroccan Market: Spices for sale in Marrakech

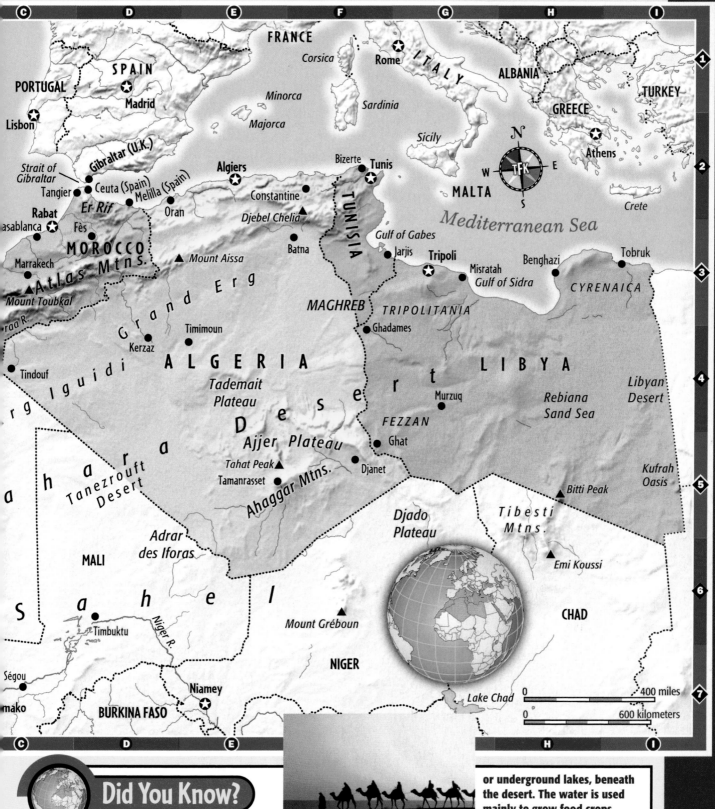

Map labels:
C D E F G H I

FRANCE
Corsica
Rome · ITALY
ALBANIA
TURKEY

SPAIN
Madrid
Minorca
Sardinia
GREECE

PORTUGAL
Lisbon
Majorca
Sicily
Athens

Gibraltar (U.K.)
Strait of Gibraltar
Tangier
Ceuta (Spain)
Melilla (Spain)
Algiers
Constantine
Bizerte · Tunis
TUNISIA
MALTA
Crete

Er Rif
Oran
Djebel Chelia ▲
Gulf of Gabes
Jarjis
Tripoli
Misratah
Gulf of Sidra
Benghazi
Tobruk
Mediterranean Sea

Rabat
Fès
Casablanca
MOROCCO
Batna
MAGHREB
TRIPOLITANIA
CYRENAICA

Marrakech
Atlas Mtns.
▲ Mount Aissa
Ghadames

Mount Toubkal ▲
raa R.
Grand Erg
ALGERIA
LIBYA
Libyan Desert

Tindouf
Timimoun
Tademait Plateau
Murzuq
Rebiana Sand Sea

Erg Iguidi
Kerzaz
Sahara Desert
FEZZAN
Kufrah Oasis

Ajjer Plateau
Ghat
Tahat Peak ▲
Tamanrasset
Ahaggar Mtns.
Djanet
Tibesti Mtns.
▲ Bitti Peak

Tanezrouft Desert
Adrar des Iforas
Djado Plateau
▲ Emi Koussi

Sahel
MALI
CHAD

Timbuktu
Niger R.
Mount Gréboun ▲
NIGER

Ségou
mako
Niamey
BURKINA FASO
Lake Chad

0 — 400 miles
0 — 600 kilometers

N W E S TFK

Did You Know?

Nomadic tribes travel on camels.

● Not all of the Sahara Desert is covered in sand dunes. There are areas thousands of miles wide with nothing but rocks and pebbles.

● The deserts of Algeria and Libya are home to oil rigs and natural-gas pipelines that enrich their economies. With the Great Man-Made River project, begun in 1984, Libya tapped into aquifers,

or underground lakes, beneath the desert. The water is used mainly to grow food crops.

● A town in the desert built around a source of water is called an oasis. Kerzaz, an oasis in the Algerian Sahara, has outdoor walkways with roofs for shade. It is surrounded by sand dunes up to 160 ft (50 m) high.

● A hot, dusty, unpleasant wind that blows from the Libyan desert toward Italy is called a sirocco.

Western Africa

Bustling Beach: Fishing boats land at a harbor in Ghana.

Canary Islands (Spain)
el Aai

Santa Antao
Sal
Mindela
CAPE VERDE
Boa Vista
São Tiago
Praia
600 miles   50 miles

The western edge of Africa looks like a puzzle piece that would fit snugly against the eastern side of South America, across the Atlantic. And in fact, the two continents used to be one, until they broke up and drifted apart about 200 million years ago.

West Africa includes the southern stretch of the Sahara Desert and, just south of it, a vast swath of grasslands called the Sahel. The Sahel has been overfarmed and plagued by drought. The coastal regions of West Africa—from Senegal to the Niger River delta—have rain forests and crops of coffee, cotton, rubber and cacao.

Cape Blanc   Atar

Nouakchott

Senegal R.

Saint Louis
Dakar
Cape Verde   **SENEGAL**

GAMBIA
Banjul

Gambia R.

GUINEA- BISSAU   Bissau

Conakry

Freetown

Data Bank

BENIN
AREA: 43,483 sq mi (112,620 sq km)
POPULATION: 7,862,944
CAPITAL: Porto-Novo
LANGUAGES: French (official), African languages

BURKINA FASO
AREA: 105,870 sq mi (274,200 sq km)
POPULATION: 13,902,972
CAPITAL: Ouagadougou
LANGUAGES: French (official), African languages

CAPE VERDE
AREA: 1,557 sq mi (4,033 sq km)
POPULATION: 420,979
CAPITAL: Praia
LANGUAGES: Portuguese, Crioulo

CÔTE D'IVOIRE
AREA: 124,502 sq mi (322,460 sq km)
POPULATION: 17,654,843
CAPITAL: Yamoussoukro
LANGUAGES: French (official), African languages

GAMBIA
AREA: 4,363 sq mi (11,300 sq km)
POPULATION: 1,641,564
CAPITAL: Banjul
LANGUAGES: English (official), native languages

GHANA
AREA: 92,456 sq mi (239,460 sq km)
POPULATION: 22,409,572
CAPITAL: Accra
LANGUAGES: English (official), African languages

GUINEA
AREA: 94,925 sq mi (245,857 sq km)
POPULATION: 9,690,222
CAPITAL: Conakry
LANGUAGES: French (official), native languages

GUINEA-BISSAU
AREA: 13,946 sq mi (36,120 sq km)
POPULATION: 1,442,029
CAPITAL: Bissau
LANGUAGES: Portuguese (official), Crioulo, African languages

LIBERIA
AREA: 43,000 sq mi (111,370 sq km)
POPULATION: 3,042,004
CAPITAL: Monrovia
LANGUAGES: English (official), tribal dialects

MALI
AREA: 478,764 sq mi (1,240,000 sq km)
POPULATION: 11,716,829
CAPITAL: Bamako
LANGUAGES: French (official), Bambara

MAURITANIA
AREA: 397,953 sq mi (1,030,700 sq km)
POPULATION: 3,177,388
CAPITAL: Nouakchott
LANGUAGES: Hassaniya Arabic, Wolof (both official), Pulaar, Soninke, French

NIGER
AREA: 489,189 sq mi (1,267,000 sq km)
POPULATION: 12,525,094
CAPITAL: Niamey
LANGUAGES: French (official), Hausa, Djerma

The Great Mosque in Djenné, Mali, is made of mud.

NIGERIA
AREA: 356,700 sq mi (923,770 sq km)
POPULATION: 131,859,731
CAPITAL: Abuja
LANGUAGES: English (official), Hausa, Yoruba, Igbo, others

SENEGAL
AREA: 75,749 sq mi (196,190 sq km)
POPULATION: 11,987,121
CAPITAL: Dakar
LANGUAGES: French (official), Wolof, Pulaar

SIERRA LEONE
AREA: 27,699 sq mi (71,740 sq km)
POPULATION: 6,005,250
CAPITAL: Freetown
LANGUAGES: English (official), Mende, Temne, Krio

TOGO
AREA: 21,925 sq mi (56,785 sq km)
POPULATION: 5,548,702
CAPITAL: Lomé
LANGUAGES: French (official), Éwé, Mina, Kabyé, Dagomba

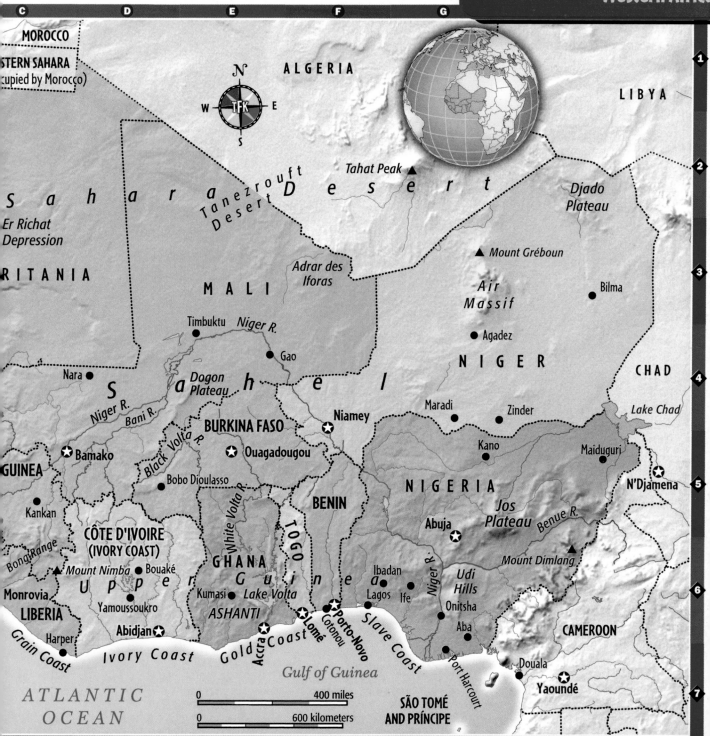

MOROCCO

WESTERN SAHARA
(occupied by Morocco)

ALGERIA

LIBYA

S a h a r a **Desert**
Tanezrouft Desert

▲ Tahat Peak

Djado Plateau

Er Richat Depression

▲ Mount Gréboun

MAURITANIA

MALI

Adrar des Iforas

Air Massif

● Bilma

● Agadez

● Timbuktu   *Niger R.*

● Gao

N I G E R

CHAD

Lake Chad

● Nara

S a h e l

Dogon Plateau

Niger R.   *Bani R.*

● Maradi   ● Zinder

BURKINA FASO

⬟ Niamey

GUINEA

⬟ Bamako

Black Volta R.

⬟ Ouagadougou

● Kano

● Maiduguri

⬟ N'Djamena

● Bobo Dioulasso

BENIN

N I G E R I A

● Kankan

CÔTE D'IVOIRE
(IVORY COAST)

White Volta R.

GHANA

T O G O

⬟ Abuja

Jos Plateau

Benue R.

Bong Range

G u i n e a

▲ Mount Nimba   ● Bouaké

● Kumasi   *Lake Volta*

● Ibadan

● Ife

Niger R.

Udi Hills

▲ Mount Dimlang

U p p e r

ASHANTI

⬟ Accra

● Lagos

● Onitsha

● Monrovia

● Yamoussoukro

⬟ Abidjan

⬟ Lomé

● Cotonou

⬟ Porto-Novo

Slave Coast

● Aba

CAMEROON

LIBERIA

● Harper

Ivory Coast

Gold Coast

● Port Harcourt

● Douala

⬟ Yaoundé

Grain Coast

Gulf of Guinea

SÃO TOMÉ
AND PRÍNCIPE

ATLANTIC OCEAN

0 ——— 400 miles
0 ——— 600 kilometers

Did You Know?

Sunset on the Niger River

● In 1986, Nigerian Wole Soyinka became the first African to win the Nobel Prize for Literature.

● The Niger River flows east from Guinea through Mali and Niger and south to Nigeria. At 2,600 mi (4,181 km) long, it is West Africa's most vital river.

● Ghana is famous for its kente cloth. It was first woven in 12th century Ghana, and clothing made from it was worn by African royalty during ceremonial events. Its name comes from *kenten*, which means "basket," because its design resembles a woven basket.

● Independent from France since 1960, the Côte d'Ivoire has a 500-year history of trading in elephant tusks, which were used to make ivory jewelry and piano keys. Today, elephants are protected, and the ivory trade is illegal.

● In 1822, freed slaves from the United States began returning to Africa. They set up the first republic on the continent in 1847, which they named Liberia from the Latin word for "free."

Central Africa

A boy swims in the Congo River.

River towns bustling with markets, untouched wilderness areas where lowland gorillas and forest elephants roam, barren deserts and dry grassland are all found in Central Africa. The Congo River and its tributaries form a lifeline for the people of Congo and the Democratic Republic of the Congo. Riverboats navigate the waters bringing people, food and trade.

Much of northern Chad is desert land. In recent years, long periods of drought have taken a heavy toll on the country and its people. The Sahara Desert is growing and moving southward. The Sahel, a semiarid grassland that stretches across south-central Chad, is expanding into neighboring savannas. To the south of Chad lies the Central African Republic, which forms a transitional area between the sub-Saharan zone in Chad and the equatorial zone to the south.

Dense forests cover large parts of Central African Republic, Congo, Democratic Republic of the Congo, Equatorial Guinea and Gabon. These countries lie near the equator, and their climate is hot and humid. Monkeys, baboons, gorillas, lions, leopards and a vast array of birds make their home in the jungle. Although natural resources are abundant in some of these lands, poverty, disease, government corruption and warfare are sad facts of daily life for the people.

Data Bank

CAMEROON
AREA: 183,567 sq mi (475,440 sq km)
POPULATION: 17,340,702
CAPITAL: Yaoundé
LANGUAGES: African languages; English, French (both official)

CENTRAL AFRICAN REPUBLIC
AREA: 240,534 sq mi (622,984 sq km)
POPULATION: 4,303,356
CAPITAL: Bangui
LANGUAGES: French (official), Sangho, tribal languages

CHAD
AREA: 495,752 sq mi (1,284,000 sq km)
POPULATION: 9,944,201
CAPITAL: N'Djamena
LANGUAGES: French, Arabic (both official), Sara, African languages

CONGO (REPUBLIC OF THE)
AREA: 132,046, sq mi (342,000 sq km)
POPULATION: 3,702,314
CAPITAL: Brazzaville
LANGUAGES: French (official), Lingala, Monokutuba, other African languages

CONGO (DEMOCRATIC REPUBLIC OF THE)
AREA: 905,562 sq mi (2,345,410 sq km)
POPULATION: 62,660,551
CAPITAL: Kinshasa
LANGUAGES: French, Lingala, Kingwana, Kikongo, other African languages

EQUATORIAL GUINEA
AREA: 10,830 sq mi (28,051 sq km)
POPULATION: 540,109
CAPITAL: Malabo
LANGUAGES: Spanish, French (both official), pidgin English, Fang

GABON
AREA: 103,347 sq mi (267,667 sq km)
POPULATION: 1,424,906
CAPITAL: Libreville
LANGUAGES: French (official), Fang, Myene, Nzebi, Bapounou/Eschira, Bandjabi

SÃO TOMÉ AND PRÍNCIPE
AREA: 386 sq mi (1,001 sq km)
POPULATION: 193,413
CAPITAL: São Tomé
LANGUAGES: Portuguese

Woman in Mokolo, Cameroon

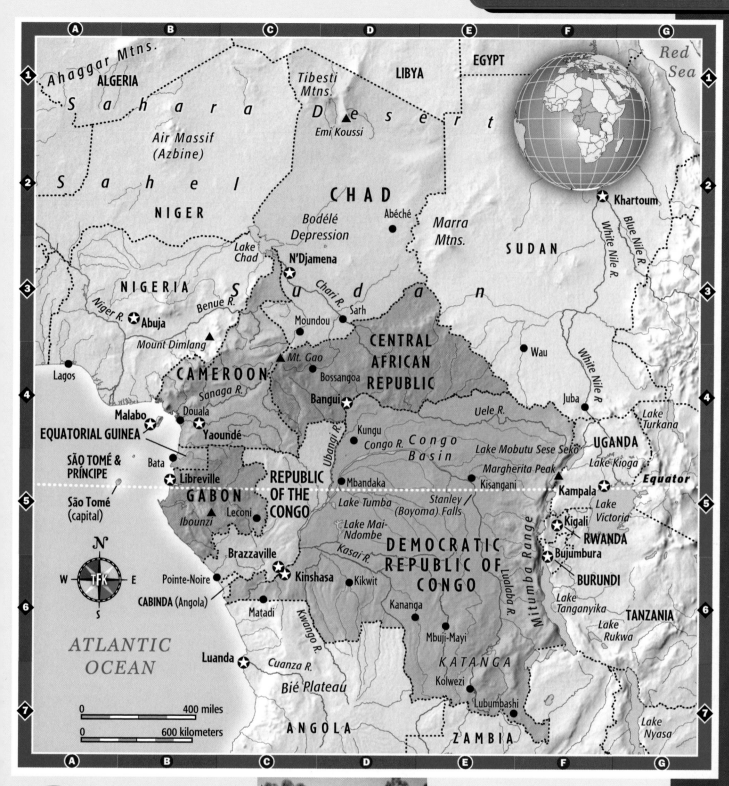

A B C D E F G

1 Ahaggar Mtns.
ALGERIA
LIBYA
EGYPT
Red Sea

S a h a r a D e s e r t
Tibesti Mtns.
▲ Emi Koussi

2 S a h e l
Air Massif (Azbine)
NIGER
CHAD
Bodélé Depression
Abéché
Marra Mtns.
SUDAN
☆ Khartoum

3 NIGERIA
Lake Chad
☆ N'Djamena
Chari R.
Sarh
Moundou
S u d a n
Wau
White Nile R.
Blue Nile R.
White Nile R.
Niger R.
☆ Abuja
Benue R.
Mount Dimlang ▲
▲ Mt. Gao
CENTRAL AFRICAN REPUBLIC

4 Lagos
CAMEROON
Sanaga R.
Bossangoa
Bangui ☆
Uele R.
Juba
Lake Turkana
Douala
Kungu
Congo R.
Congo Basin
Lake Mobutu Sese Seko
Malabo
☆ Yaoundé
Ubangi R.
Margherita Peak ▲
UGANDA
Lake Kioga
EQUATORIAL GUINEA
SÃO TOMÉ & PRÍNCIPE
Bata
☆ Libreville
Mbandaka
Kisangani
Kampala ☆
Equator

5 São Tomé (capital)
GABON
Ibounzi ▲
Leconi
REPUBLIC OF THE CONGO
Lake Tumba
Stanley / (Boyoma) Falls
Lake Victoria
☆ Kigali
RWANDA
Lake Mai-Ndombe
DEMOCRATIC REPUBLIC OF CONGO
Mitumba Range
Bujumbura
Kasai R.
Lualaba R.

6 Brazzaville
Pointe-Noire
☆ Kinshasa
Kikwit
Kananga
Lake Tanganyika
BURUNDI
Lake Rukwa
TANZANIA
CABINDA (Angola)
Matadi
Kwango R.
Mbuji-Mayi
KATANGA
Lake Nyasa

7 ATLANTIC OCEAN
Luanda ☆
Cuanza R.
Bié Plateau
A N G O L A
Kolwezi
Lubumbashi
Z A M B I A

N W E S — TFK

0 ——— 400 miles
0 ——— 600 kilometers

A B C D E F G

Watusi dancers in the Democratic Republic of Congo

Did You Know?

- Pygmies, a group of people found in Central Africa, are an average height of 4 ft (120 cm).

- The Kota people of the Central African Republic believe that their ancestors help them communicate with God.

- Name game: Equatorial Guinea was formerly known as Spanish Guinea. The Democratic Republic of the Congo was once known as the Belgian Congo. It was called Zaïre from 1971 to 1997. The country is often referred to as Congo (Kinshasa), while the other Congo is called Congo (Brazzaville).

East Central Africa

Spectacular highlands, rolling plains dotted with acacia trees, lush grasslands teeming with wildlife and sparkling freshwater and saltwater lakes are the prominent features of this part of Africa. Clustered around Lake Victoria, which is the continent's largest lake, are Uganda, Kenya and Tanzania. Africa's deepest lake, Lake Tanganyika, lies at the western edge of Tanzania and Burundi. The small, landlocked country of Rwanda shares borders with Burundi, Tanzania and Uganda.

A group of Masai women

East Central Africa has many lakes, but water is still considered a precious gift. Kenyans often greet one another by asking, "Does it rain where you live?" For many of the region's people, years of drought, grinding poverty, government corruption, ethnic rivalries and an AIDS epidemic have combined to make everyday life difficult.

In 1964, Tanganyika joined with the island of Zanzibar to form the country of Tanzania. South of Zanzibar, in the Indian Ocean, are the small island nations of Comoros and Seychelles. Still further south is Madagascar, the fourth-largest island in the world.

Heads Up: Serengeti National Park, in Tanzania, is home to these giraffes.

Data Bank

BURUNDI
AREA: 10,745 sq mi (27,830 sq km)
POPULATION: 8,090,068
CAPITAL: Bujumbura
LANGUAGES: Kirundi, French (both official), Swahili

COMOROS
AREA: 838 sq mi (2,170 sq km)
POPULATION: 690,948
CAPITAL: Moroni
LANGUAGES: Arabic, French (both official), Shikomoro

KENYA
AREA: 224,960 sq mi (582,650 sq km)
POPULATION: 34,707,817
CAPITAL: Nairobi
LANGUAGES: English, Kiswahili (both official), native languages

MADAGASCAR
AREA: 226,660 sq mi (587,040 sq km)
POPULATION: 18,595,469
CAPITAL: Antananarivo
LANGUAGES: Malagasy, French (both official)

MALAWI
AREA: 45,745 sq mi (118,480 sq km)
POPULATION: 13,013,926
CAPITAL: Lilongwe
LANGUAGES: English, Chichewa (both official)

MAURITIUS
AREA: 788 sq mi (2,040 sq km)
POPULATION: 1,240,827
CAPITAL: Port Louis
LANGUAGES: English, French (both official), Creole, Hindi, Urdu

MOZAMBIQUE
AREA: 309,494 sq mi (801,590 sq km)
POPULATION: 19,686,505
CAPITAL: Maputo
LANGUAGES: Portuguese (official), Bantu languages

RWANDA
AREA: 10,169 sq mi (26,338 sq km)
POPULATION: 8,648,248
CAPITAL: Kigali
LANGUAGES: Kinyarwanda, French, English (all official), Bantu, Kiswahili

SEYCHELLES
AREA: 176 sq mi (455 sq km)
POPULATION: 81,541
CAPITAL: Victoria
LANGUAGES: English, French (both official), Creole

TANZANIA
AREA: 364,898 sq mi (945,087 sq km)
POPULATION: 37,445,392
CAPITAL: Dar es Salaam
LANGUAGES: Kiswahili, English (both official), Arabic

UGANDA
AREA: 91,135 sq mi (236,040 sq km)
POPULATION: 28,195,754
CAPITAL: Kampala
LANGUAGES: English (official), Ganda, other native languages

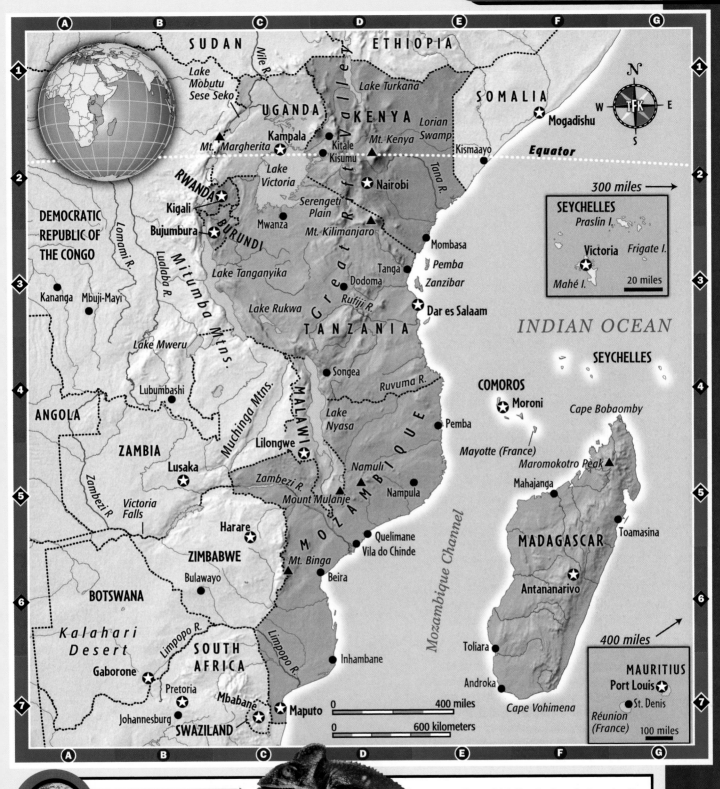

East Central Africa Map

SUDAN
ETHIOPIA
Lake Mobutu Sese Seko
Nile R.
Lake Turkana
SOMALIA
Mogadishu
UGANDA
▲ Mt. Margherita
Kampala ★
Kitale ●
Kisumu ●
Mt. Kenya ▲
Lorian Swamp
Kismaayo ●
Equator
N W TFK E S
RWANDA
Lake Victoria
Serengeti Plain
Nairobi ★
Tana R.
DEMOCRATIC REPUBLIC OF THE CONGO
Lomani R.
Kigali ★
BURUNDI
Bujumbura ★
Mwanza ●
Mt. Kilimanjaro ▲
300 miles
Lualaba R.
Mitumba Mtns.
Lake Tanganyika
Dodoma ●
Tanga ●
Mombasa ●
Pemba
Zanzibar
SEYCHELLES
Praslin I.
Victoria ★
Frigate I.
Mahé I.
20 miles
Kananga ●
Mbuji-Mayi ●
Lake Rukwa
Rufiji R.
Dar es Salaam ★
TANZANIA
INDIAN OCEAN
Lake Mweru
Great Rift Valley
Songea ●
Ruvuma R.
SEYCHELLES
Lubumbashi ●
Muchinga Mtns.
MALAWI
Lake Nyasa
COMOROS
Moroni ★
Cape Bobaomby
ANGOLA
ZAMBIA
Lilongwe ★
Namuli ▲
Pemba ●
Mayotte (France)
Maromokotro Peak ▲
Mahajanga ●
Lusaka ★
Zambezi R.
Mount Mulanje ▲
Nampula ●
Zambezi R.
Victoria Falls
Harare ★
MOZAMBIQUE
Mt. Binga ▲
Beira ●
Quelimane ●
Vila do Chinde ●
Mozambique Channel
MADAGASCAR
Toamasina ●
ZIMBABWE
Bulawayo ●
Antananarivo ★
BOTSWANA
400 miles
Kalahari Desert
Limpopo R.
SOUTH AFRICA
Limpopo R.
Inhambane ●
Toliara ●
Androka ●
Cape Vohimena
MAURITIUS
Port Louis ★
St. Denis ●
Réunion (France)
100 miles
Gaborone ●
Pretoria ★
Mbabane ★
Johannesburg ●
Maputo ★
SWAZILAND
0   400 miles
0   600 kilometers

Did You Know?

● Scientists believe that our earliest human ancestors lived in Kenya.

● The coelacanth (see-la-canth), an ancient type of fish, was believed to be extinct. In 1938, one was found swimming in the Indian Ocean, near Comoros.

● Gorillas, which live in the rain forests of equatorial Africa, are the world's largest primates. A male gorilla can weigh up to 441 lbs (200 kg).

● A giraffe can run as fast as 32 mph (56 kph), and a stampeding elephant can cover 12 mi (19 km) in 30 minutes.

● Madagascar is a haven for chameleons. Half of the chameleons in the world are found on the island.

Southern Africa

Johannesburg, South Africa

Spotted cheetahs, lumbering elephants, magnificent lions and hundreds of bird species—these are the hallmarks of southern Africa. The region's vast savannas, mountains and plateaus host an astonishing array of plant and animal life. Tourists come from around the world to take safaris, adventures whose name means "journey" in Swahili. The southern part of Africa is rich in natural resources, such as diamonds, gold and copper, as well as physical beauty. At Zimbabwe's spectacular Victoria Falls, the Zambezi River plunges nearly 355 ft (108 m) into a rain-forested gorge. Thundering over the rocks is some 33,000 cubic ft (935 cubic m) of water per second!

The richest, most modern country on the continent is South Africa. Comprising more than 30 ethnic groups, the country has undergone many political and social changes. For hundreds of years, a small white minority ruled a mostly black population. Following the country's first free election in 1994, South Africa entered a new era of equality and cooperation.

Data Bank

ANGOLA
AREA: 481,350 sq mi (1,246,700 sq km)
POPULATION: 12,127,071
CAPITAL: Luanda
LANGUAGES: Portuguese (official), Bantu, other African languages

BOTSWANA
AREA: 231,800 sq mi (600,370 sq km)
POPULATION: 1,639,833
CAPITAL: Gaborone
LANGUAGES: English (official), Setswana

LESOTHO
AREA: 11,720 sq mi (30,355 sq km)
POPULATION: 2,022,331
CAPITAL: Maseru
LANGUAGES: Sesotho (southern Sotho), English (official), Zulu, Xhosa

NAMIBIA
AREA: 318,694 sq mi (825,418 sq km)
POPULATION: 2,044,147
CAPITAL: Windhoek
LANGUAGES: English (official), Afrikaans, native languages

SOUTH AFRICA
AREA: 471,008 sq mi (1,219,912 sq km)
POPULATION: 44,187,637
CAPITAL: Pretoria (administrative capital), Cape Town (legislative capital)
LANGUAGES: Afrikaans, English, Ndebele, Pedi, Sotho, Swazi, Tsonga, Tswana, Venda, Xhosa, Zulu (all official)

SWAZILAND
AREA: 6,704 sq mi (17,363 sq km)
POPULATION: 1,136,334
CAPITAL: Mbabane
LANGUAGES: siSwati, English (both official)

ZAMBIA
AREA: 290,583 sq mi (752,614 sq km)
POPULATION: 11,502,010
CAPITAL: Lusaka
LANGUAGES: English (official), Bemba, Kaonda, Lozi, Lunda, other native languages

ZIMBABWE
AREA: 150,802 sq mi (390,580 sq km)
POPULATION: 12,236,805
CAPITAL: Harare
LANGUAGES: English (official), Shona, Sindebele, native languages

Victoria Falls

Map labels:

A B C D E F G
1 2 3 4 5 6 7

Kinshasa
CABINDA (Angola)
DEMOCRATIC REPUBLIC OF THE CONGO
Lualaba R.
Mitumba Mtns.
Lake Tanganyika
N W E S TFK
Zanzibar
Dar es Salaam
Lower Guinea
Malanje Highlands
Bihé Plateau
Luanda
Benguela
Mt. Moco
Huambo
ANGOLA
Lubumbashi
Ndola
ZAMBIA
Zambezi R.
Lusaka
Muchinga Mtns.
Lilongwe
MALAWI
Lake Nyasa
TANZANIA
Pemba
MOZAMBIQUE
Huíla Plateau
Neriquinha
Zambezi R.
Lake Kariba
Victoria Falls
Harare
ZIMBABWE
Mount Inyangani
Mutare
Cunene R.
Etosha Pan
Mt. Aha
Okavango Delta
Bulawayo
Beira
Save R.
Mozambique Channel
Skeleton Coast
Namib Desert
NAMIBIA
Mt. Brand
Francistown
Selebi Phikwe
Limpopo R.
Limpopo R.
Walvis Bay
Windhoek
BOTSWANA
Gaborone
Kalahari Desert
Pretoria
SWAZILAND
Maputo
INDIAN OCEAN
Molopo R.
Johannesburg
Mbabane
GREAT NAMAQUALAND
Great Karas Mtns.
Orange R.
Vaal R.
Kimberley
Maseru
Mt. Thabana Ntlenyana
Pietermaritzburg
Durban
Diamond Coast
LITTLE NAMAQUALAND
Bloemfontein
LESOTHO
Drakensberg
ATLANTIC OCEAN
SOUTH AFRICA
Great Karoo
East London
Cape Town
Port Elizabeth
Cape of Good Hope

0   400 miles
0   600 kilometers

Did You Know?

● Victoria Falls is about twice as wide and deep as Niagara Falls.

● South Africa is nicknamed the Rainbow Nation for its amazing mix of people and cultures.

● Swaziland's King Mswati III is one of the world's last absolute monarchs.

● Angola is the second-largest oil-producing country in sub-Saharan Africa.

● The Namib Desert, in Namibia, is said to be the oldest desert in the world. Namibia is home to the largest population of cheetahs.

● Botswana boasts more than 70 species of snakes!

Australia and the Pacific Islands

The Great Barrier Reef includes nearly 3,000 reefs.

Australia is the smallest, flattest and—with the exception of Antarctica—the driest continent. It is also a region with many different landscapes: parched deserts, vast grasslands, tropical rain forests and plains dotted with mammoth rocks.

Located between the Indian and Pacific Oceans, Australia is relatively isolated from other continents. It is home to unusual plant and animal life, including the only egg-laying mammals on earth, the platypus and the echidna. Off Australia's northeast coast, the Great Barrier Reef contains an unparalleled treasure of brilliant corals and marine life.

To the east of Australia lie the Pacific Islands, a collection of more than 10,000 islands, atolls and islets. The largest of this group are New Zealand and New Guinea. New Guinea is the world's second-largest island, after Greenland. Half the island forms part of Indonesia; the other half is the independent country Papua New Guinea.

The Pacific Islands are known for their natural beauty. In New Zealand alone, the terrain ranges from snowy glaciers and sparkling fjords to active volcanoes, temperate rainforests and sandy beaches.

Regional Facts

AREA, AUSTRALIA:
2,967,893 sq mi (7,686,850 sq km)

LAND AREA, PACIFIC ISLANDS:
317,700 sq mi (822,800 sq km)

NUMBER OF COUNTRIES: 13 countries—
Fiji, Kiribati, Marshall Islands, Micronesia, Nauru, New Zealand, Palau, Papua New Guinea, Somoa, Solomon Islands, Tonga, Tuvalu, Vanuatu

HIGHEST POINT: Mount Wilhelm, Papua New Guinea, 14,793 ft (4,509 m)

LOWEST POINT: Lake Eyre, Australia, 49 ft (15 m) below sea level

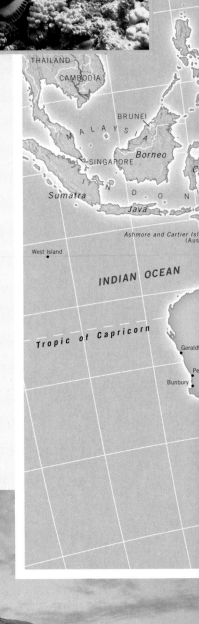

Uluru (Ayers Rock) is the world's largest monolith.

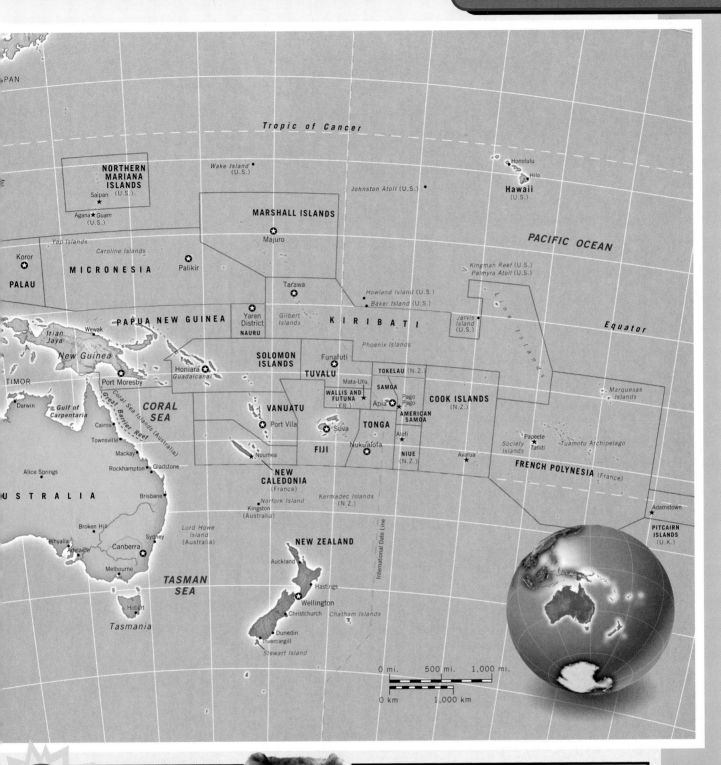

PAN

Tropic of Cancer

NORTHERN MARIANA ISLANDS (U.S.)
Saipan ★

Agana ★ *Guam*
(U.S.)

Wake Island •
(U.S.)

Johnston Atoll (U.S.) •

Honolulu •
Hilo •
Hawaii
(U.S.)

PACIFIC OCEAN

Yap Islands
Caroline Islands

Koror
✪
PALAU

M I C R O N E S I A
Palikir ✪

MARSHALL ISLANDS
Majuro ✪

Tarawa ✪

Kingman Reef (U.S.)
Palmyra Atoll (U.S.)

PAPUA NEW GUINEA
Irian Jaya
Wewak •
New Guinea

Yaren
District ✪
NAURU

Gilbert Islands

Howland Island (U.S.) •
Baker Island (U.S.) •

K I R I B A T I

Jarvis
Island
(U.S.) •

Line Islands

Equator

TIMOR

Port Moresby •
✪

Darwin •
Gulf of Carpentaria

Honiara ✪
Guadalcanal

SOLOMON ISLANDS

Phoenix Islands

Funafuti ✪

TUVALU

TOKELAU (N.Z.)

Mata-Utu ★

SAMOA

Pago
Pago

COOK ISLANDS
(N.Z.)

Marquesas Islands

Coral Sea Islands (Australia)

Cairns •

Townsville •

CORAL SEA

VANUATU
Port Vila ✪

WALLIS AND FUTUNA (F.R.)

Apia ✪

AMERICAN SAMOA

Suva ✪

TONGA

Nuku'alofa ✪

Alofi ★
NIUE
(N.Z.)

Avarua ★

Society Islands
Papeete •
Tahiti ★

Tuamotu Archipelago

Mackay •

Rockhampton • Gladstone •

Noumea ★

FIJI

FRENCH POLYNESIA (France)

Alice Springs •

A U S T R A L I A

Brisbane •

NEW CALEDONIA
(France)

Norfork Island
Kingston
(Australia) •

Kermadec Islands
(N.Z.)

Broken Hill •

Whyalla •

Sydney •

Adelaide • Canberra •

Lord Howe Island
(Australia) •

NEW ZEALAND

Auckland •

Adamstown ★

PITCAIRN ISLANDS
(U.K.)

Melbourne •

TASMAN SEA

Hobart •

Tasmania

Hastings •

Wellington •

Christchurch • *Chatham Islands*

Dunedin •

Invercargill •

Stewart Island

International Date Line

0 mi.	500 mi.	1,000 mi.

0 km	1,000 km

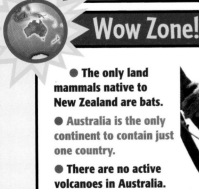

Wow Zone!

● The only land mammals native to New Zealand are bats.

● Australia is the only continent to contain just one country.

● There are no active volcanoes in Australia.

● Koalas are not bears. They are marsupials. They carry their young in a pouch.

● Fiji contains more than 800 islands and islets spread across 1,000,000 sq mi (3,000,000 sq km). Only 100 of Fiji's islands are inhabited.

● In 1789, sailors on the British ship *Bounty* took over the vessel and set their captain, William Bligh, adrift in a small boat. The incident was made famous in the novel—and subsequent movies—*Mutiny on the Bounty*. Bligh and 18 shipmates survived and traveled more than 3,600 mi (5,800 km) before arriving at the island of Java.

Australia and Papua New Guinea

Sydney Harbor: The majestic peaked roofs belong to the Sydney Opera House.

Australia is a hot, dry country of stunning sunsets and vast plains. Known for its unusual animals and colorful birds, the land Down Under is home to kangaroos, koalas, lorikeets and rosellas. Australia stretches across almost 3 million sq mi (8 million sq km), making it the world's sixth-largest country. It is almost as big as the United States, but its population is less than one-tenth the size of the United States' population. Most of Australia's interior, which is called the Outback, has so little water that hardly anyone can live there. Most Australians—some 70% of the population—live in the country's large coastal cities. Sydney has 4 million residents and is Australia's largest urban center. The island of Tasmania is located off Australia's southern coast. It is the only place on earth where you will find the fierce little mammal aptly named Tasmanian devil.

Off the northern coast of Australia lies Papua New Guinea. This rugged country occupies the eastern half of the island of New Guinea (the other half of the island belongs to Indonesia). Papua New Guinea was an Australian territory until it gained independence in 1975.

A Tasmanian devil gets ready to let out a screech.

Mother kangaroo and her baby near Adelaide, Australia

Data Bank

AUSTRALIA
AREA: 2,967,893 sq mi (7,686,850 sq km)
POPULATION: 20,264,082
CAPITAL: Canberra
LANGUAGES: English, native languages

PAPUA NEW GUINEA
AREA: 178,703 sq mi (462,840 sq km)
POPULATION: 5,670,544
CAPITAL: Port Moresby
LANGUAGES: Motu, other native languages, English

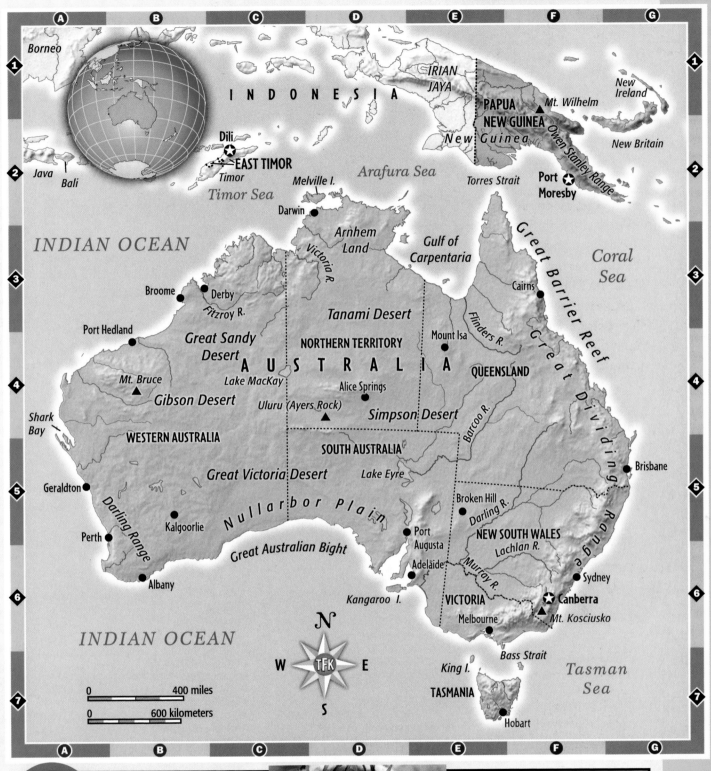

Australia and Papua New Guinea map with grid references A–G (columns) and 1–7 (rows).

Labels on map:

Borneo, Java, Bali, INDONESIA, IRIAN JAYA, New Ireland, Mt. Wilhelm, PAPUA NEW GUINEA, New Guinea, New Britain, Dili, EAST TIMOR, Timor, Arafura Sea, Torres Strait, Port Moresby, Owen Stanley Range, Timor Sea, Melville I., Darwin, INDIAN OCEAN, Arnhem Land, Victoria R., Gulf of Carpentaria, Coral Sea, Broome, Derby, Fitzroy R., Cairns, Great Barrier Reef, Tanami Desert, Port Hedland, Great Sandy Desert, NORTHERN TERRITORY, Mount Isa, Flinders R., Mt. Bruce, AUSTRALIA, Lake MacKay, Alice Springs, QUEENSLAND, Gibson Desert, Uluru (Ayers Rock), Simpson Desert, Great Dividing Range, Barcoo R., Shark Bay, WESTERN AUSTRALIA, SOUTH AUSTRALIA, Great Victoria Desert, Lake Eyre, Brisbane, Geraldton, Nullarbor Plain, Broken Hill, Darling R., Darling Range, Kalgoorlie, Port Augusta, NEW SOUTH WALES, Lachlan R., Perth, Great Australian Bight, Adelaide, Murray R., Sydney, Albany, Kangaroo I., VICTORIA, Canberra, Mt. Kosciusko, Melbourne, Bass Strait, King I., Tasman Sea, TASMANIA, Hobart

N W E S compass rose (TFK)

0   400 miles
0   600 kilometers

Did You Know?

● There are 30 million kangaroos in Australia. That's almost two kangaroos per person!

● Australia is home to the world's largest rock, called Uluru or Ayers Rock. The 1,142-ft (9,348-m) monolith is sacred to the Aborigines, Australia's native people.

A dancer at a sing-sing or gathering, in Papua New Guinea

● About 700 different languages are spoken in Papua New Guinea.

● Australia is called the land Down Under because it lies below the equator.

● The Great Barrier Reef—the world's largest coral reef—lies off Australia's northeastern coast. Stretching 1,250 mi (2,000 km), this brilliant coral garden contains nearly 3,000 reefs and as many as 2,000 species of fish.

New Zealand and the Pacific Islands

A beach scene in Samoa

More than 10,000 coral and volcanic islands dot the vast central Pacific Ocean. Within the Pacific Islands, also known as Oceania, are three groups: Melanesia, Polynesia and Micronesia. Oceania—with its coral reefs, blue lagoons, soaring volcanic mountains and mild climate—is one of the most beautiful places in the world.

Most Pacific Island nations include many small islands—Micronesia has more than 600 islands and islets, Fiji has more than 800—and all share a similar mild climate. The people of Oceania speak dozens of different languages.

New Guinea and the islands of New Zealand make up 90% of the Pacific Islands' land area.

The kiwi is native to New Zealand.

Data Bank

FIJI
AREA: 7,054 sq mi (18,270 sq km)
POPULATION: 905,949
CAPITAL: Suva
LANGUAGES: English (official), Fijian, Hindustani

KIRIBATI
AREA: 313 sq mi (811 sq km)
POPULATION: 105,432
CAPITAL: Tarawa
LANGUAGES: English (official), I-Kiribati

MARSHALL ISLANDS
AREA: 70 sq mi (181 sq km)
POPULATION: 60,422
CAPITAL: Majuro
LANGUAGES: Marshallese, English (both official), Japanese

MICRONESIA
AREA: 271 sq mi (702 sq km)
POPULATION: 108,004
CAPITAL: Palikir
LANGUAGES: English (official), Trukese, Pohnpeian, Yapese, other native languages

NEW ZEALAND
AREA: 103,737 sq mi (268,680 sq km)
POPULATION: 4,076,140
CAPITAL: Wellington
LANGUAGES: English, Maori (both official)

SOLOMON ISLANDS
AREA: 10,985 sq mi (28,450 sq km)
POPULATION: 552,438
CAPITAL: Honiara
LANGUAGES: English, Solomon Pidgin, Melanesian languages

VANUATU
AREA: 4,719 sq mi (12,200 sq km)
POPULATION: 208,869
CAPITAL: Port-Vila
LANGUAGES: English, French, Bislama (all official), others

NAURU
AREA: 8 sq mi (21 sq km)
POPULATION: 13,287
CAPITAL: Yaren District
LANGUAGES: Nauruan, English

PALAU
AREA: 177 sq mi (458 sq km)
POPULATION: 20,579
CAPITAL: Koror
LANGUAGES: English, Palauan, Sonsoralese, Tobi, others

SAMOA
AREA: 1,136 sq mi (2,944 sq km)
POPULATION: 176,908
CAPITAL: Apia
LANGUAGES: Samoan (Polynesian), English

TONGA
AREA: 289 sq mi (748 sq km)
POPULATION: 114,689
CAPITAL: Nuku'alofa
LANGUAGES: Tongan, English

TUVALU
AREA: 10 sq mi (26 sq km)
POPULATION: 11,810
CAPITAL: Funafuti
LANGUAGES: Tuvalulan, English, Somoan, Kiribati

Map labels: CHINA, TAIWAN, PHILIPPINES, PALAU, Iwo (Japan), Okinawa (Japan), North Mariana Islands (U.S.), Guam (U.S.), Yap, INDONESIA, AUSTRALIA

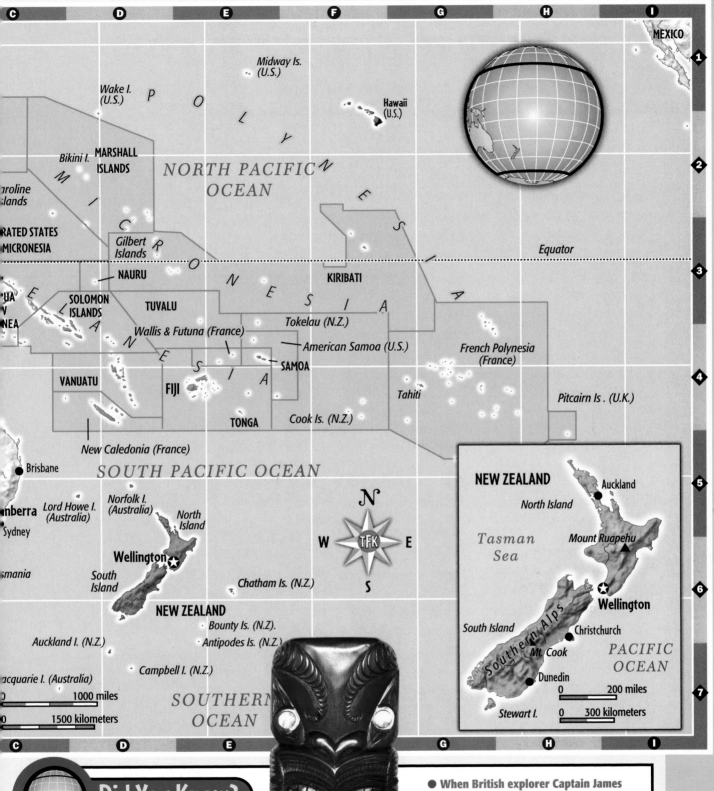

C D E F G H I

MEXICO

Midway Is.
(U.S.)

Wake I.
(U.S.)

P O L Y N E S I A

Hawaii
(U.S.)

Bikini I. MARSHALL
ISLANDS

NORTH PACIFIC
OCEAN

aroline
Islands

M I C R O N E S I A

RATED STATES
MICRONESIA

Gilbert
Islands

Equator

NAURU

KIRIBATI

UA
V
NEA

SOLOMON
ISLANDS

TUVALU

Tokelau (N.Z.)

Wallis & Futuna (France)

American Samoa (U.S.)

French Polynesia
(France)

M
E
L
A
N
E
S
I
A

VANUATU

SAMOA

FIJI

Tahiti

Pitcairn Is . (U.K.)

New Caledonia (France)

TONGA

Cook Is. (N.Z.)

Brisbane

SOUTH PACIFIC OCEAN

Norfolk I.
(Australia)

NEW ZEALAND

nberra

Lord Howe I.
(Australia)

North
Island

North Island

Auckland

Sydney

N

Tasman
Sea

Mount Ruapehu ▲

W TFK E

Wellington

smania

South
Island

Chatham Is. (N.Z.)

S

South Island

Southern Alps

Christchurch

Mt. Cook

PACIFIC
OCEAN

NEW ZEALAND

Auckland I. (N.Z.)

Bounty Is. (N.Z.)

Antipodes Is. (N.Z.)

Dunedin

acquarie I. (Australia)

Campbell I. (N.Z.)

SOUTHERN
OCEAN

0 1000 miles

0 1500 kilometers

Stewart I.

0 200 miles

0 300 kilometers

Did You Know?

● There are several extinct
volcanoes within the borders of
Auckland, New Zealand.

● New Zealand was the first
country to give women the vote.

● Flightless kiwi birds live only in New Zealand.
"Kiwi" has become a friendly nickname for a
person from New Zealand.

Maori tribal masks often feature
tongues sticking out.

● When British explorer Captain James
Cook first discovered New Zealand, the
native Maori men stuck out their tongues
at him. He learned that this was intended to
scare him off. Eventually, he and the Maori
people became friendly.

● Copra (dried coconut meat) is a food
product throughout Oceania.

● The people of Oceania are well known for their
music, dance and art. Their masks, costumes and
sculptures are in museums all around the world.

Antarctica

Antarctica is the highest, driest, coldest and windiest place on earth. It is also the location of the South Pole—the southernmost point on earth. Almost all of Antarctica is covered by an ice sheet. The rest of the continent is barren rock. During the winter months, from June until August, the night lasts for 24 hours, and huge blizzards and windstorms sweep across the frozen plains. Yet with its soaring ice cliffs and amazing views of the aurora australis, or southern lights, Antarctica is one of the most beautiful places in the world. It is also home to an amazing array of animals, including many kinds of whales, birds, fish, insects and mammals. Penguins are probably Antarctica's most famous residents.

About 500 million years ago, the frozen land of Antarctica was located near the equator. As recently as 65 million years ago—during the age of dinosaurs—it was warm enough in Antarctica for many life forms to thrive. Now scientists are discovering amazingly well-preserved fossils of dinosaurs and other ancient life forms on the continent.

King penguins on parade

No human beings are native to Antarctica. Since the first explorers reached the South Pole in 1911, scientists and adventurers have ventured to the frozen land to learn more about it. Each year, as many as 4,000 people from 27 nations live, work and study at research centers. An additional 1,000 scientists travel to the Antarctic seas to study marine life and oceanography.

McMurdo Station is Antarctica's largest research center.

Continent Facts

NUMBER OF COUNTRIES AND TERRITORIES: There are no national governments in Antarctica. Instead, Antarctica is governed by a treaty signed by 45 nations. The treaty states that Antarctica is a free and peaceful territory. The treaty also supports open scientific exchange and protects Antarctica's natural environment.

AREA: 5,405,430 sq mi (14,000,000 sq km)

LONGEST RIVER: There are no true rivers in Antarctica. The Onyx River, a snowmelt area, is only about 18 mi (29 km) long.

LONGEST MOUNTAIN RANGE: The Transantarctic Mountains are 3,000 mi long (4,800 km).

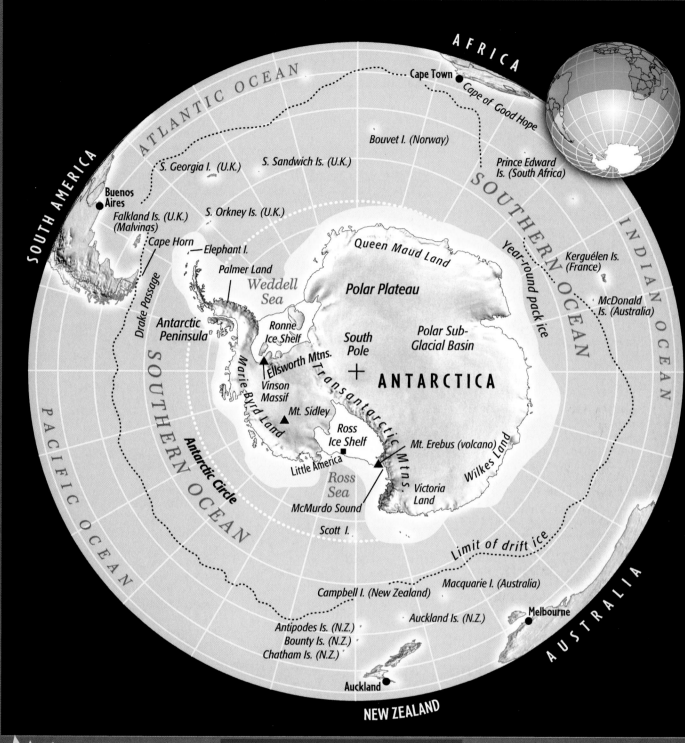

AFRICA

Cape Town

Cape of Good Hope

ATLANTIC OCEAN

Bouvet I. (Norway)

SOUTHERN OCEAN

INDIAN OCEAN

S. Georgia I. (U.K.)

S. Sandwich Is. (U.K.)

Prince Edward Is. (South Africa)

SOUTH AMERICA

Buenos Aires

Falkland Is. (U.K.) (Malvinas)

S. Orkney Is. (U.K.)

Kerguélen Is. (France)

Year-round pack ice

Cape Horn

Elephant I.

Queen Maud Land

McDonald Is. (Australia)

Drake Passage

Palmer Land

Weddell Sea

Polar Plateau

Antarctic Peninsula

Ronne Ice Shelf

South Pole

Polar Sub-Glacial Basin

PACIFIC OCEAN

Marie Byrd Land

Ellsworth Mtns.

Transantarctic Mtns.

+ **ANTARCTICA**

SOUTHERN OCEAN

Vinson Massif

Mt. Sidley

Ross Ice Shelf

Mt. Erebus (volcano)

Wilkes Land

Antarctic Circle

Little America

Ross Sea

Victoria Land

McMurdo Sound

Scott I.

Limit of drift ice

Campbell I. (New Zealand)

Macquarie I. (Australia)

AUSTRALIA

Antipodes Is. (N.Z.)

Auckland Is. (N.Z.)

Melbourne

Bounty Is. (N.Z.)

Chatham Is. (N.Z.)

Auckland

NEW ZEALAND

Wow Zone!

The Antarctic landscape

● On December 14, 1911, Norwegian Roald Amundsen became the first person to reach the South Pole.

● Ice and snow cover 98% of Antarctica—that's 80% of the ice in the world! The remaining 2% of the continent is rock.

● Antarctica gets less than 2 in (5 cm) of rain or snow per year. It is the world's biggest desert.

● Scientists in Antarctica recorded the coldest temperature on earth: −128.6°F (−88.0°C)!

● The biggest hole in Earth's ozone layer is located over Antarctica.

World-at-a-Glance

AFGHANISTAN
AREA: 249,999 sq mi (647,500 sq km)
POPULATION: 31,056,997
CAPITAL: Kabul
LANGUAGES: Pashtu, Afghan Persian (Dari), other Turkic languages
GOVERNMENT: Transitional
RELIGIONS: Sunni Muslim, Shi'a Muslim
LITERACY RATE: 36%
CURRENCY: Afghani
MAIN EXPORTS: Fruits and nuts, carpets, wool, cotton, hides and pelts, precious and semi-precious gems

ALBANIA
AREA: 11,100 sq mi (28,748 sq km)
POPULATION: 3,581,655
CAPITAL: Tirana
LANGUAGES: Albanian (Tosk is the official dialect), Greek
GOVERNMENT: Emerging democracy
RELIGIONS: Muslim, Albanian Orthodox, Roman Catholic
LITERACY RATE: 87%
CURRENCY: Lek
MAIN EXPORTS: Textiles and footwear, asphalt, metals, crude oil, vegetables, fruits, tobacco

ALGERIA
AREA: 919,586 sq mi (2,381,740 sq km)
POPULATION: 32,930,091
CAPITAL: Algiers
LANGUAGES: Arabic (official), French, Berber dialects
GOVERNMENT: Republic
RELIGION: Sunni Muslim
LITERACY RATE: 70%
CURRENCY: Algerian dinar
MAIN EXPORTS: Petroleum, natural gas, petroleum products

ANDORRA
AREA: 181 sq mi (468 sq km)
POPULATION: 71,201
CAPITAL: Andorra la Vella
LANGUAGES: Catalan (official), French, Castilian, Portuguese
GOVERNMENT: Parliamentary democracy
RELIGION: Roman Catholic

LITERACY RATE: 100%
CURRENCY: Euro
MAIN EXPORTS: Tobacco products, furniture

ANGOLA
AREA: 481,350 sq mi (1,246,700 sq km)
POPULATION: 12,127,071
CAPITAL: Luanda
LANGUAGES: Portuguese (official), Bantu and other African languages
GOVERNMENT: Republic, nominally a multiparty democracy
RELIGIONS: Native beliefs, Roman Catholic, Protestant
LITERACY RATE: 67%
CURRENCY: Kwanza
MAIN EXPORTS: Crude oil, diamonds, refined petroleum products, gas, coffee, sisal, fish, timber, cotton

ANTIGUA AND BARBUDA
AREA: 171 sq mi (443 sq km)
POPULATION: 69,108
CAPITAL: Saint John's
LANGUAGES: English (official), local dialects
GOVERNMENT: Constitutional monarchy
RELIGIONS: Protestant, Roman Catholic
LITERACY RATE: 86%
CURRENCY: East Caribbean dollar
MAIN EXPORTS: Petroleum products, machinery and transport equipment, food and live animals

ARGENTINA
AREA: 1,068,296 sq mi (2,766,890 sq km)
POPULATION: 39,921,833
CAPITAL: Buenos Aires
LANGUAGES: Spanish (official), English, Italian, German
GOVERNMENT: Republic
RELIGIONS: Roman Catholic, Protestant, Jewish
LITERACY RATE: 97%
CURRENCY: Argentine peso
MAIN EXPORTS: Edible oils, fuels and energy, cereals, feed, motor vehicles

ARMENIA
AREA: 11,500 sq mi (29,800 sq km)
POPULATION: 2,976,372
CAPITAL: Yerevan

LANGUAGES: Armenian, Russian
GOVERNMENT: Republic
RELIGIONS: Armenian Apostolic, other Christian, Yezidi
LITERACY RATE: 99%
CURRENCY: Dram
MAIN EXPORTS: Diamonds, mineral products, foodstuffs, energy

AUSTRALIA
AREA: 2,967,893 sq mi (7,686,850 sq km)
POPULATION: 20,264,082
CAPITAL: Canberra
LANGUAGES: English, native languages
GOVERNMENT: Democracy
RELIGIONS: Protestant, Roman Catholic, other
LITERACY RATE: 99%
CURRENCY: Australian dollar
MAIN EXPORTS: Coal, gold, meat, wool, alumina, iron ore, wheat, machinery and transport equipment

AUSTRIA
AREA: 32,375 sq mi (83,858 sq km)
POPULATION: 8,192,880
CAPITAL: Vienna
LANGUAGES: German
GOVERNMENT: Republic
RELIGIONS: Roman Catholic, Protestant, Muslim
LITERACY RATE: 98%
CURRENCY: Euro
MAIN EXPORTS: Machinery, motor vehicles and parts, paper, metal goods, chemicals, iron, steel

AZERBAIJAN
AREA: 33,400 sq mi (86,000 sq km)
POPULATION: 7,961,619
CAPITAL: Baku
LANGUAGES: Azerbaijani (Azeri), Russian, Armenian
GOVERNMENT: Republic
RELIGIONS: Muslim, Russian Orthodox, Armenian Orthodox
LITERACY RATE: 99%
CURRENCY: Azerbaijani manat
MAIN EXPORTS: Oil and gas, machinery, cotton, foodstuffs

BAHAMAS

AREA: 5,380 sq mi (13,940 sq km)

POPULATION: 303,770

CAPITAL: Nassau

LANGUAGE: English

GOVERNMENT: Parliamentary democracy

RELIGIONS: Protestant, Roman Catholic

LITERACY RATE: 96%

CURRENCY: Bahamian dollar

MAIN EXPORTS: Fish, rum, salt, chemicals, fruit and vegetables

BAHRAIN

AREA: 257 sq mi (665 sq km)

POPULATION: 698,585

CAPITAL: Manama

LANGUAGES: Arabic, English, Farsi, Urdu

GOVERNMENT: Constitutional hereditary monarchy

RELIGIONS: Shi'a Muslim, Sunni Muslim

LITERACY RATE: 89%

CURRENCY: Bahraini dinar

MAIN EXPORTS: Petroleum and petroleum products, aluminum, textiles

BANGLADESH

AREA: 55,598 sq mi (144,000 sq km)

POPULATION: 147,365,352

CAPITAL: Dhaka

LANGUAGES: Bangla (official), English

GOVERNMENT: Parliamentary democracy

RELIGIONS: Muslim, Hindu

LITERACY RATE: 43%

CURRENCY: Taka

MAIN EXPORTS: Clothing, jute, leather, frozen fish and seafood

BARBADOS

AREA: 166 sq mi (431 sq km)

POPULATION: 279,912

CAPITAL: Bridgetown

LANGUAGE: English

GOVERNMENT: Parliamentary democracy

RELIGIONS: Protestant, Roman Catholic

LITERACY RATE: 100%

CURRENCY: Barbadian dollar

MAIN EXPORTS: Sugar and molasses, rum, foodstuffs, chemicals, electrical components

BELARUS

AREA: 80,154 sq mi (207,600 sq km)

POPULATION: 10,293,011

CAPITAL: Minsk

LANGUAGES: Belarusian, Russian

GOVERNMENT: Republic

RELIGIONS: Eastern Orthodox, Roman Catholic, Protestant, Jewish, Muslim

LITERACY RATE: 100%

CURRENCY: Belarusian ruble

MAIN EXPORTS: Machinery and equipment, mineral products, chemicals, metals, textiles, foodstuffs

BELGIUM

AREA: 11,781 sq mi (30,510 sq km)

POPULATION: 10,379,067

CAPITAL: Brussels

LANGUAGES: Dutch, French, German (all official)

GOVERNMENT: Federal parliamentary democracy under a constitutional monarch

RELIGIONS: Roman Catholic, Protestant

LITERACY RATE: 99%

CURRENCY: Euro

MAIN EXPORTS: Machinery and equipment, chemicals, diamonds, metals and metal products, foodstuffs

BELIZE

AREA: 8,865 sq mi (22,966 sq km)

POPULATION: 287,730

CAPITAL: Belmopan

LANGUAGES: English (official), Spanish, Mayan, Garifuna (Carib)

GOVERNMENT: Parliamentary democracy

RELIGIONS: Roman Catholic, Protestant

LITERACY RATE: 94%

CURRENCY: Belizean dollar

MAIN EXPORTS: Sugar, bananas, citrus, clothing, fish products, molasses, wood

BENIN

AREA: 43,483 sq mi (112,620 sq km)

POPULATION: 7,862,944

CAPITAL: Porto-Novo

LANGUAGES: French (official), African languages

GOVERNMENT: Republic under multiparty democratic rule

RELIGIONS: Native beliefs, Christian, Muslim

LITERACY RATE: 34%

CURRENCY: Communauté Financière Africaine franc

MAIN EXPORTS: Cotton, crude oil, palm products, cocoa

BHUTAN

AREA: 18,147 sq mi (47,000 sq km)

POPULATION: 2,279,723

CAPITAL: Thimphu

LANGUAGES: Dzongkha (official)

GOVERNMENT: Monarchy

RELIGIONS: Buddhist, Hindu

LITERACY RATE: 47%

CURRENCY: Ngultrum and Indian rupee

MAIN EXPORTS: Electricity, cardamom, gypsum, timber, handicrafts, cement, fruit, precious stones, spices

BOLIVIA

AREA: 424,162 sq mi (1,098,580 sq km)

POPULATION: 8,989,046

CAPITAL: La Paz (seat of government); Sucre (legal capital)

LANGUAGES: Spanish, Quechua, and Aymara (all official)

GOVERNMENT: Republic

RELIGIONS: Roman Catholic, Protestant

LITERACY RATE: 87%

CURRENCY: Boliviano

MAIN EXPORTS: Soybeans, natural gas, zinc, gold, wood

BOSNIA AND HERZEGOVINA

AREA: 19,741 sq mi (51,129 sq km)

POPULATION: 4,498,976

CAPITAL: Sarajevo

LANGUAGES: Croatian, Serbian, Bosnian

GOVERNMENT: Emerging democracy

RELIGIONS: Muslim, Orthodox, Roman Catholic, Protestant

LITERACY RATE: 95%

CURRENCY: Marka

MAIN EXPORTS: Metals, clothing, wood products

BOTSWANA

AREA: 231,800 sq mi (600,370 sq km)

POPULATION: 1,639,833

CAPITAL: Gaborone

LANGUAGES: English (official), Setswana

GOVERNMENT: Parliamentary republic

RELIGIONS: Native beliefs, Christian

LITERACY RATE: 80%

CURRENCY: Pula

MAIN EXPORTS: Diamonds, copper, nickel, soda ash, meat, textiles

BRAZIL

AREA: 3,286,470 sq mi (8,511,965 sq km)

POPULATION: 188,078,227

CAPITAL: Brasília

LANGUAGES: Portuguese (official), Spanish, English, French

GOVERNMENT: Federative republic

RELIGION: Roman Catholic

LITERACY RATE: 86%

CURRENCY: Real

MAIN EXPORTS: Transport equipment, iron ore, soybeans, footwear, coffee, motor vehicles

BRUNEI
AREA: 2,228 sq mi (5,770 sq km)
POPULATION: 379,444
CAPITAL: Bandar Seri Begawan
LANGUAGES: Malay (official), English, Chinese
GOVERNMENT: Constitutional sultanate
RELIGIONS: Muslim, Buddhist, Christian, other
LITERACY RATE: 91%
CURRENCY: Bruneian dollar
MAIN EXPORTS: Crude oil, natural gas, refined products

BULGARIA
AREA: 48,822 sq mi (110,910 sq km)
POPULATION: 7,385,367
CAPITAL: Sofia
LANGUAGES: Bulgarian
GOVERNMENT: Parliamentary democracy
RELIGIONS: Orthodox, Muslim, Roman Catholic, Protestant
LITERACY RATE: 99%
CURRENCY: Lev
MAIN EXPORTS: Clothing, footwear, iron and steel, machinery and equipment, fuels

BURKINA FASO
AREA: 105,870 sq mi (274,200 sq km)
POPULATION: 13,902,972
CAPITAL: Ouagadougou
LANGUAGES: French (official), African languages
GOVERNMENT: Parliamentary republic
RELIGIONS: Native beliefs, Muslim, Christian
LITERACY RATE: 27%
CURRENCY: Communauté Financière Africaine franc
MAIN EXPORTS: Cotton, livestock, gold

BURUNDI
AREA: 10,745 sq mi (27,830 sq km)
POPULATION: 8,090,068
CAPITAL: Bujumbura
LANGUAGES: Kirundi, French (both official), Swahili
GOVERNMENT: Republic
RELIGION: Roman Catholic, Protestant, native beliefs, Muslim
LITERACY RATE: 52%
CURRENCY: Burundi franc
MAIN EXPORTS: Coffee, tea, sugar, cotton

CAMBODIA
AREA: 69,900 sq mi (181,040 sq km)
POPULATION: 13,881,427
CAPITAL: Phnom Penh

LANGUAGES: Khmer (official), French, English
GOVERNMENT: Multiparty democracy under a constitutional monarchy
RELIGIONS: Buddhist, other
LITERACY RATE: 74%
CURRENCY: Riel
MAIN EXPORTS: Timber, garments, rubber, rice, fish

CAMEROON
AREA: 183,567 sq mi (475,440 sq km)
POPULATION: 17,340,702
CAPITAL: Yaoundé
LANGUAGES: African languages; English and French (both official)
GOVERNMENT: Unitary republic
RELIGIONS: Native beliefs, Christian, Muslim
LITERACY RATE: 79%
CURRENCY: Communauté Financière Africaine franc
MAIN EXPORTS: Crude oil and petroleum products, lumber, cocoa beans, aluminum

CANADA
AREA: 3,855,085 sq mi (9,984,670 sq km)
POPULATION: 33,098,932
CAPITAL: Ottawa
LANGUAGES: English and French (both official), other
GOVERNMENT: Confederation with parliamentary democracy
RELIGIONS: Roman Catholic, Protestant, others
LITERACY RATE: 99%
CURRENCY: Canadian dollar
MAIN EXPORTS: Motor vehicles, machinery, aircraft, chemicals, plastics, fertilizers, wood pulp, timber, crude petroleum

CAPE VERDE
AREA: 1,557 sq mi (4,033 sq km)
POPULATION: 420,979
CAPITAL: Praia
LANGUAGES: Portuguese, Crioulo
GOVERNMENT: Republic
RELIGIONS: Roman Catholic, Protestant
LITERACY RATE: 77%
CURRENCY: Cape Verdean escudo
MAIN EXPORTS: Fuel, shoes, garments, fish

CENTRAL AFRICAN REPUBLIC
AREA: 240,534 sq mi (622,984 sq km)
POPULATION: 4,303,356
CAPITAL: Bangui
LANGUAGES: French (official), Sangho, tribal languages
GOVERNMENT: Republic
RELIGIONS: Native beliefs, Protestant, Roman Catholic, Muslim
LITERACY RATE: 51%

CURRENCY: Communauté Financière Africaine franc
MAIN EXPORTS: Diamonds, timber, cotton, coffee, tobacco

CHAD
AREA: 495,752 sq mi (1,284,000 sq km)
POPULATION: 9,944,201
CAPITAL: N'Djamena
LANGUAGES: French and Arabic (both official), Sara, African languages
GOVERNMENT: Republic
RELIGIONS: Muslim, Chrisitian, animist, others
LITERACY RATE: 48%
CURRENCY: Communauté Financière Africaine franc
MAIN EXPORTS: Cotton, cattle, gum arabic

CHILE
AREA: 292,258 sq mi (756,950 sq km)
POPULATION: 16,134,219
CAPITAL: Santiago
LANGUAGE: Spanish
GOVERNMENT: Republic
RELIGIONS: Roman Catholic, Protestant, Jewish
LITERACY RATE: 96%
CURRENCY: Chilean peso
MAIN EXPORTS: Copper, fish, fruits, paper and pulp, chemicals

CHINA
AREA: 3,705,386 sq mi (9,596,960 sq km)
POPULATION: 1,313,973,713
CAPITAL: Beijing
LANGUAGES: Chinese (Mandarin), local dialects
GOVERNMENT: Communist state
RELIGIONS: Daoist (Taoist), Buddhist, Muslim, Christian
LITERACY RATE: 91%
CURRENCY: Yuan
MAIN EXPORTS: Machinery and equipment, textiles and clothing, footwear, toys, sporting goods, mineral fuels

COLOMBIA
AREA: 439,733 sq mi (1,138,910 sq km)
POPULATION: 43,593,035
CAPITAL: Bogotá
LANGUAGE: Spanish
GOVERNMENT: Republic
RELIGION: Roman Catholic
LITERACY RATE: 93%
CURRENCY: Colombian peso
MAIN EXPORTS: Petroleum, coffee, coal, clothing, bananas, flowers

COMOROS
AREA: 838 sq mi (2,170 sq km)
POPULATION: 690,948

CAPITAL: Moroni
LANGUAGES: Arabic and French (both official), Shikomoro
GOVERNMENT: Independent republic
RELIGIONS: Sunni Muslim, Roman Catholic
LITERACY RATE: 57%
CURRENCY: Comoran franc
MAIN EXPORTS: Vanilla, ylang-ylang, cloves, perfume oil, copra

CONGO, DEMOCRATIC REPUBLIC OF THE
AREA: 905,562 sq mi (2,345,410 sq km)
POPULATION: 62,660,551

CAPITAL: Kinshasa
LANGUAGES: French (official), Lingala, Kingwana, Kikongo, other African languages
GOVERNMENT: Dictatorship
RELIGIONS: Roman Catholic, Protestant, Kimbanguist, Muslim, native beliefs
LITERACY RATE: 66%
CURRENCY: Congolese franc
MAIN EXPORTS: Diamonds, copper, crude oil, coffee, cobalt

CONGO, REPUBLIC OF THE
AREA: 132,046 sq mi (342,000 sq km)
POPULATION: 3,702,314

CAPITAL: Brazzaville
LANGUAGES: French (official), Lingala and Monokutuba, other African languages
GOVERNMENT: Republic
RELIGIONS: Christian, animist, Muslim
LITERACY RATE: 84%
CURRENCY: Communauté Financière Africaine franc
MAIN EXPORTS: Petroleum, lumber, plywood, sugar, cocoa, coffee, diamonds

COSTA RICA
AREA: 19,730 sq mi (51,100 sq km)
POPULATION: 4,075,261

CAPITAL: San José
LANGUAGE: Spanish (official)
GOVERNMENT: Democratic republic
RELIGIONS: Roman Catholic, Protestant, other
LITERACY RATE: 96%
CURRENCY: Costa Rican colón
MAIN EXPORTS: Coffee, bananas, sugar, pineapples, textiles, electronic components, medical equipment

CÔTE D'IVOIRE
AREA: 124,502 sq mi (322,460 sq km)
POPULATION: 17,654,843

CAPITAL: Yamoussoukro
LANGUAGES: French (official), African languages
GOVERNMENT: Republic
RELIGION: Muslim, Christian
LITERACY RATE: 51%
CURRENCY: Communauté Financière Africaine franc
MAIN EXPORTS: Cocoa, coffee, timber, petroleum, cotton, bananas, pineapples

CROATIA
AREA: 21,829 sq mi (56,542 sq km)
POPULATION: 4,494,749

CAPITAL: Zagreb
LANGUAGE: Croatian
GOVERNMENT: Presidential/parliamentary democracy
RELIGIONS: Roman Catholic, Orthodox, Muslim
LITERACY RATE: 99%
CURRENCY: Kuna
MAIN EXPORTS: Transport equipment, textiles, chemicals, foodstuffs, fuels

CUBA
AREA: 42,803 sq mi (110,860 sq km)
POPULATION: 11,382,820

CAPITAL: Havana
LANGUAGE: Spanish
GOVERNMENT: Communist state
RELIGION: Roman Catholic, Protestant
LITERACY RATE: 97%
CURRENCY: Cuban peso
MAIN EXPORTS: Sugar, nickel, tobacco, fish, medical products, citrus, coffee

CYPRUS
AREA: 3,572 sq mi (9,250 sq km)
POPULATION: 784,301

CAPITAL: Nicosia
LANGUAGES: Greek, Turkish, English
GOVERNMENT: Republic
RELIGIONS: Greek Orthodox, Muslim, Maronite, Armenian Apostolic
LITERACY RATE: 98%
CURRENCY: Cypriot pound, Turkish lira
MAIN EXPORTS: Citrus, potatoes, pharmaceuticals, cement, textiles

CZECH REPUBLIC
AREA: 30,450 sq mi (78,866 sq km)
POPULATION: 10,235,455

CAPITAL: Prague
LANGUAGE: Czech
GOVERNMENT: Parliamentary democracy
RELIGIONS: Roman Catholic, Protestant
LITERACY RATE: 99%
CURRENCY: Koruna
MAIN EXPORTS: Machinery and transport equipment, chemicals, raw materials, fuel

DENMARK
AREA: 16,639 sq mi (43,094 sq km)
POPULATION: 5,450,661

CAPITAL: Copenhagen
LANGUAGES: Danish, Faroese, Greenlandic, German
GOVERNMENT: Constitutional monarchy
RELIGIONS: Protestant, Roman Catholic, Muslim
LITERACY RATE: 99%
CURRENCY: Krone
MAIN EXPORTS: Machinery and instruments, meat, dairy products, fish, chemicals, furniture, ships, windmills

DJIBOUTI
AREA: 8,800 sq mi (23,000 sq km)
POPULATION: 486,530

CAPITAL: Djibouti
LANGUAGES: French and Arabic (both official), Somali, Afar
GOVERNMENT: Republic
RELIGIONS: Muslim, Christian
LITERACY RATE: 68%
CURRENCY: Djiboutian franc
MAIN EXPORTS: Re-exports, hides and skins, coffee

DOMINICA
AREA: 290 sq mi (754 sq km)
POPULATION: 68,910

CAPITAL: Roseau
LANGUAGES: English (official), French patois
GOVERNMENT: Parliamentary democracy
RELIGIONS: Roman Catholic, Protestant
LITERACY RATE: 94%
CURRENCY: East Caribbean dollar
MAIN EXPORTS: Bananas, soap, bay oil, vegetables, grapefruit, oranges

DOMINICAN REPUBLIC
AREA: 18,815 sq mi (48,730 sq km)
POPULATION: 9,183,984

CAPITAL: Santo Domingo
LANGUAGE: Spanish
GOVERNMENT: Representative democracy
RELIGION: Roman Catholic
LITERACY RATE: 85%
CURRENCY: Dominican peso
MAIN EXPORTS: Ferronickel, sugar, gold, silver, coffee, cocoa, tobacco, meats

EAST TIMOR
AREA: 5,814 sq mi (15,007 sq km)
POPULATION: 1,062,777
CAPITAL: Dili
LANGUAGES: Tetum, Portuguese (both official), Indonesian, English
GOVERNMENT: Republic
RELIGIONS: Roman Catholic, Muslim, Protestant
LITERACY RATE: 59%
CURRENCY: US dollar
MAIN EXPORTS: Coffee, sandalwood, marble

ECUADOR
AREA: 109,483 sq mi (283,560 sq km)
POPULATION: 13,547,510
CAPITAL: Quito
LANGUAGES: Spanish (official), Amerindian languages
GOVERNMENT: Republic
RELIGION: Roman Catholic
LITERACY RATE: 93%
CURRENCY: US dollar
MAIN EXPORTS: Petroleum, bananas, shrimp, coffee, cocoa, flowers, fish

EGYPT
AREA: 386,660 sq mi (1,001,450 sq km)
POPULATION: 78,887,007
CAPITAL: Cairo
LANGUAGE: Arabic (official)
GOVERNMENT: Republic
RELIGIONS: Muslim (mostly Sunni), Coptic Christian
LITERACY RATE: 58%
CURRENCY: Egyptian pound
MAIN EXPORTS: Crude oil and petroleum products, cotton, textiles, metal products

EL SALVADOR
AREA: 8,124 sq mi (21,040 sq km)
POPULATION: 6,822,378
CAPITAL: San Salvador
LANGUAGES: Spanish, Nahua
GOVERNMENT: Republic
RELIGION: Roman Catholic
LITERACY RATE: 80%
CURRENCY: US dollar
MAIN EXPORTS: Offshore assembly exports, coffee, sugar, shrimp, textiles, chemicals, electricity

EQUATORIAL GUINEA
AREA: 10,830 sq mi (28,051 sq km)
POPULATION: 540,109
CAPITAL: Malabo
LANGUAGES: Spanish and French (both official), pidgin English, Fang

---

GOVERNMENT: Republic
RELIGION: Christian
LITERACY RATE: 86%
CURRENCY: Communauté Financière Africaine franc
MAIN EXPORTS: Petroleum, methanol, timber, cocoa

ERITREA
AREA: 46,842 sq mi (121,320 sq km)
POPULATION: 4,786,994
CAPITAL: Asmara
LANGUAGES: Afar, Arabic, Tigre, Kunama, other languages
GOVERNMENT: Transitional
RELIGIONS: Muslim, Coptic Christian, Roman Catholic, Protestant
LITERACY RATE: 59%
CURRENCY: Nakfa
MAIN EXPORTS: Livestock, sorghum, textiles, food, small manufactures

ESTONIA
AREA: 17,462 sq mi (45,226 sq km)
POPULATION: 1,324,333
CAPITAL: Tallinn
LANGUAGES: Estonian (official), Russian, Ukrainian, Finnish
GOVERNMENT: Parliamentary republic
RELIGIONS: Protestant, Russian Orthodox, Estonian Orthodox
LITERACY RATE: 100%
CURRENCY: Estonian kroon
MAIN EXPORTS: Machinery and equipment, wood and paper, textiles, food products, furniture, metals

ETHIOPIA
AREA: 485,184 sq mi (1,127,127 sq km)
POPULATION: 74,777,981
CAPITAL: Addis Ababa
LANGUAGES: Amharic, Tigrinya, Oromigna, other local languages
GOVERNMENT: Federal republic
RELIGIONS: Muslim, Ethiopian Orthodox, animist
LITERACY RATE: 43%
CURRENCY: Birr
MAIN EXPORTS: Coffee, qat, gold, leather products, live animals, oilseeds

FIJI
AREA: 7,054 sq mi (18,270 sq km)
POPULATION: 905,949
CAPITAL: Suva
LANGUAGES: English (official), Fijian, Hindustani
GOVERNMENT: Republic
RELIGIONS: Christian, Hindu, Muslim
LITERACY RATE: 94%

CURRENCY: Fijian dollar
MAIN EXPORTS: Sugar, garments, gold, timber, fish, molasses, coconut oil

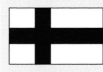

FINLAND
AREA: 130,127 sq mi (337,030 sq km)
POPULATION: 5,231,372
CAPITAL: Helsinki
LANGUAGES: Finnish and Swedish (both official)
GOVERNMENT: Republic
RELIGIONS: Evangelical Lutheran, Russian Orthodox
LITERACY RATE: 100%
CURRENCY: Euro
MAIN EXPORTS: Machinery and equipment, chemicals, metals, timber, paper, pulp

FRANCE
AREA: 211,208 sq mi (547,030 sq km)
POPULATION: 62,752,136
CAPITAL: Paris
LANGUAGE: French
GOVERNMENT: Republic
RELIGIONS: Roman Catholic, Protestant, Jewish, Muslim
LITERACY RATE: 99%
CURRENCY: Euro
MAIN EXPORTS: Machinery and transportation equipment, aircraft, plastics, chemicals, pharmaceutical products, iron and steel, beverages

GABON
AREA: 103,347 sq mi (267,667 sq km)
POPULATION: 1,424,906
CAPITAL: Libreville
LANGUAGES: French (official), Fang, Myene, Nzebi, Bapounou/Eschira, Bandjabi
GOVERNMENT: Republic
RELIGIONS: Christian, animist, Muslim
LITERACY RATE: 63%
CURRENCY: Communauté Financière Africaine franc
MAIN EXPORTS: Crude oil, timber, manganese, uranium

THE GAMBIA
AREA: 4,363 sq mi (11,300 sq km)
POPULATION: 1,641,564
CAPITAL: Banjul
LANGUAGES: English (official), native languages
GOVERNMENT: Republic
RELIGIONS: Muslim, Christian, other
LITERACY RATE: 40%
CURRENCY: Dalasi
MAIN EXPORTS: Peanut products, fish, cotton lint, palm kernels, re-exports

GEORGIA

AREA: 26,911 sq mi (69,700 sq km)

POPULATION: 4,661,473

CAPITAL: T'bilisi

LANGUAGES: Georgian (official), Russian, Armenian, Azeri

GOVERNMENT: Republic

RELIGIONS: Georgian Orthodox, Muslim, Russian Orthodox, Armenian Apostolic

LITERACY RATE: 100%

CURRENCY: Lari

MAIN EXPORTS: Scrap metal, machinery, chemicals, fuel re-exports, citrus fruits, tea

GERMANY

AREA: 137,846 sq mi (357,021 sq km)

POPULATION: 82,422,299

CAPITAL: Berlin

LANGUAGE: German

GOVERNMENT: Federal republic

RELIGIONS: Protestant, Roman Catholic, Muslim

LITERACY RATE: 99%

CURRENCY: Euro

MAIN EXPORTS: Machinery, vehicles, chemicals, metals and manufactures, foodstuffs, textiles

GHANA

AREA: 92,456 sq mi (239,460 sq km)

POPULATION: 22,409,572

CAPITAL: Accra

LANGUAGES: English (official), African languages

GOVERNMENT: Constitutional democracy

RELIGIONS: Native beliefs, Muslim, Christian

LITERACY RATE: 75%

CURRENCY: Cedi

MAIN EXPORTS: Gold, cocoa, timber, tuna, bauxite, aluminum, diamonds

GREECE

AREA: 50,942 sq mi (131,940 sq km)

POPULATION: 10,688,058

CAPITAL: Athens

LANGUAGES: Greek (official), English, French

GOVERNMENT: Parliamentary republic

RELIGIONS: Greek Orthodox, Muslim

LITERACY RATE: 98%

CURRENCY: Euro

MAIN EXPORTS: Food and beverages, petroleum products, chemicals, textiles

GRENADA

AREA: 133 sq mi (344 sq km)

POPULATION: 89,703

CAPITAL: St. George's

LANGUAGES: English (official), French patois

GOVERNMENT: Constitutional monarchy

RELIGIONS: Roman Catholic, Protestant

LITERACY RATE: 96%

CURRENCY: East Caribbean dollar

MAIN EXPORTS: Bananas, cocoa, nutmeg, fruit and vegetables, clothing, mace

GUATEMALA

AREA: 42,042 sq mi (108,890 sq km)

POPULATION: 12,293,545

CAPITAL: Guatemala City

LANGUAGES: Spanish, Amerindian languages

GOVERNMENT: Constitutional democratic republic

RELIGIONS: Roman Catholic, Protestant, native Mayan beliefs

LITERACY RATE: 71%

CURRENCY: Quetzal, US dollar

MAIN EXPORTS: Coffee, sugar, bananas, fruits and vegetables, cardamom, meat, apparel, petroleum, electricity

GUINEA

AREA: 94,925 sq mi (245,857 sq km)

POPULATION: 9,690,222

CAPITAL: Conakry

LANGUAGES: French (official), native languages

GOVERNMENT: Republic

RELIGIONS: Muslim, Christian, Native beliefs

LITERACY RATE: 36%

CURRENCY: Guinean franc

MAIN EXPORTS: Bauxite, alumina, gold, diamonds, coffee, fish

GUINEA-BISSAU

AREA: 13,946 sq mi (36,120 sq km)

POPULATION: 1,442,029

CAPITAL: Bissau

LANGUAGES: Portuguese (official), Crioulo, African languages

GOVERNMENT: Republic

RELIGIONS: Native beliefs, Muslim, Christian

LITERACY RATE: 42%

CURRENCY: Communauté Financière Africaine franc

MAIN EXPORTS: Cashew nuts, shrimp, peanuts, palm kernels, sawn lumber

GUYANA

AREA: 83,000 sq mi (214,970 sq km)

POPULATION: 767,245

CAPITAL: Georgetown

LANGUAGES: English, Amerindian dialects, Creole, Hindi, Urdu

GOVERNMENT: Republic

RELIGIONS: Christian, Hindu, Muslim, other

LITERACY RATE: 99%

CURRENCY: Guyanese dollar

MAIN EXPORTS: Sugar, gold, rice, shrimp, bauxite/alumina, molasses, rum, timber

HAITI

AREA: 10,714 sq mi (27,750 sq km)

POPULATION: 8,308,504

CAPITAL: Port-au-Prince

LANGUAGES: French, Creole (both official)

GOVERNMENT: Elected government

RELIGIONS: Roman Catholic, Protestant, others

LITERACY RATE: 53%

CURRENCY: Gourde

MAIN EXPORTS: Manufactures, coffee, oils, cocoa

HONDURAS

AREA: 43,278 sq mi (112,090 sq km)

POPULATION: 7,326,496

CAPITAL: Tegucigalpa

LANGUAGES: Spanish, Amerindian dialects

GOVERNMENT: Democratic constitutional republic

RELIGIONS: Roman Catholic, Protestant

LITERACY RATE: 76%

CURRENCY: Lempira

MAIN EXPORTS: Coffee, bananas, shrimp, lobster, meat, zinc, lumber

HUNGARY

AREA: 35,919 sq mi (93,030 sq km)

POPULATION: 9,981,334

CAPITAL: Budapest

LANGUAGE: Hungarian

GOVERNMENT: Parliamentary democracy

RELIGIONS: Roman Catholic, Calvinist, Lutheran

LITERACY RATE: 99%

CURRENCY: Forint

MAIN EXPORTS: Machinery and equipment, other manufactures, food products, raw materials, fuels and electricity

ICELAND

AREA: 39,768 sq mi (103,000 sq km)

POPULATION: 299,388

CAPITAL: Reykjavik

LANGUAGES: Icelandic, English, Nordic languages, German

GOVERNMENT: Constitutional republic

RELIGION: Evangelical Lutheran

LITERACY RATE: 99%

CURRENCY: Icelandic krona

MAIN EXPORTS: Fish and fish products, animal products, aluminum, diatomite, ferrosilicon

127

INDIA

AREA: 1,269,338 sq mi (3,287,590 sq km)

POPULATION: 1,095,351,995

CAPITAL: New Delhi

LANGUAGES: Hindi (official), English, native languages

GOVERNMENT: Federal republic

RELIGIONS: Hindu, Muslim, Christian, Sikh

LITERACY RATE: 60%

CURRENCY: Indian rupee

MAIN EXPORTS: Textile goods, gems and jewelry, engineering goods, chemicals, leather manufactures

INDONESIA

AREA: 741,096 sq mi (1,919,440 sq km)

POPULATION: 245,452,739

CAPITAL: Jakarta

LANGUAGES: Bahasa Indonesian, English, Dutch, local dialects

GOVERNMENT: Republic

RELIGIONS: Muslim, Protestant, Roman Catholic, Hindu, Buddhist

LITERACY RATE: 88%

CURRENCY: Indonesian rupiah

MAIN EXPORTS: Oil and gas, electrical appliances, plywood, textiles, rubber

IRAN

AREA: 636,293 sq mi (1,648,000 sq km)

POPULATION: 68,688,433

CAPITAL: Tehran

LANGUAGES: Persian, Turkic, Kurdish

GOVERNMENT: Theocratic republic

RELIGIONS: Shi'a Muslim, Sunni Muslim, Zoroastrianism, Jewish, Christian

LITERACY RATE: 79%

CURRENCY: Iranian rial

MAIN EXPORTS: Petroleum, carpets, fruits and nuts, iron and steel, chemicals

IRAQ

AREA: 168,753 sq mi (437,072 sq km)

POPULATION: 26,783,383

CAPITAL: Baghdad

LANGUAGES: Arabic, Kurdish, Assyrian, Armenian

GOVERNMENT: Transitional

RELIGIONS: Muslim, Christian

LITERACY RATE: 40%

CURRENCY: Iraqi dinar

MAIN EXPORTS: Crude oil

IRELAND

AREA: 27,136 sq mi (70,280 sq km)

POPULATION: 4,062,235

CAPITAL: Dublin

LANGUAGES: English, Irish (Gaelic)

GOVERNMENT: Republic

RELIGIONS: Roman Catholic, Church of Ireland

LITERACY RATE: 99%

CURRENCY: Euro

MAIN EXPORTS: Machinery and equipment, computers, chemicals, pharmaceuticals, live animals

ISRAEL

AREA: 8,020 sq mi (20,770 sq km)

POPULATION: 6,352,117

CAPITAL: Jerusalem

LANGUAGES: Hebrew, Arabic (both official), English

GOVERNMENT: Parliamentary democracy

RELIGIONS: Jewish, Muslim, Christian

LITERACY RATE: 97%

CURRENCY: New Israeli shekel

MAIN EXPORTS: Machinery and equipment, software, cut diamonds, agricultural products, chemicals, textiles

ITALY

AREA: 116,305 sq mi (301,230 sq km)

POPULATION: 58,133,509

CAPITAL: Rome

LANGUAGES: Italian (official), German, French, Slovene

GOVERNMENT: Republic

RELIGIONS: Roman Catholic, Protestant, Jewish, Muslim

LITERACY RATE: 99%

CURRENCY: Euro

MAIN EXPORTS: Engineering products, textiles, production machinery, motor vehicles, transport equipment, chemicals, food, beverages, tobacco, minerals

JAMAICA

AREA: 4,244 sq mi (10,991 sq km)

POPULATION: 2,758,124

CAPITAL: Kingston

LANGUAGES: English, patois English

GOVERNMENT: Constitutional parliamentary democracy

RELIGIONS: Protestant, Roman Catholic

LITERACY RATE: 88%

CURRENCY: Jamaican dollar

MAIN EXPORTS: Alumina, bauxite, sugar, bananas, rum

JAPAN

AREA: 145,882 sq mi (377,835 sq km)

POPULATION: 127,463,611

CAPITAL: Tokyo

LANGUAGE: Japanese

GOVERNMENT: Constitutional monarchy with a parliamentary government

RELIGION: Shinto and Buddhist

LITERACY RATE: 99%

CURRENCY: Yen

MAIN EXPORTS: Motor vehicles, semi-conductors, office machinery, chemicals

JORDAN

AREA: 35,637 sq mi (92,300 sq km)

POPULATION: 5,906,760

CAPITAL: Amman

LANGUAGES: Arabic (official), English

GOVERNMENT: Constitutional monarchy

RELIGIONS: Sunni Muslim, Christian

LITERACY RATE: 91%

CURRENCY: Jordanian dinar

MAIN EXPORTS: Phosphates, fertilizers, potash, agricultural products, manufactures, pharmaceuticals

KAZAKHSTAN

AREA: 1,049,150 sq mi (2,717,300 sq km)

POPULATION: 16,798,552

CAPITAL: Astana

LANGUAGES: Russian (official), Kazakh

GOVERNMENT: Republic

RELIGIONS: Muslim, Russian Orthodox, Protestant

LITERACY RATE: 98%

CURRENCY: Tenge

MAIN EXPORTS: Oil and oil products, ferrous metals, chemicals, machinery, grain, wool, meat, coal

KENYA

AREA: 224,960 sq mi (582,650 sq km)

POPULATION: 32,021,856

CAPITAL: Nairobi

LANGUAGES: English and Kiswahili (both official), native languages

GOVERNMENT: Republic

RELIGIONS: Protestant, Roman Catholic, native beliefs

LITERACY RATE: 85%

CURRENCY: Kenyan shilling

MAIN EXPORTS: Tea, horticultural products, coffee, petroleum products, fish

KIRIBATI

AREA: 313 sq mi (811 sq km)

POPULATION: 100,798

CAPITAL: Tarawa

LANGUAGES: English (official), I-Kiribati

GOVERNMENT: Republic

RELIGIONS: Roman Catholic, Protestant, Muslim, Baha'i

LITERACY RATE: NA

CURRENCY: Australian dollar

MAIN EXPORTS: Copra, coconuts, seaweed

KOREA, NORTH
AREA: 46,540 sq mi (120,540 sq km)
POPULATION: 22,697,553
CAPITAL: Pyongyang
LANGUAGE: Korean
GOVERNMENT: Authoritarian socialist
RELIGIONS: Buddhist, Confucianist, Christian, Chondogyo (Religion of the Heavenly Way)
LITERACY RATE: 99%
CURRENCY: North Korean won
MAIN EXPORTS: Minerals, fish products

KOREA, SOUTH
AREA: 38,023 sq mi (98,480 sq km)
POPULATION: 48,598,175
CAPITAL: Seoul
LANGUAGE: Korean
GOVERNMENT: Republic
RELIGIONS: Christian, Buddhist, Confucianist, Shamanist, Chondogyo
LITERACY RATE: 98%
CURRENCY: South Korean won
MAIN EXPORTS: Electronic products, machinery and equipment, cars, steel, ships, clothing, footwear, fish

KUWAIT
AREA: 6,880 sq mi (17,820 sq km)
POPULATION: 2,257,549
CAPITAL: Kuwait
LANGUAGES: Arabic (official), English
GOVERNMENT: Nominal constitutional monarchy
RELIGIONS: Muslim, Christian, Hindu, Parsi
LITERACY RATE: 84%
CURRENCY: Kuwaiti dinar
MAIN EXPORTS: Oil and refined products

KYRGYZSTAN
AREA: 76,641 sq mi (198,500 sq km)
POPULATION: 4,965,081
CAPITAL: Bishkek
LANGUAGES: Kyrgyz and Russian (both official)
GOVERNMENT: Republic
RELIGIONS: Muslim, Russian Orthodox
LITERACY RATE: 97%
CURRENCY: Kyrgyzstani som
MAIN EXPORTS: Cotton, wool, meat, tobacco, gold, mercury, uranium

LAOS
AREA: 91,429 sq mi (236,800 sq km)
POPULATION: 6,068,117
CAPITAL: Vientiane
LANGUAGES: Lao (official), French, English, ethnic languages
GOVERNMENT: Communist state
RELIGIONS: Buddhist, animist, Christian
LITERACY RATE: 53%
CURRENCY: Kip
MAIN EXPORTS: Wood products, clothes, electricity, coffee, tin

LATVIA
AREA: 24,938 sq mi (64,589 sq km)
POPULATION: 2,332,078
CAPITAL: Riga
LANGUAGES: Latvian (official), Lithuanian, Russian
GOVERNMENT: Parliamentary democracy
RELIGIONS: Lutheran, Roman Catholic, Russian Orthodox
LITERACY RATE: 100%
CURRENCY: Latvian lat
MAIN EXPORTS: Wood and wood products, machinery and equipment

LEBANON
AREA: 4,015 sq mi (10,400 sq km)
POPULATION: 3,777,218
CAPITAL: Beirut
LANGUAGES: Arabic (official), French, English, Armenian
GOVERNMENT: Republic
RELIGIONS: Muslim, Christian
LITERACY RATE: 87%
CURRENCY: Lebanese pound
MAIN EXPORTS: Foodstuffs, tobacco, textiles, chemicals, precious stones

LESOTHO
AREA: 11,720 sq mi (30,355 sq km)
POPULATION: 1,865,040
CAPITAL: Maseru
LANGUAGES: Sesotho (southern Sotho), English (official), Zulu, Xhosa
GOVERNMENT: Parliamentary constitutional monarchy
RELIGIONS: Christian, native beliefs
LITERACY RATE: 85%
CURRENCY: Loti, South African rand
MAIN EXPORTS: Manufactured clothing, road vehicles, footwear, wool and mohair

LIBERIA
AREA: 43,000 sq mi (111,370 sq km)
POPULATION: 3,390,635
CAPITAL: Monrovia
LANGUAGES: English (official), tribal dialects
GOVERNMENT: Republic
RELIGIONS: Native beliefs, Christian, Muslim
LITERACY RATE: 58%
CURRENCY: Liberian dollar
MAIN EXPORTS: Rubber, timber, iron, diamonds, cocoa, coffee

LIBYA
AREA: 679,358 sq mi (1,759,540 sq km)
POPULATION: 5,631,585
CAPITAL: Tripoli
LANGUAGES: Arabic, Italian, English
GOVERNMENT: Military dictatorship
RELIGION: Sunni Muslim
LITERACY RATE: 83%
CURRENCY: Libyan dinar
MAIN EXPORTS: Crude oil, refined petroleum products

LIECHTENSTEIN
AREA: 62 sq mi (160 sq km)
POPULATION: 33,436
CAPITAL: Vaduz
LANGUAGES: German (official), Alemannic dialect
GOVERNMENT: Hereditary constitutional monarchy
RELIGIONS: Roman Catholic, Protestant
LITERACY RATE: 100%
CURRENCY: Swiss franc
MAIN EXPORTS: Parts for motor vehicles, dental products, prepared foodstuffs

LITHUANIA
AREA: 25,174 sq mi (65,200 sq km)
POPULATION: 3,584,836
CAPITAL: Vilnius
LANGUAGES: Lithuanian (official), Polish, Russian
GOVERNMENT: Parliamentary democracy
RELIGIONS: Roman Catholic, Protestant, Russian Orthodox, Muslim, Jewish
LITERACY RATE: 100%
CURRENCY: Litas
MAIN EXPORTS: Mineral products, textiles, clothing, machinery and equipment

LUXEMBOURG
AREA: 998 sq mi (2,586 sq km)
POPULATION: 462,690
CAPITAL: Luxembourg
LANGUAGES: Luxembourgish, German, French
GOVERNMENT: Constitutional monarchy
RELIGIONS: Roman Catholic, Protestant, Jewish, Muslim
LITERACY RATE: 100%
CURRENCY: Euro
MAIN EXPORTS: Machinery and equipment, steel products, chemicals

MACEDONIA
AREA: 9,781 sq mi (25,333 sq km)
POPULATION: 2,071,210
CAPITAL: Skopje
LANGUAGES: Macedonian, Albanian, Turkish, Serbo-Croatian
GOVERNMENT: Parliamentary democracy
RELIGIONS: Macedonian Orthodox, Muslim
LITERACY RATE: NA
CURRENCY: Denar
MAIN EXPORTS: Food, beverages, tobacco, iron and steel

MADAGASCAR

AREA: 226,660 sq mi (587,040 sq km)
POPULATION: 18,595,469
CAPITAL: Antananarivo
LANGUAGES: Malagasy and French (both official)
GOVERNMENT: Republic
RELIGIONS: Native beliefs, Christian, Muslim
LITERACY RATE: 69%
CURRENCY: Malagasy franc
MAIN EXPORTS: Coffee, vanilla, shellfish, sugar, cotton, cloth, petroleum products

MALAWI

AREA: 45,745 sq mi (118,480 sq km)
POPULATION: 13,013,926
CAPITAL: Lilongwe
LANGUAGES: English and Chichewa (both official)
GOVERNMENT: Multiparty democracy
RELIGIONS: Protestant, Roman Catholic, Muslim, native beliefs
LITERACY RATE: 63%
CURRENCY: Malawian kwacha
MAIN EXPORTS: Tobacco, tea, sugar, cotton, coffee, peanuts, wood products, clothing

MALAYSIA

AREA: 127,316 sq mi (329,750 sq km)
POPULATION: 24,385,858
CAPITAL: Kuala Lumpur
LANGUAGES: Bahasa Melayu (official), English, Chinese, Tamil, Telugu, Malayalam
GOVERNMENT: Constitutional monarchy
RELIGIONS: Muslim, Buddhist, Daoist, Hindu, Christian
LITERACY RATE: 89%
CURRENCY: Ringgit
MAIN EXPORTS: Electronic equipment, petroleum and liquefied natural gas, wood and wood products, palm oil, rubber

MALDIVES

AREA: 116 sq mi (300 sq km)
POPULATION: 359,008
CAPITAL: Malé
LANGUAGES: Dhivehi, English
GOVERNMENT: Republic
RELIGION: Sunni Muslim
LITERACY RATE: 97%
CURRENCY: Maldivian rufiyaa
MAIN EXPORTS: Fish, clothing

MALI

AREA: 478,764 sq mi (1,240,000 sq km)
POPULATION 11,716,829
CAPITAL: Bamako
LANGUAGES: French (official), Bambara

GOVERNMENT: Republic
RELIGIONS: Muslim, Native beliefs, Christian
LITERACY RATE: 46%
CURRENCY: Communauté Financière Africaine franc
MAIN EXPORTS: Cotton, gold, livestock

MALTA

AREA: 122 sq mi (316 sq km)
POPULATION: 400,214
CAPITAL: Valletta
LANGUAGES: Maltese and English (both official)
GOVERNMENT: Republic
RELIGION: Roman Catholic
LITERACY RATE: 93%
CURRENCY: Maltese lira
MAIN EXPORTS: Machinery, transportation equipment

MARSHALL ISLANDS

AREA: 70 sq mi (181 sq km)
POPULATION: 60,422
CAPITAL: Majuro
LANGUAGES: Marshallese and English (both official), Japanese
GOVERNMENT: Constitutional government
RELIGION: Christian
LITERACY RATE: 94%
CURRENCY: US dollar
MAIN EXPORTS: Copra cake, coconut oil, handcrafts, fish

MAURITANIA

AREA: 397,953 sq mi (1,030,700 sq km)
POPULATION: 3,177,388
CAPITAL: Nouakchott
LANGUAGES: Hassaniya Arabic and Wolof (both official), Pulaar, Soninke, French
GOVERNMENT: Republic
RELIGION: Muslim
LITERACY RATE: 42%
CURRENCY: Ouguiya
MAIN EXPORTS: Iron ore, fish and fish products, gold

MAURITIUS

AREA: 788 sq mi (2,040 sq km)
POPULATION: 1,240,827
CAPITAL: Port Louis
LANGUAGES: English and French (both official), Creole, Hindi, Urdu
GOVERNMENT: Parliamentary democracy
RELIGIONS: Hindu, Roman Catholic, Protestant, Muslim
LITERACY RATE: 86%
CURRENCY: Mauritian rupee
MAIN EXPORTS: Clothing and textiles, sugar, cut flowers, molasses

---

MEXICO

AREA: 761,600 sq mi (1,972,550 sq km)
POPULATION: 107,449,525
CAPITAL: Mexico City
LANGUAGES: Spanish, Mayan, Nahuatl and other native languages
GOVERNMENT: Federal republic
RELIGIONS: Roman Catholic, Protestant
LITERACY RATE: 94%
CURRENCY: Mexican peso
MAIN EXPORTS: Manufactured goods, oil and oil products, silver, fruit, vegetables

MICRONESIA

AREA: 271 sq mi (702 sq km)
POPULATION: 108,004
CAPITAL: Palikir
LANGUAGES: English (official), Trukese, Pohnpeian, Yapese, other native languages
GOVERNMENT: Constitutional government
RELIGIONS: Roman Catholic, Protestant
LITERACY RATE: 89%
CURRENCY: US Dollar
MAIN EXPORTS: Fish, garments, bananas, black pepper

MOLDOVA

AREA: 13,067 sq mi (33,843 sq km)
POPULATION: 4,466,706
CAPITAL: Chisinau
LANGUAGES: Moldovan (official), Russian, Gagauz
GOVERNMENT Republic
RELIGIONS: Eastern Orthodox, Jewish, Baptist
LITERACY RATE: 99%
CURRENCY: Moldovan leu
MAIN EXPORTS: Foodstuffs, textiles, machinery

MONACO

AREA: .75 sq mi (1.95 sq km)
POPULATION: 32,543
CAPITAL: Monaco
LANGUAGES: French (official), English, Italian, Monégasque
GOVERNMENT: Constitutional monarchy
RELIGION: Roman Catholic
LITERACY RATE: 99%
CURRENCY: Euro
MAIN EXPORTS: NA

MONGOLIA

AREA: 604,250 sq mi (1,565,000 sq km)
POPULATION: 2,832,224
CAPITAL: Ulaanbaatar
LANGUAGES: Khalkha Mongol, Turkic, Russian
GOVERNMENT: Parliamentary

RELIGIONS: Tibetan Buddhist, Lamaism, Muslim, Shamanism, Christian
LITERACY RATE: 98%
CURRENCY: Togrog/tugrik
MAIN EXPORTS: Copper, livestock, animal products, cashmere, wool, hides, fluorspar

MONTENEGRO
AREA: 5,415 sq mi (14,026 sq km)
POPULATION: 630,548
CAPITAL: Podgorica
LANGUAGES: Serbian, Bosnian, Albanian, Croatian
GOVERNMENT: Republic
RELIGIONS: Orthodox, Muslim, Roman Catholic
LITERACY RATE: 96.4%
CURRENCY: Euro
MAIN EXPORTS: Manufactured goods, food and live animals, raw materials

MOROCCO
AREA: 172,413 sq mi (446,550 sq km)
POPULATION: 33,241,259
CAPITAL: Rabat
LANGUAGES: Arabic (official), Berber dialects, French
GOVERNMENT: Constitutional monarchy
RELIGIONS: Muslim, Christian, Jewish
LITERACY RATE: 52%
CURRENCY: Dirham
MAIN EXPORTS: Clothing, fish, inorganic chemicals, transistors, crude minerals, fertilizers, petroleum products, fruit

MOZAMBIQUE
AREA: 309,494 sq mi (801,590 sq km)
POPULATION: 19,686,505
CAPITAL: Maputo
LANGUAGES: Portuguese (official), Bantu languages
GOVERNMENT: Republic
RELIGIONS: Native beliefs, Christian, Muslim
LITERACY RATE: 48%
CURRENCY: Metical
MAIN EXPORTS: Aluminum, prawns, cashews, cotton, sugar, citrus, timber

MYANMAR (BURMA)
AREA: 261,969 sq mi (678,500 sq km)
POPULATION: 47382633
CAPITAL: Rangoon
LANGUAGES: Burmese, minority languages
GOVERNMENT: Military regime
RELIGIONS: Buddhist, Baptist, Roman Catholic, Muslim, animist
LITERACY RATE: 85%
CURRENCY: Kyat
MAIN EXPORTS: Gas, wood products, pulses, beans, fish, rice

NAMIBIA
AREA: 318,694 sq mi (825,418 sq km)
POPULATION: 2,044,147
CAPITAL: Windhoek
LANGUAGES: English (official), Afrikaans, German, native languages
GOVERNMENT: Republic
RELIGIONS: Christian, native beliefs
LITERACY RATE: 84%
CURRENCY: Namibian dollar; South African rand
MAIN EXPORTS: Diamonds, copper, gold, zinc, lead, uranium, cattle, processed fish

NAURU
AREA: 8 sq mi (21 sq km)
POPULATION: 13,287
CAPITAL: Yaren District
LANGUAGES: Nauruan, English
GOVERNMENT: Republic
RELIGIONS: Protestant, Roman Catholic
LITERACY RATE: NA
CURRENCY: Australian dollar
MAIN EXPORT: Phosphates

NEPAL
AREA: 54,363 sq mi (140,800 sq km)
POPULATION: 28,287,147
CAPITAL: Kathmandu
LANGUAGES: Nepali, English
GOVERNMENT: Parliamentary democracy, constitutional monarchy
RELIGIONS: Hinduism, Buddhism, Muslim
LITERACY RATE: 49%
CURRENCY: Nepalese rupee
MAIN EXPORTS: Carpets, clothing, leather goods, jute goods, grain

THE NETHERLANDS
AREA: 16,033 sq mi (41,526 sq km)
POPULATION: 16,491,461
CAPITAL: Amsterdam
LANGUAGES: Dutch and Frisian (both official)
GOVERNMENT: Constitutional monarchy
RELIGIONS: Roman Catholic, Protestant, Muslim
LITERACY RATE: 99%
CURRENCY: Euro
MAIN EXPORTS: Machinery and equipment, chemicals, fuels, foodstuffs

NEW ZEALAND
AREA: 103,737 sq mi (268,680 sq km)
POPULATION: 4,076,140
CAPITAL: Wellington
LANGUAGES: English and Maori (both official)

GOVERNMENT: Parliamentary democracy
RELIGIONS: Protestant, Roman Catholic
LITERACY RATE: 99%
CURRENCY: New Zealand dollar
MAIN EXPORTS: Dairy products, meat, wood and wood products, fish, machinery

NICARAGUA
AREA: 49,998 sq mi (129,494 sq km)
POPULATION: 5,570,129
CAPITAL: Managua
LANGUAGE: Spanish (official)
GOVERNMENT: Republic
RELIGIONS: Roman Catholic, Protestant
LITERACY RATE: 68%
CURRENCY: Gold cordoba
MAIN EXPORTS: Coffee, shrimp and lobster, cotton, tobacco, bananas, beef

NIGER
AREA: 489,189 sq mi (1,267,000 sq km)
POPULATION: 12,525,094
CAPITAL: Niamey
LANGUAGES: French (official), Hausa, Djerma
GOVERNMENT: Republic
RELIGIONS: Muslim, native beliefs, Christian
LITERACY RATE: 18%
CURRENCY: Communauté Financière Africaine franc
MAIN EXPORTS: Uranium ore, livestock, cowpeas, onions

NIGERIA
AREA: 356,700 sq mi (923,770 sq km)
POPULATION: 131,859,731
CAPITAL: Abuja
LANGUAGES: English (official), Hausa, Yoruba, Igbo, others
GOVERNMENT: Republic transitioning from military to civilian rule
RELIGIONS: Muslim, Christian, native beliefs
LITERACY RATE: 68%
CURRENCY: Naira
MAIN EXPORTS: Petroleum and petroleum products, cocoa, rubber

NORWAY
AREA: 125,181 sq mi (324,220 sq km)
POPULATION: 4,610,820
CAPITAL: Oslo
LANGUAGE: Norwegian (official)
GOVERNMENT: Constitutional monarchy
RELIGIONS: Protestant, Roman Catholic
LITERACY RATE: 100%
CURRENCY: Norwegian krone
MAIN EXPORTS: Petroleum and petroleum products, machinery and equipment, metals, chemicals, ships, fish

OMAN
AREA: 82,030 sq mi (212,460 sq km)
POPULATION: 3,102,229
CAPITAL: Muscat
LANGUAGES: Arabic (official), English, Indian languages
GOVERNMENT: Monarchy
RELIGIONS: Ibadhi Muslim, Sunni Muslim, Shi'a Muslim, Hindu
LITERACY RATE: 76%
CURRENCY: Omani rial
MAIN EXPORTS: Petroleum, fish, metals, textiles

PAKISTAN
AREA: 310,400 sq mi (803,940 sq km)
POPULATION: 165,803,560
CAPITAL: Islamabad
LANGUAGES: Urdu (official), Punjabi, Sindhi, Siraiki, Pashtu, others
GOVERNMENT: Federal republic
RELIGIONS: Muslim, Christian, Hindu
LITERACY RATE: 49%
CURRENCY: Pakistani rupee
MAIN EXPORTS: Textiles, rice, leather, sports goods, carpets

PALAU
AREA: 177 sq mi (458 sq km)
POPULATION: 20,579
CAPITAL: Koror
LANGUAGES: English, Palauan, Sonsoralese, Tobi, others
GOVERNMENT: Constitutional government
RELIGIONS: Roman Catholic, Protestant
LITERACY RATE: 92%
CURRENCY: US Dollar
MAIN EXPORTS: Shellfish, tuna, copra, garments

PANAMA
AREA: 30,193 sq mi (78,200 sq km)
POPULATION: 3,191,319
CAPITAL: Panama City
LANGUAGES: Spanish (official), English
GOVERNMENT: Constitutional democracy
RELIGIONS: Roman Catholic, Protestant
LITERACY RATE: 93%
CURRENCY: Balboa; US dollar
MAIN EXPORTS: Bananas, shrimp, sugar, coffee, clothing

PAPUA NEW GUINEA
AREA: 178,703 sq mi (462,840 sq km)
POPULATION: 5,670,544
CAPITAL: Port Moresby
LANGUAGES: Motu, other native languages, English
GOVERNMENT: Constitutional monarchy with parliamentary democracy
RELIGIONS: Roman Catholic, Protestant, native beliefs
LITERACY RATE: 65%
CURRENCY: Kina
MAIN EXPORTS: Oil, gold, copper ore, logs, palm oil, coffee, cocoa, crayfish, prawns

PARAGUAY
AREA: 157,046 sq mi (406,750 sq km)
POPULATION: 6,506,464
CAPITAL: Asunción
LANGUAGES: Spanish and Guarani (both official)
GOVERNMENT: Constitutional republic
RELIGIONS: Roman Catholic, Protestant
LITERACY RATE: 94%
CURRENCY: Guaraní
MAIN EXPORTS: Soybeans, feed, cotton, meat, edible oils, electricity

PERU
AREA: 496,223 sq mi (1,285,220 sq km)
POPULATION: 28,302,603
CAPITAL: Lima
LANGUAGES: Spanish and Quechua (both official), Aymara
GOVERNMENT: Constitutional republic
RELIGION: Roman Catholic
LITERACY RATE: 88%
CURRENCY: Nuevo sol
MAIN EXPORTS: Fish and fish products, gold, copper, zinc, crude petroleum, lead, coffee, sugar, cotton

THE PHILIPPINES
AREA: 115,830 sq mi (300,000 sq km)
POPULATION: 89,468,677
CAPITAL: Manila
LANGUAGES: Filipino and English (both official), Tagalog, other native languages
GOVERNMENT: Republic
RELIGIONS: Roman Catholic, Protestant, Muslim, Buddhist
LITERACY RATE: 93%
CURRENCY: Philippine peso
MAIN EXPORTS: Electronic equipment, machinery and transport equipment, garments, coconut products, chemicals

POLAND
AREA: 120,727 sq mi (312,685 sq km)
POPULATION: 38,536,869
CAPITAL: Warsaw
LANGUAGE: Polish
GOVERNMENT: Republic
RELIGIONS: Roman Catholic, Eastern Orthodox, Protestant
LITERACY RATE: 100%
CURRENCY: Zloty
MAIN EXPORTS: Machinery and transport equipment, manufactured goods, food

PORTUGAL
AREA: 35,672 sq mi (92,391 sq km)
POPULATION: 10,605,870
CAPITAL: Lisbon
LANGUAGE: Portuguese
GOVERNMENT: Parliamentary democracy
RELIGIONS: Roman Catholic, Protestant
LITERACY RATE: 93%
CURRENCY: Euro
MAIN EXPORTS: Clothing and footwear, machinery, chemicals, cork and paper products, hides

QATAR
AREA: 4,416 sq mi (11,437 sq km)
POPULATION: 885,359
CAPITAL: Doha
LANGUAGES: Arabic (official), English
GOVERNMENT: Monarchy
RELIGION: Muslim
LITERACY RATE: 89%
CURRENCY: Qatari rial
MAIN EXPORTS: Petroleum products, fertilizers, steel

ROMANIA
AREA: 91,700 sq mi (237,500 sq km)
POPULATION: 22,303,552
CAPITAL: Bucharest
LANGUAGES: Romanian (official), Hungarian, German
GOVERNMENT: Republic
RELIGIONS: Eastern Orthodox, Protestant, Catholic
LITERACY RATE: 98%
CURRENCY: Leu
MAIN EXPORTS: Textiles and footwear, metals and metal products, machinery and equipment, minerals, fuels

RUSSIA
AREA: 6,592,735 sq mi (17,075,200 sq km)
POPULATION: 142,893,540
CAPITAL: Moscow
LANGUAGES: Russian, others
GOVERNMENT: Federation
RELIGIONS: Russian Orthodox, Muslim
LITERACY RATE: 100%
CURRENCY: Russian ruble
MAIN EXPORTS: Petroleum and petroleum products, natural gas, wood and wood products, metals, chemicals

RWANDA
AREA: 10,169 sq mi (26,338 sq km)
POPULATION: 8,648,248
CAPITAL: Kigali
LANGUAGES: Kinyarwanda, French and English (all official); Bantu, Kiswahili
GOVERNMENT: Republic
RELIGIONS: Roman Catholic, Protestant, Muslim, native beliefs
LITERACY RATE: 70%
CURRENCY: Rwandan franc
MAIN EXPORTS: Coffee, tea, hides, tin ore

SAINT KITTS AND NEVIS
AREA: 101 sq mi (261 sq km)
POPULATION: 39,129
CAPITAL: Basseterre
LANGUAGE: English
GOVERNMENT: Constitutional monarchy
RELIGIONS: Protestant, Roman Catholic
LITERACY RATE: 98%
CURRENCY: East Caribbean dollar
MAIN EXPORTS: Machinery, food, electronics, beverages, tobacco

SAINT LUCIA
AREA: 238 sq mi (616 sq km)
POPULATION: 168,458
CAPITAL: Castries
LANGUAGES: English (official), French patois
GOVERNMENT: Parliamentary democracy
RELIGIONS: Roman Catholic, Protestant
LITERACY RATE: 90%
CURRENCY: East Caribbean dollar
MAIN EXPORTS: Bananas, clothing, cocoa, vegetables, fruits, coconut oil

SAINT VINCENT AND THE GRENADINES
AREA: 150 sq mi (389 sq km)
POPULATION: 117,848
CAPITAL: Kingstown
LANGUAGES: English, French patois
GOVERNMENT: Parliamentary democracy
RELIGIONS: Protestant, Roman Catholic, Hindu
LITERACY RATE: 96%
CURRENCY: East Caribbean dollar
MAIN EXPORTS: Bananas, eddoes and dasheen (taro), arrowroot starch, tennis racquets

SAMOA
AREA: 1,136 sq mi (2,944 sq km)
POPULATION: 176,908
CAPITAL: Apia
LANGUAGES: Samoan (Polynesian), English

GOVERNMENT: Constitutional monarchy under native chief
RELIGIONS: Protestant, Roman Catholic
LITERACY RATE: 100%
CURRENCY: Tala
MAIN EXPORTS: Fish, coconut oil and cream, copra, taro, garments, beer

SAN MARINO
AREA: 24 sq mi (61 sq km)
POPULATION: 29,251
CAPITAL: San Marino
LANGUAGE: Italian
GOVERNMENT: Independent republic
RELIGION: Roman Catholic
LITERACY RATE: 96%
CURRENCY: Euro
MAIN EXPORTS: Building stone, lime, wood, chestnuts, wheat, wine, hides

SÃO TOMÉ AND PRÍNCIPE
AREA: 386 sq mi (1,001 sq km)
POPULATION: 193,413
CAPITAL: São Tomé
LANGUAGE: Portuguese
GOVERNMENT: Republic
RELIGION: Christian
LITERACY RATE: 79%
CURRENCY: Dobra
MAIN EXPORTS: Cocoa, copra, coffee, palm oil

SAUDI ARABIA
AREA: 756,981 sq mi (1,960,582 sq km)
POPULATION: 27,019,731
CAPITAL: Riyadh
LANGUAGE: Arabic
GOVERNMENT: Monarchy
RELIGION: Muslim
LITERACY RATE: 79%
CURRENCY: Saudi riyal
MAIN EXPORTS: Petroleum and petroleum products

SENEGAL
AREA: 75,749 sq mi (196,190 sq km)
POPULATION: 11,987,121
CAPITAL: Dakar
LANGUAGES: French (official), Wolof, Pulaar
GOVERNMENT: Republic under multiparty democratic rule
RELIGIONS: Muslim, indigenous beliefs, Christian
LITERACY RATE: 40%
CURRENCY: Communauté Financière Africaine franc
MAIN EXPORTS: Fish, groundnuts (peanuts), petroleum products, phosphates, cotton

SERBIA
AREA: 34,116 sq mi (88,361 sq km)
POPULATION: 10,663,022
CAPITAL: Belgrade
LANGUAGES: Serbian (official), Romanian, Hungarian, Slovak, Ukrainian, Croatian, Albanian
GOVERNMENT: Republic
RELIGIONS: Serbian Orthodox, Muslim, Roman Catholic, Protestant
LITERACY RATE: 96%
CURRENCY: Serbian Dinar
MAIN EXPORTS: Manufactured goods, food and live animals, machinery and transport equipment

SEYCHELLES
AREA: 176 sq mi (455 sq km)
POPULATION: 81,541
CAPITAL: Victoria
LANGUAGES: English and French (both official), Creole
GOVERNMENT: Republic
RELIGIONS: Roman Catholic, Anglican, other Christian
LITERACY RATE: 92%
CURRENCY: Seychelles rupee
MAIN EXPORTS: Canned tuna, frozen fish, cinnamon bark, copra, petroleum products

SIERRA LEONE
AREA: 27,699 sq mi (71,740 sq km)
POPULATION: 6,005,250
CAPITAL: Freetown
LANGUAGES: English (official), Mende, Temne, Krio
GOVERNMENT: Constitutional democracy
RELIGIONS: Muslim, native beliefs, Christian
LITERACY RATE: 30%
CURRENCY: Leone
MAIN EXPORTS: Diamonds, rutile, cocoa, coffee, fish

SINGAPORE
AREA: 267 sq mi (692 sq km)
POPULATION: 4,492,150
CAPITAL: Singapore
LANGUAGES: Malay, Chinese, Tamil, English (all official)
GOVERNMENT: Parliamentary republic
RELIGIONS: Buddhist, Muslim, Christian, Hindu, Sikh, Taoist, Confucianist
LITERACY RATE: 93%
CURRENCY: Singapore dollar
MAIN EXPORTS: Machinery and equipment (including electronics), consumer goods, chemicals, mineral fuels

SLOVAKIA
AREA: 18,859 sq mi (48,845 sq km)
POPULATION: 5,439,448
CAPITAL: Bratislava
LANGUAGES: Slovak (official), Hungarian
GOVERNMENT: Parliamentary republic
RELIGIONS: Roman Catholic, Protestant, Orthodox
LITERACY RATE: 100%
CURRENCY: Slovak koruna
MAIN EXPORTS: Machinery and transport equipment, chemicals

SLOVENIA
AREA: 7,827 sq mi (20,273 sq km)
POPULATION: 2,010,347
CAPITAL: Ljubljana
LANGUAGES: Slovenian, Serbo-Croatian
GOVERNMENT: Parliamentary democratic republic
RELIGIONS: Roman Catholic, Lutheran, Muslim
LITERACY RATE: 100%
CURRENCY: Tolar
MAIN EXPORTS: Manufactured goods, machinery and transport equipment

SOLOMON ISLANDS
AREA: 10,985 sq mi (28,450 sq km)
POPULATION: 552,438
CAPITAL: Honiara
LANGUAGES: English, Solomon Pidgin, Melanesian languages
GOVERNMENT: Parliamentary republic tending toward anarchy
RELIGIONS: Anglican, Roman Catholic, Protestant, native beliefs
LITERACY RATE: NA
CURRENCY: Solomon Islands dollar
MAIN EXPORTS: Timber, fish, copra, palm oil, cocoa

SOMALIA
AREA: 246,199 sq mi (637,657 sq km)
POPULATION: 8,863,338
CAPITAL: Mogadishu
LANGUAGES: Somali (official), Arabic, English, Italian
GOVERNMENT: Transitional parliamentary
RELIGION: Sunni Muslim
LITERACY RATE: 38%
CURRENCY: Somali shilling
MAIN EXPORTS: Livestock, bananas, hides, fish, charcoal, scrap metal

SOUTH AFRICA
AREA: 471,008 sq mi (1,219,912 sq km)
POPULATION: 44,187,637
CAPITAL: Pretoria
LANGUAGES: Afrikaans, English, Ndebele, Pedi, Sotho, Swazi, Tsonga, Tswana, Venda, Xhosa, Zulu (all official)
GOVERNMENT: Republic
RELIGIONS Christian, Muslim, Hindu, native beliefs, animist
LITERACY RATE: 86%
CURRENCY: Rand
MAIN EXPORTS: Gold, diamonds, platinum, machinery and equipment

SPAIN
AREA: 194,896 sq mi (504,782 sq km)
POPULATION: 40,397,842
CAPITAL: Madrid
LANGUAGES: Castilian Spanish, Catalan, Galician, Basque
GOVERNMENT: Parliamentary monarchy
RELIGION: Roman Catholic
LITERACY RATE: 98%
CURRENCY: Euro
MAIN EXPORTS: Machinery, motor vehicles, foodstuffs, other consumer goods

SRI LANKA
AREA: 23,332 sq mi (65,610 sq km)
POPULATION: 20,222,240
CAPITAL: Colombo
LANGUAGES: Sinhala (official), Tamil, English
GOVERNMENT: Republic
RELIGIONS: Buddhist, Hindu, Christian, Muslim
LITERACY RATE: 92%
CURRENCY: Sri Lankan rupee
MAIN EXPORTS: Textiles and apparel, tea, diamonds, coconut products

SUDAN
AREA: 967,493 sq mi (2,505,810 sq km)
POPULATION: 41,236,378
CAPITAL: Khartoum
LANGUAGES: Arabic, Nubian, dialects of Nilotic, Nilo-Hamitic, Sudanic languages, English
GOVERNMENT: Authoritarian regime
RELIGIONS: Sunni Muslim, native beliefs, Christian
LITERACY RATE: 61%
CURRENCY: Sudanese dinar
MAIN EXPORTS: Oil and petroleum products, cotton, sesame, livestock

SURINAME
AREA: 63,039 sq mi (163,270 sq km)
POPULATION: 439,117
CAPITAL: Paramaribo
LANGUAGES: Dutch (official), Surinamese, English
GOVERNMENT: Constitutional democracy
RELIGIONS: Hindu, Muslim, Roman Catholic, Protestant, native beliefs
LITERACY RATE: 88%
CURRENCY: Surinamese guilder
MAIN EXPORTS: Alumina, crude oil, lumber, shrimp and fish, rice, bananas

SWAZILAND
AREA: 6,704 sq mi (17,363 sq km)
POPULATION: 1,136,334
CAPITAL: Mbabane
LANGUAGES: siSwati, English (both official)
GOVERNMENT: Monarchy
RELIGIONS: Zionist, Roman Catholic, Muslim, Anglican, Bahai, Methodist
LITERACY RATE: 82%
CURRENCY: Lilangeni
MAIN EXPORTS: Soft drink concentrates, sugar, wood pulp, cotton yarn

SWEDEN
AREA: 173,731 sq mi (449,964 sq km)
POPULATION: 9,016,596
CAPITAL: Stockholm
LANGUAGE: Swedish
GOVERNMENT: Constitutional monarchy
RELIGIONS: Lutheran, Roman Catholic, Orthodox, Baptist, Muslim, Jewish
LITERACY RATE: 99%
CURRENCY: Swedish krona
MAIN EXPORTS: Machinery, motor vehicles, paper products, pulp and wood

SWITZERLAND
AREA: 15,942 sq mi (41,290 sq km)
POPULATION: 7,523,934
CAPITAL: Bern
LANGUAGES: German, French, Italian, Romansch (all official)
GOVERNMENT: Federal republic
RELIGIONS: Roman Catholic, Protestant
LITERACY RATE: 99%
CURRENCY: Swiss franc
MAIN EXPORTS: Machinery, chemicals, metals, watches, agricultural products

SYRIA
AREA: 71,498 sq mi (185,180 sq km)
POPULATION: 18,881,361
CAPITAL: Damascus
LANGUAGES: Arabic (official), French, English
GOVERNMENT: Republic under military regime
RELIGIONS: Sunni Muslim, Alawite, Druze, and other Muslim sects, Christian, Jewish
LITERACY RATE: 77%
CURRENCY: Syrian pound
MAIN EXPORTS: Crude oil, petroleum products, fruits and vegetables, cotton fiber, clothing, meat and live animals

TAIWAN
AREA: 13,892 sq mi (35,980 sq km)
POPULATION: 23,036,087
CAPITAL: Taipei
LANGUAGES: Chinese (Mandarin), Taiwanese, Hakka dialects
GOVERNMENT: Multiparty democratic regime
RELIGIONS: Buddhist, Confucian, and Taoist, Christian
LITERACY RATE: 96%
CURRENCY: New Taiwan dollar
MAIN EXPORTS: Machinery and electrical equipment, metals, textiles, plastics

TAJIKISTAN
AREA: 55,251 sq mi (143,100 sq km)
POPULATION: 7,320,815
CAPITAL: Dushanbe
LANGUAGES: Tajik (official), Russian
GOVERNMENT: Republic
RELIGIONS: Sunni Muslim, Shi'a Muslim
LITERACY RATE: 99%
CURRENCY: Somoni
MAIN EXPORTS: Aluminum, electricity, cotton, fruits, vegetable oil, textiles

TANZANIA
AREA: 364,898 sq mi (945,087 sq km)
POPULATION: 37,445,392
CAPITAL: Dar es Salaam
LANGUAGES: Kiswahili and English (both official), Arabic
GOVERNMENT: Republic
RELIGIONS: Christian, Muslim, native beliefs
LITERACY RATE: 78%
CURRENCY: Tanzanian shilling
MAIN EXPORTS: Gold, coffee, cashew nuts, manufactures, cotton

THAILAND
AREA: 198,455 sq mi (514,000 sq km)
POPULATION: 64,631,595
CAPITAL: Bangkok
LANGUAGES: Thai, English
GOVERNMENT: Constitutional democracy
RELIGIONS: Buddhism, Muslim, Christianity, Hinduism
LITERACY RATE: 93%
CURRENCY: Baht
MAIN EXPORTS: Computers, transistors, seafood, clothing, rice

TOGO
AREA: 21,925 sq mi (56,785 sq km)
POPULATION: 5,548,702
CAPITAL: Lomé
LANGUAGES: French (official), Éwé, Mina, Kabyé, Dagomba
GOVERNMENT: Republic under transition to democratic rule
RELIGIONS: Native beliefs, Christian, Muslim
LITERACY RATE: 61%
CURRENCY: Communauté Financière Africaine franc
MAIN EXPORTS: Cotton, phosphates, coffee, cocoa

TONGA
AREA: 289 sq mi (748 sq km)
POPULATION: 114,689
CAPITAL: Nuku'alofa
LANGUAGES: Tongan, English
GOVERNMENT: Constitutional monarchy
RELIGION: Christian
LITERACY RATE: 99%
CURRENCY: Pa'anga
MAIN EXPORTS: Squash, fish, vanilla beans, root crops

TRINIDAD AND TOBAGO
AREA: 1,980 sq mi (5,128 sq km)
POPULATION: 1,065,842
CAPITAL: Port-of-Spain
LANGUAGES: English (official), Hindi, French, Spanish, Chinese
GOVERNMENT: Parliamentary democracy
RELIGIONS: Roman Catholic, Hindu, Protestant, Muslim, other
LITERACY RATE: 99%
CURRENCY: Trinidad and Tobago dollar
MAIN EXPORTS: Petroleum and petroleum products, chemicals, steel products

TUNISIA
AREA: 63,170 sq mi (163,610 sq km)
POPULATION: 10,032,050
CAPITAL: Tunis
LANGUAGES: Arabic (official), French
GOVERNMENT: Republic
RELIGION: Muslim
LITERACY RATE: 74%
CURRENCY: Tunisian dinar
MAIN EXPORTS: Textiles, mechanical goods, phosphates and chemicals, agricultural products, hydrocarbons

TURKEY
AREA: 301,381 sq mi (780,580 sq km)
POPULATION: 68,893,918
CAPITAL: Ankara
LANGUAGES: Turkish (official), Kurdish, Arabic, Armenian, Greek
GOVERNMENT: Republican parliamentary democracy
RELIGION: Muslim
LITERACY RATE: 87%
CURRENCY: Turkish lira
MAIN EXPORTS: Clothing, foodstuffs, textiles, metal manufactures

TURKMENISTAN
AREA: 188,455 sq mi (488,100 sq km)
POPULATION: 4,863,169
CAPITAL: Ashgabat
LANGUAGES: Turkmen, Russian, Uzbek, other
GOVERNMENT: Republic
RELIGIONS: Muslim, Eastern Orthodox
LITERACY RATE: 98%
CURRENCY: Turkmen manat
MAIN EXPORTS: Gas, oil, cotton, textiles

TUVALU
AREA: 10 sq mi (26 sq km)
POPULATION: 11,468
CAPITAL: Funafuti
LANGUAGES: Tuvaluan, English, Samoan, Kiribati
GOVERNMENT: Constitutional monarchy with a parliamentary democracy
RELIGION: Protestant
LITERACY RATE: NA
CURRENCY: Australian dollar; Tuvaluan dollar
MAIN EXPORTS: Copra, fish

UGANDA
AREA: 91,135 sq mi (236,040 sq km)
POPULATION: 26,404,543
CAPITAL: Kampala
LANGUAGES: English (official), Ganda, other native languages
GOVERNMENT: Republic
RELIGIONS: Roman Catholic, Protestant, Muslim, native beliefs
LITERACY RATE: 70%
CURRENCY: Ugandan shilling
MAIN EXPORTS: Coffee, fish and fish products, tea, gold, cotton, flowers

UKRAINE
AREA: 233,088 sq mi (603,700 sq km)
POPULATION: 47,732,079
CAPITAL: Kiev
LANGUAGES: Ukrainian, Russian, Romanian, Polish, Hungarian
GOVERNMENT: Republic
RELIGIONS: Ukrainian Orthodox, Ukrainian Catholic, Protestant, Jewish
LITERACY RATE: 100%
CURRENCY: Hryvnia
MAIN EXPORTS: Ferrous and non-ferrous metals, fuel and petroleum products, chemicals, machinery and transport

UNITED ARAB EMIRATES
AREA: 32,000 sq mi (82,880 sq km)
POPULATION: 2,523,915
CAPITAL: Abu Dhabi
LANGUAGES: Arabic (official), Persian, English, Hindi, Urdu
GOVERNMENT: Federation
RELIGIONS: Muslim, Christian, Hindu, others
LITERACY RATE: 78%
CURRENCY: Emirati dirham
MAIN EXPORTS: Crude oil, natural gas, re-exports, dried fish, dates

UNITED KINGDOM
AREA: 94,525 sq mi (244,820 sq km)
POPULATION: 60,270,708
CAPITAL: London
LANGUAGES: English, Welsh, Gaelic
GOVERNMENT: Constitutional monarchy
RELIGIONS: Anglican, Roman Catholic, Protestant, Muslim, Sikh, Hindu, Jewish
LITERACY RATE: 99%
CURRENCY: British pound
MAIN EXPORTS: Manufactured goods, fuels, chemicals, food, beverages, tobacco

UNITED STATES
AREA: 3,717,776 sq mi (9,629,091 sq km)
POPULATION: 293,027,571
CAPITAL: Washington, D.C.
LANGUAGES: English, Spanish
GOVERNMENT: Federal republic
RELIGIONS: Protestant, Roman Catholic, Jewish, others
LITERACY RATE: 97%
CURRENCY: US dollar
MAIN EXPORTS: Capital goods, automobiles, industrial supplies and raw materials, consumer goods

URUGUAY
AREA: 68,038 sq mi (176,220 sq km)
POPULATION: 3,440,205
CAPITAL: Montevideo
LANGUAGES: Spanish, Portunol
GOVERNMENT: Republic
RELIGIONS: Roman Catholic, Protestant, Jewish, others
LITERACY RATE: 98%
CURRENCY: Uruguayan peso
MAIN EXPORTS: Meat, rice, leather products, wool, vehicles, dairy products

UZBEKISTAN
AREA: 172,740 sq mi (447,400 sq km)
POPULATION: 26,410,416
CAPITAL: Tashkent
LANGUAGES: Uzbek, Russian, Tajik, others
GOVERNMENT: Republic
RELIGIONS: Muslim, Eastern Orthodox, others
LITERACY RATE: 99%
CURRENCY: Uzbekistani sum
MAIN EXPORTS: Cotton, gold, energy products, mineral fertilizers, ferrous metals, textiles, food products, automobiles

VANUATU
AREA: 4,719 sq mi (12,200 sq km)
POPULATION: 202,609
CAPITAL: Port-Vila
LANGUAGES: English, French and Bislama (all official), others
GOVERNMENT: Parliamentary repubilc
RELIGIONS: Protestant, Roman Catholic, native beliefs
LITERACY RATE: 53%
CURRENCY: Vatu
MAIN EXPORTS: Copra, beef, cocoa, timber, kava, coffee

VATICAN CITY (HOLY SEE)
AREA: .17 sq mi (.44 sq km)
POPULATION: 890
CAPITAL: None
LANGUAGES: Latin, Italian, others
GOVERNMENT: Ecclesiastical
RELIGION: Roman Catholic
LITERACY RATE: 100%
CURRENCY: Euro
MAIN EXPORTS: NA

VENEZUELA
AREA: 352,141 sq mi (912,050 sq km)
POPULATION: 25,017,387
CAPITAL: Caracas
LANGUAGES: Spanish (official), native dialects
GOVERNMENT: Federal republic
RELIGIONS: Roman Catholic, Protestant, others
LITERACY RATE: 93%
CURRENCY: Bolivar
MAIN EXPORTS: Petroleum, bauxite and aluminum, steel, chemicals, agricultural products

VIETNAM
AREA: 127,243 sq mi (329,560 sq km)
POPULATION: 82,689,518
CAPITAL: Hanoi
LANGUAGES: Vietnamese (official), English, French, Chinese, Khmer, others
GOVERNMENT: Communist state
RELIGIONS: Buddhist, Hoa Hao, Cao Dai, Roman Catholic, Protestant, others
LITERACY RATE: 94%
CURRENCY: Dong
MAIN EXPORTS: Crude oil, marine products, rice, coffee, rubber, tea, garments, shoes

YEMEN
AREA: 203,848 sq mi (527,970 sq km)
POPULATION: 20,024,867
CAPITAL: Sanaa
LANGUAGE: Arabic
GOVERNMENT: Republic
RELIGION: Muslim
LITERACY RATE: 50%
CURRENCY: Yemeni rial
MAIN EXPORTS: Crude oil, coffee, dried and salted fish

ZAMBIA
AREA: 290,583 sq mi (752,614 sq km)
POPULATION: 10,462,436
CAPITAL: Lusaka
LANGUAGES: English (official), Bemba, Kaonda, Lozi, Lunda, other native languages
GOVERNMENT: Republic
RELIGIONS: Christian, Muslim, Hindu, native beliefs
LITERACY RATE: 81%
CURRENCY: Zambian kwacha
MAIN EXPORTS: Copper, cobalt, electricity, tobacco, flowers, cotton

ZIMBABWE
AREA: 150,802 sq mi (390,580 sq km)
POPULATION: 12,671,860
CAPITAL: Harare
LANGUAGES: English (official), Shona, Sindebele, native languages
GOVERNMENT: Parliamentary democracy
RELIGIONS: Syncretic, Christian, Muslim, others
LITERACY RATE: 91%
CURRENCY: Zimbabwean dollar
MAIN EXPORTS: Tobacco, gold, ferroalloys, textiles/clothing

Index

Illustration and Photo Credits

All maps: Joe LeMonnier, Joe Lertola, Jean Wisenbaugh

8–9: NASA (earth); www.Shutterstock.com (lithosphere, hydrosphere, clouds, boy, dinosaur). **10–15:** www.Shutterstock.com. **16–17:** www.Shutterstock.com (ice fishing, Niagara Falls); iStockphoto.com/Photawa (Rideau Canal). **18–23:** www.Shutterstock.com. **24–25:** www.Shutterstock.com (Liberty Bell, New York, Chesapeake Bay); Library of Congress, Prints and Photographs Division (Statue of Liberty). **26–27:** www.Shutterstock.com. **28–29:** www.Shutterstock.com (horses, riverboat); U.S. Fish and Wildlife Service (panther). **30–31:** NASA (Mission Control); www.Shutterstock.com (Montezuma Castle, Chapel of San Miguel). **32–33:** www.Shutterstock.com. **34–35:** iStockphoto.com/Combttiphoto (Santa Prisca); www.Shutterstock.com (Tikal, Arenal). **36–41:** www.Shutterstock.com. **42–43:** age fotostock/SuperStock, Inc. (woman); www.Shutterstock.com (tamarin, Rio de Janeiro); iStockphoto.com/stevegeer. **44–51:** www.Shutterstock.com. **52–53:** iStockphoto.com/raiwa (La Sagrada Familia); www.Shutterstock.com (flamenco, Mezquita, Gibraltar). **54–69:** www.Shutterstock.com. **70–71:** www.Shutterstock.com (Latvian Freedom Monument, Tallinn, Mir Castle); SuperStock/Ernest Manewal (Latvian girl). **72–105:** www.Shutterstock.com. **106–107:** www.Shutterstock.com (Ghana); iStockphoto.com/alantobey (Djenne, Niger River). **108–109:** www.Shutterstock.com (boy); SuperStock, Inc. (woman, Watusi dancers). **110–115:** www.Shutterstock.com. **116–117:** www.Shutterstock.com (Sydney Opera House, Tasmanian devil, kangaroo); SuperStock, Inc./Holton Collection. **118–119:** www.Shutterstock.com (Samoa); iStockphoto.com/junjun (Maori mask); iStockphoto.com/keeweeboy (kiwi bird). **120–121:** National Science Foundation (McMurdo station); www.Shutterstock.com (Penguins, Antarctic landscape).